£36,50   Enslin
£12,

Liberalism beyond Justice

───────────────

Liberalism beyond Justice

CITIZENS, SOCIETY, AND THE
BOUNDARIES OF POLITICAL THEORY

John Tomasi

PRINCETON UNIVERSITY PRESS

PRINCETON AND OXFORD

Library of Congress Cataloging-in-Publication Data

Tomasi, John, 1961–
Liberalism beyond justice : citizens, society, and the boundaries
of political theory / John Tomasi.
p.cm.
Includes bibliographical references and index.
ISBN 0-691-04968-8 — ISBN 0-691-04969-6 (pbk)
1. Liberalism. 2. Social justice. I. Title.
JC574.T66 2000
320.51'3—dc21   00-058486

This book has been composed in Janson

The paper used in this publication meets the minimum requirements
of ANSI/NISO Z39.48-1992 (R1997) (*Permanence of Paper*)

www.pup.princeton.edu

Printed in the United States of America

1 3 5 7 9 10 8 6 4 2
1 3 5 7 9 10 8 6 4 2
(Pbk.)

For Amy

CONTENTS

viii   CONTENTS

ACKNOWLEDGMENTS

I FIRST STARTED THINKING about the way politcal values shape personal relationships because of a conversation I had long ago with Amy Seybolt in Winona, Arizona. I have had wonderful institutional support for this project. I spent a year as a visiting fellow at the University Center for Human Values in Princeton in 1994. I greatly appreciated the intellectual welcome extended to me by Amy Gutmann, and the confidence she has shown in this project ever since. I am also indebted to George Kateb and Alan Ryan and to the other fellows that year, Francis Kamm, Peter Euben, Samuel Freeman, and Julia Driver. I spent a marvelous year teaching in Stanford's Ethics in Society Program, under the direction of Susan Okin. Susan has been a steady friend, and valued critic. I began the formal writing phase of this book during a semester as a Visiting Fellow at the Social Philosophy and Policy Center at Bowling Green State University in 1996. I am indebted to Jeff Paul and Fred Miller for making my stay possible and, especially, to Loren Lomasky, Ray Frey, and Danny Shapiro for stimulating conversation. I finished the first complete draft of the manuscript during my year as a Fellow in Ethics in Harvard's Program in Ethics and the Professions in 1998–99. Arthur Applbaum and my fellow fellows, Walter Sinnott Armstrong, Leora Bilsky, Annabelle Lever, Walter Robinson, and Steve Behnke politely endured my obsession with this project. I am pleased to record my special debt to Dennis Thompson for all his advice and encouragement.

I have presented versions of this argument to many audiences, and so here mention just a few. Walter Grinder invited me to discuss my account of citizenship at a seminar sponsored by the Institute for Civil Society. Ken Winston and his colleagues at the Austinian Society at Harvard's John F. Kennedy School gave me a good grilling on my proposals about civic education. Marty Zupan at the Institute for Humane Studies organized a bracing day-long workshop on my account of political liberalism: Charles Larmore and Eamonn Callan provided direct responses; Bill Galston, Richard Flathman, Robert Fullinwider, Susan Wolf, and Michael Slote were discussants; and Jeremy Shearmur graciously chaired. I am especially fortunate to have participated for the past four years in a series of seminars held in a remote monastery in Arrabida, Portugal, where I tried out many of these ideas for the first time. I profited enormously from my visits to Arrabida, and especially from my conversations there with Steven Lukes, John Gray, David Miller, Gordon Wood, Bill Galston, Miriam Galston,

Steven Macedo, Cliff Orwin, Chandran Kukathas, Joao Rosas, Len Goodman, and my dear friend Joao Carlos Espada. I presented bits and pieces of this manuscript at many American Political Science Association panels. The APSA panel that most deeply marked my thinking was a roundtable on Steven Macedo's book *Diversity and Distrust: Civic Education in a Multicultural Democracy* (my co-panelists were Amy Gutmann, Ronald Beiner, Melissa Williams, and Macedo). Steve and I look in the same direction but see very different things. He does not know even now what a model he has been to me, with the thoughtful and broadminded way he has always-responded to my challenges.

I am indebted to many individuals as well. Bernard Williams, G. A. Cohen, Will Kymlicka, Tony Laden, Lucas Swaine, Joseph Coleman, Patrick Durning, David Stevens, Robert Reich, and David Siu all wrote comments on various parts. David Estlund has responded to many dozens of e-mails from me with technical questions about Rawlsian political liberalism, all with his characteristic precision and care. Two reviewers for Princeton University Press, David Schmidtz and Bill Galston, backed my project even when it was in rough form. Amy Gutmann, Eamonn Callan, and Dave Estlund each wrote detailed comments on a late draft of the whole. Many of these people disagree with me still about political liberalism and the nature of liberal citizenship; I have learned from them all. I thank Mahasin Abuwi and Bryan McGraw for putting the manuscript together for the Press and Cindy Crumrine for her skillful copyediting. My editors at Princeton, Ann Wald and Ian Malcom, have shown patience nonpareil.

I owe a special debt to my colleagues in the Department of Political Science at Brown University, where I have recently been promoted to the rank of Associate Professor. On my first day at Brown, Jim Morone encouraged me to take a risk and write the book he knew I had in mind, even if that meant it might not be finished by the time the tenure bell rang. Darrell West, as Department chair, took the same view and generously granted me far more than my fair share of research leaves. My greatest debt at Brown, by far, is to Nancy Rosenblum. Nancy has set a high example for me of genuine engagement with political ideas. "I write for myself," she once declared, and I have taken that as encouragement that I could do the same. Nancy has been not only my champion, but my friend. I thank her for the friendship most of all.

I was a first-year graduate student at the time and wrote up my idea as a seminar paper, my first ever in political theory. That paper grew into one of my first articles ("Individual Rights and Community Virtues" *Ethics* 101, no. 2), then into my Oxford B.Phil. thesis and onward in the form of my D.Phil. dissertation. That same idea appears here, greatly compressed, in chapter 3. It is the seed from which this book grew. Amy has been discussing these ideas with me right from that first day. We have since been married, earned graduate degrees, and set out on the wondrous adventure of raising our two small children, Peter and Lydia. I dedicate this book to Amy with love.

My final acknowledgment is less personal. I wish to thank Friedrich Nietzsche, who said at least one thing that I believe: philosophy should be *unsettling*.

J.T.

INTRODUCTION

IMAGINE A society in a box. The box is closed and thus you know nothing about this society—nothing, that is, but one thing: Whatever else may be true of this society, it is one in which a liberal conception of justice has been legitimately achieved. This society, then, is just. Indeed, imagine that it is *completely just*, such that in this liberal society there is no significant social injustice whatsoever.

What would it mean for a society to be just? Let's say that a liberal society is just insofar as the institutions of democratic self-rule within it honor basic rights and secure a fair distribution of benefits and burdens among citizens. Of course, different liberals have different views about what rights people have and about which distributions are fair. They might thus have very different ideas about what a just society would look like. At one extreme are those who think liberal justice calls for an extensive system of positive entitlements—state-backed guarantees regarding employment, housing, medical care, higher education, funding for the arts, culture, aesthetic zoning ordinances, and more. At the other extreme are those who think liberal justice requires something more like a night-watchman state, the main role of which is to protect private property and enforce the contracts into which citizens voluntarily enter. But whatever conception of justice you think is the correct or most reasonable one for liberals, imagine that in this society the institutional requirements of that conception of justice have been realized.

Imagine also that when this state wields its power in pursuit of justice, it does so *legitimately*. Let's say that a state exercises its political power legitimately when the authority of the state elicits the free assent of many citizens for the right reasons.[1] So in this society the strictures of justice are not simply imposed by government officials upon an unwilling citizenry. Instead, the people living here affirm social justice as a great good. They are freely and firmly committed to seeing the requirements of social justice fulfilled in their society.

But now, allow me ask you the first of two questions about this society. Knowing only that this society has achieved justice in this way, do you think this would likely be an *attractive* society? For example, do you think this might be a society in which you yourself would want to live?

If you are not a liberal, you might have a ready answer to this question: no. You might believe, as many critics of liberalism have believed, that there is something inherently unattractive in any liberal societal ideal, with its anemic grounds of shared meanings, and the priority given to rights and the litigious conception of interpersonal relations associated with them. What is such a society *for*? such critics, from their various perspectives, have traditionally asked. Critics believe that a society where liberal principles have been freely affirmed and instantiated, whatever its other attractions, is already deeply bankrupt. We will return to this fundamental disagreement below, but for now let's say "fair enough" and go on. What if you *are* a liberal? How do you answer?

Some liberals considering this question might be concerned, understandably, that this society not be one in which goods were desperately scarce—perhaps because of some recent environmental, biological, or military disaster. But I am asking you to imagine that there is no such crisis in this society. When I say that this imaginary (but still-hidden) society is *just*, I assume that this is a society in which the circumstances of justice obtain. So, in this society is characterized by a moderate scarcity of the sort that David Hume famously described.[2] Strictly in terms of material resources, this is a society roughly like present-day England, Canada, Australia, or the United States. But now, imagining that these moderately scarce resources were to come to be distributed in way that was completely just (by your own preferred conception of liberal justice)—and knowing nothing else about this society—do you think you might like to live in this society?

There is a strong impulse among people attracted to the liberal view to give a quick answer to this question: Would I want to live in a perfectly just society? Yes! There are good reasons for this impulse. In a just liberal society, people are treated with equal concern and respect. Further, as a condition of legitimacy, people are freely and firmly committed to treating one another that way. This state of affairs is a very great good. Still, this first question is meant to help us to pause and begin thinking about the role of liberal justice vis-à-vis other values that we think might make a social world attractive.

For example, an important set of thoughts one could entertain during that pause might concern the personality traits and nonpublic virtues that might characterize people in such a society, no matter how *just* they or the basic structure of their society might be. What does it matter, one might consider, if a society is perfectly just, but the people there turn out to lack many other personal virtues besides the virtue of being "just people"? At the extreme, what if one's fellow citizens were just, but nothing more. What would it be like to live among humans where everyone was *just* just? Of course, in addition to having a clear and freely given commitment to social justice, the people who are to be living with you in this society *might* have many of the dispositions and interpersonal attitudes that you think would make a social world attractive—dispositions that might make this society a supportive "home" for whatever worldview you affirm. That is, in their nonpublic lives, some people in this imaginary society might exhibit high degrees of religious piety, personal generosity, marital commitment, or virtues such as kindness or humility, to name a few possibilities. But, by hypothesis, you do not know whether any people in this society do or do not have personal virtues such as these.[3] Knowing only, as you do, that the society is *just*, this first question is meant as a way for us to begin considering how important you might think it is for a social world to be just when you do not know these other things about it.

But this question about the relation of liberal political values to other social values leads us to a second, more fundamental, question. If you knew only that this society is one in which (your preferred conception of) liberal justice has been legitimately achieved, do you think that would be sufficient for this society to fulfill all the normative ambitions relevant to it as a liberal society? This is not a first-personal question about the role of social justice within your own view of what makes a form of human living-together attractive overall. Rather, it is a question about the role of social justice within *liberalism* and thus about the range of normative criteria that are relevant to liberal theory. It is a question, if you like, put to you in your role as a liberal citizen. Simply stated, would the legitimate instantiation of liberal principles of justice itself make a society a *success* as a liberal society?

There is a powerful current in contemporary thought suggesting that the answer to this second question must, again, be yes. Liberals take freedom and equality seriously, and liberal accounts of justice, in their various ways, give societal primacy to those concerns. What's more, the recent emphasis given by liberal thinkers to problems of legitimacy may seem to incorporate the first-personal question I initially asked, or at least to incorporate all elements of that question that are relevant to *political* theory. After all, a system of liberal governance is not legitimate unless it can win the free assent of many citizens. This involves imagining would-be citizens satisfying themselves at least to some degree regarding whether they personally find a just society an attractive place in which to live.

Certainly most contemporary political theorists proceed as though a concern for legitimacy and the democratic pursuit of justice exhausts the concerns properly addressed by them. Indeed, most liberal theorists write as though for them to address a social concern within their theory *simply means* to talk about that concern in terms of justice and the legitimacy of state coercive action (or in terms of a narrow band of deliberative dispositions—e.g., the much ballyhooed "sense of justice"—immediately attendant to those concepts). If a liberal, as a liberal, cares about some value, then her concern for that value should be expressed in her account of liberal public life. Once one has worked out one's account of justice and the immediately attendant democratic values, there are no other values for liberal theorists, writing as such, to be concerned about. Most writers, to varying degrees, thus affirm the coextensivity of what would count as an adequate theoretical defense of *liberalism* with what would count as an adequate theoretical defense of a liberal *justified coercion*. The project of justifying liberalism, of giving liberalism its fullest and most powerful defense, is taken to be identical to the project of justifying the authority of the liberal state.

In this book, I mean to question those assumptions. I believe that a different answer to that second question is the right one for liberals generally, and for liberals in the emerging tradition of political liberalism in particular: Would I, as a liberal citizen, want to live in a society where democratic justice has been legitimately achieved? *I have no idea.* At the very least, I shall try to convince you that, however in the end you decide to answer, a long and important pause in the face of that question is not only appropriate but actually required by your commitment to liberalism. I aim to demonstrate that the normative domain of liberal theory construction is importantly wider than the domain of public, deliberative value. For political liberals in particular, there is important work for liberal theorists to attend to beyond their current fixation on questions of legitimacy and justification. As I put it, there is liberalism beyond justice.

My book is in six chapters. In the first, I describe the conceptual crisis that motivated the development of political liberalism. While still in its infancy, political liberalism has already proven itself as a radical new development in terms of its justificatory structure. But I believe that political liberalism is radical in other ways as well, ways that its early defenders have not themselves foreseen. To see why, I introduce the idea of an ethical background culture. A society's ethical background culture serves as a kind of map of meaning, a map that influences the way anyone making a life within that society finds the world morally intelligible. A society's public values unavoidably influence that society's background culture, thus informally influencing how well the social world in practice delivers or makes available many personal, nonpublic payoffs. Political liberals admit that their view cannot prevent "spillovers" from public to nonpublic spheres of life. I show that this admission has theoretical consequences they have not anticipated.

In chapter 2 I set out a series of questions that citizens in a diverse society might reasonably ask about spillovers between public and nonpublic domains. I show that political liberals, by their own motivational foundations, must answer many more of their citizens' questions about the liberal nonpublic world than they have so far recognized. In some cases, they must answer their citizens' questions for reasons that are not reducible to any concern about justice or legitimacy (the concerns that political liberals usually think of themselves as being exclusively bound to consider).

In chapter 3, I offer an account of liberal nonpublic reason. This is the general form of reasoning shared by all citizens who make lives for themselves in a world structured by liberal political institutions. I then examine the resources available to liberals in answering their citizens' questions about the unintended social effects of liberal politics. There are resources within this realm of nonpublic reason that can be affirmed by liberals in a way that fully respects the architecture of public reason.

In chapter 4 I ask what formal place these resources directed at well-being might have within the boundaries of political theory. I suggest that this machinery be understood as providing a new, more normatively ambitious ideal of good citizen conduct. A freely given commitment to just institutions is not all that a liberal theory asks of its members as citizens. People are called upon as citizens to tend to matters at the very core of their lives, not just to matters that protect life's outer frame. Good citizenship, in a free society, is a matter of living well.

Taking care to respect the architecture of public reason, I then explore the institutional implications of this well-being-directed conception of liberal citizenship. In chapter 5, I reconsider the formative project implied by political liberalism, the account of free motivational development relevant to it and, crucially, the form of civic schooling political liberalism requires. At the level of actual policy making concerning school design and many other issues as well, public reason often runs out. When that happens, political liberals must attend to their distinctively broadened range of civic ambitions when giving advice about the specific design of (politically permissible) laws and policies. In all these areas, I show the dramatic divergence between political and ethical liberalism, both in theory and in practice.

In chapter 6, finally, I examine the content of liberal justice itself. I explain how the political liberal expansion of the range of the politically reasonable disrupts the best known comprehensive liberal arguments for justice as fairness. This points to the need for liberals to develop a less materially ambitious and more socially nuanced conception of justice than any they have so far considered. At this level as well, the emergence of political liberalism changes everything.

Political liberalism is a radical view. It is a form of human living-together that invites citizens to aim higher than even its most ardent defenders have suggested. It is often said that the politicization of justice cuts political philosophers off from questions about ethical well-being. But I argue that an acceptance of the political form of justification makes discussion of ethical questions central to liberal theorizing—it simply relocates those concerns to a different part of the theory. Rather than signaling any philosophical contraction or retreat, the move toward a political form of justification urgently requires that the boundaries of liberal theory construction be *expanded*, and expanded in nonpublic directions.

Of course, this is not the orthodox view of political liberalism. Most people see political liberalism as a mere technical development, its significance confined to justificatory matters. They accept the idea that liberals can adopt a new broader foundation but go on living in pretty much the same old house. So it may seem as if we have a very long way to go to get to any rival view of liberalism such as the one I am proposing. To get there we must begin at the beginning, with an examination of the motivational foundations of political liberalism.

Liberalism beyond Justice

Chapter One

POLITICAL LIBERALISM

Motivational Foundations

Every political view includes a principle of legitimacy, a principle, that is, which explains when and why the exercise of political power is justified. To fully exposit a political view, it is not enough to simply set out an account of how people should order their public institutions, an account, that is, of social justice. Justification of state power should also include an account of the reasons the persons who live there have, or should have, for affirming those particular institutions. The principle of legitimacy provides that extra element.

Not surprisingly, there are as many rival principles of legitimacy as there are rival political views. Theocrats, for example, say the use of political power is justified in the end by otherworldly considerations, such as the salvation of citizens' souls. Fascists have seen political power as justified by the needs of the state as an organic entity; communists, by the historic imperatives of a society's economic development.

The liberal principle of legitimacy—like each of the others—reflects what its proponents believe is most important in human social life. For liberals, this is the idea that in the conditions of pluralism that mark modern societies, *individual citizens* must be recognized as the ultimate arbiters of what gives value to their own lives. Political power must be justifiable in principle to each of them. For liberals, the justification of social structures must be provided not in the unified terms of any single religious doctrine, story of nation, or all-encompassing economic theory. Rather, justification must proceed in terms of whatever questions citizens themselves think fit to ask. The liberal principle of legitimacy says that a system of social order is justified only if it is conducted on the basis of principles that citizens might be expected to endorse after asking their questions and considering the best answers the defenders of that social order might give.[1]

Political liberalism was born out of a crisis in this principle of legitimacy. The ambition underlying all versions of liberalism has long been to define the common good of political association in terms of a minimal moral conception—that is, a basic value or set of values that most citizens share despite even their many important differences.[2] Political principles are neutral—and thus satisfy the liberal principle of legitimacy—insofar as they can be justified by reference to such shared values, without assuming the validity or truth of any particular (controversial) conception of the good life.

This liberal principle of legitimacy does not require that every person must agree with every particular rule, policy, or court decision that is enforced by the liberal state. Rather, the idea is that if many people agree to have some set of foundational principles regulate the basic structure of their society, including the processes by which particular policies and laws will be arrived at, then they affirm the use of political coercion even regarding the particular outcomes they dislike.

In the seminal formulations of Kant and Mill, the liberal commitment to state neutrality was justified ultimately by reference to a particular view of human moral nature—one championing autonomy (for Kant, a life lived according to rational will) or individualism (for Mill, an experimental attitude toward one's projects). Both Kant and Mill, each for his own reasons and in his own way, affirmed the idea that the liberal state should not seek to impose any particular view of the good life on its citizens. Rather, these liberals argued that forms of life have their value to people because, and only when, individuals freely come to affirm those ways of life for themselves. Some contemporary liberals—Ronald Dworkin, Will Kymlicka, and Joseph Raz prominent among them—continue to defend liberal politics firmly within this tradition. These contemporary "ethical" liberals, and Raz in particular, have defended more expansive or even communitarian conceptions of autonomy—for example, conceptions of autonomy that give increasing place to the demands of a person's history or (unchosen) social context of choice. But what liberal citizens are said to share, on all the many variants of this broad approach, is a commitment to the moral importance of individual choice-making rather than to any particular outcome of choice. It is upon this shared ideal of individualism that a liberal rights-based politics can be built.

However, many other liberal theorists have come to worry that even a broadened ideal of individualism is something on which people may reasonably disagree. Charles Larmore, for example, traces a Romantic movement from Herder to Alasdair MacIntyre and Michael Sandel in our day, one central strand of which has been a critique of precisely those moral ideals associated with Kant and Mill. In opposition to the traditional liberal emphasis on reflective individualism as a philosophy of life—the idea that people should always maintain a contingent allegiance, revisable on reflection, to their own view of the good life—thinkers in this Romantic tradition have stressed the values of belonging and custom.[3] For these people, Larmore says, "such ways of life (shared customs, ties of place and language, and religious orthodoxies) shape the sense of value on the basis of which we make whatever choices we do." These commitments reach to the foundations of people's nature as moral beings. "They are so integral to our very conception of ourselves as moral beings that to imagine them as objects of choice would be to imagine ourselves as without any guiding sense of morality."[4] From this perspective of the nature of moral value, the individualistic philosophy of ethical liberalism has seemed bound to destroy the roots of morality itself.

Whatever in the end one might oneself come to think of this view of moral personality and value, many theorists have come to see that this is a view that many citizens of modern societies do hold. The Romantic ideal is as much a part of Western culture as the contrary ideals of autonomy and individuality described by Kant and Mill.[5] For a growing number of contemporary theorists, these forms of enthusiasm for custom seem to be incompatible with any single ideal of moral personality on which liberal politics might be directly founded.

However, if any recognizably liberal ideal of individualism or autonomy is itself subject to irresolvable controversy, no such ideal can serve as the minimal moral conception on which liberal politics has long hoped to rely. Any liberal theory that is founded on a controversial view of moral personality would be overly restrictive, and in an illegitimating way. Many citizens will consistently object to the state coercively enforcing liberal strictures against them. For example, such citizens may object to judicial decisions protecting heretical or blasphemous speech in the name of personal freedom, or to decisions disallowing devotional Bible study in public schools based on a similar rationale. Crucially, such people will object not just to the particular rulings but to the justificatory foundation of the public decision-making system itself, a foundation made up of an autonomy-affirming philosophy of life that they themselves reject for moral reasons.[6] If traditional versions of liberalism must invoke moral notions of autonomy or individualism that are incompatible with the ethical outlooks of many of these Romantic citizens, then the acceptance of Romanticism as a way of life undercuts the traditional justification of liberal politics.

John Rawls, who has given by far the most detailed account of political liberalism, sees the motivational foundations of this emerging version of liberalism just this way—though Rawls describes the crisis of legitimacy as arising internally to his own argument for justice as fairness. If state-backed coercion in the name of some set of principles of justice is to be justified, according to Rawls, it must be shown that those principles matter to citizens in a first-personal and moral way. Rawls calls this the test of stability.

In the third part of *A Theory of Justice* (henceforth *Theory*), Rawls describes how people who have once acquired a sense of justice could reasonably be expected to regard justice not just as a constraint on their actions but as a good in itself for them. "The desire to act justly and the desire to express our nature as free moral persons turn out to specify what is practically speaking the same desire."[7] Rawls was confident that this congruence would obtain because of the way the principles of justice were themselves derived. Those principles were derived from a device called the original position, a device that in *Theory* is sometimes described as representing an important fact about people: people's true moral nature is to be free. A conception of justice derived from a particular view of human nature—if the view hit upon were true—could then reasonably be expected to be recognized by people as reflecting who they really are. Insofar as people desire to express their true moral nature, and thus avoid giving way to "the contingencies and accidents of the world," they could be expected to see that acting according to those principles would be congruent with their own good.[8] Coercive power exercised on the basis of principles derived that way could thus satisfy the liberal principle of legitimacy.

However, as Rawls came later to see, "*Theory* relies on a premise the realization of which its principles of justice rule out."[9] The premise is that all good citizens must converge on the particular view of human moral nature that the original position was said to model: the true moral nature of people lies in their capacity for freedom. But that particular view of human nature—as much as the individualism of Mill or Kant—is something on which many citizens of goodwill, and Romantic "citizens of faith" in particular, disagree. Indeed, disagreement about the true character of human moral nature is particularly likely in a society that gives central place to associative and deliberative liberties, the hallmarks of a liberal society. Liberal principles of justice support precisely the institutional conditions that undercut (or make unrealistic) the comprehensive form of justification upon which Rawls's argument in *Theory* depended. Some citizens who grow up in a free society may reasonably be expected to ask questions that no reference to the individualist ideals of Kant or Mill (or to the modified conceptions of autonomy of Dworkin, Kymlicka, or Raz) can satisfy. And citizens may ask these questions while still very much wishing to take part in political association with (diverse) others on terms that all can accept. How might liberal forms of state coercion be justified to "politically reasonable" citizens such as these?

On the traditional or "comprehensive" liberal approach the hope has been to defend some suitably general liberal view about true human moral nature against critics by means of philosophical argumentation. The critics having been confronted and their beliefs about human moral nature shown to be false, philosophers could then use their own true view of moral personality as a shared moral basis for liberal politics. But accepting the fact of reasonable value pluralism requires that liberals now abandon all such philosophical ambitions. In conditions of institutional freedom, convergence on a single conception of human moral nature is unlikely, no matter how long or cleverly philosophers argue. A new trailhead must be considered: perhaps liberals should begin looking for the shared moral basis for liberal politics merely in the cluster of moral ideas that people in Western democracies already hold, however inchoately, regarding their *political* lives.

Political liberals, thus propose two major adjustments to the traditional liberal paradigm. First, political liberals recast their arguments for state neutrality as arguments that appeal only to people's beliefs about politics itself. For example, Rawls recasts his basic argument for justice as fairness in *Theory* as a freestanding *political* conception of justice. Instead of reading the original position as representing any particular view about the true moral nature of persons, a reading that was strongly implied in the text of *Theory*, Rawls says that we should instead view that device—and his other arguments for justice as fairness in *Theory*—as based on the shared elements of the public life of a democratic culture. Rawls sets aside questions about the truth of the (various) foundations of those shared public elements. He emphasizes instead the formative role of liberal institutions in leading otherwise diverse people to share a common set of political ideas—central among them the shared idea that whatever their differences, all people in liberal societies should be respected as free and equal for political purposes.

This first adjustment, a change in the way the liberal conception of justice is justified, is known as the *politicization of justice*.[10] The politicization of justice in turn forces many other changes and, in particular, calls for the development of a whole cluster of theoretical concepts that had not been needed by liberal philosophers before. These ideas are needed to show how a conception of justice constructed merely from people's political views could meet the first-personal stability test I described above. After all, moral and religious convictions typically matter more to people then even their most basic political beliefs. So, people might accept principles justified in this political way as a general matter, and yet reject such principles whenever they conflicted with their own religious or comprehensive moral beliefs. To remedy this requires the second major adjustment of political liberalism: the addition to liberal theory of further stages of justification, stages concerned not with justice but with legitimacy.

If coercion in the name of some conception of justice is to be justified in a social world marked by reasonable value pluralism, liberals think that citizens must be able to affirm those shared political principles on the basis of their own views of what gives life its ultimate meaning and value. They must be able to embed the political conceptions within their own comprehensive conceptions of the good, and thus achieve "full individual justification."

A Catholic, for example, might embed certain basic liberal political principles within her own comprehensive doctrine through the doctrine of free faith—a doctrine that is essential to the Catholic account of each person's relation to Jesus Christ. She adopts core liberal principles out of her concern for her own Catholicity.[11] Rather than thinking that philosophical argument must lead all reasonable persons to affirm liberal principles for the same set of moral reasons (the view suggested by *Theory*), political liberalism operates from the more modest hope that different groups may come to affirm some common set of principles for their own diverse sets of reasons.[12] For example, an atheist might join the Catholic in affirming political protections of free faith, though do so purely out of concern for his own very different moral belief system. He is concerned, as an atheist, that he will be able to live his own life atheistically, even while sharing a social world with Catholics and others who personally reject his worldview.

If people who have achieved full individual justification in a plural society find that they do share a political conception of justice, then an "overlapping consensus" forms and an even further level of justification—"public justification by political society—has been achieved. In that event, the conditions of liberal legitimacy have been met.[13] Political liberal theory has provided us with an argument for a particular conception of justice *and* an account of how it is possible that such a conception could be enforced legitimately even in a society that contains citizens of faith as well as autonomous individualists.

The general idea of a political conception of liberalism—while still in its infancy—has proven tremendously attractive and is rapidly gaining adherents.[14] Political liberalism holds out the possibility of a form of political union that is accommodating to a wide range of social diversity—moral, philosophical, and religious—while avoiding the bitter fights about deep moral value that have historically dogged liberal theory. If the political face of liberalism can indeed be detached from any particular comprehensive view of moral life, then political liberalism may prove to be more accommodating than even the most capacious variant of ethical liberalism. Political liberalism might be thought of as an attempt to fulfill the broadminded promise at the heart of Locke's famous *Letter Concerning Toleration*: to find a moral form of human living-together for people who see the point of their lives in irresolvably different ways but are committed to sharing a social world with one another.

Still, this nascent view is controversial, and has already come under attack. Some question whether political liberalism can succeed on its own terms. When we look closely, such critics say, political liberalism rests on foundations that cannot really abstain from controversies about the good life.

Ethical liberals explicitly base their politics on a theory of true moral personality. But critics claim that political liberals do just the same thing—they just do it indirectly, through their moralized account of the citizen. Political liberals, whatever they say, do take as basic, and as fixed, a partially comprehensive conception of moral personality—the part of moral personality relevant to politics. But, this objection continues, if political liberalism

does surreptitiously rely on a conception of the person, then the two allegedly different patterns of justification—one ethical, the other political—
turn out on close examination to be indistinguishable. Beneath all the technical camouflage, political liberalism is merely a species of comprehensive
liberalism. The politicization of justice does not allow liberals to bypass
the old moral disputes after all. Political liberalism inherits all the difficulties (and has only the same strengths) of the traditional liberal view.[15]

I do not find this line of criticism compelling. Political liberalism does
not start with any fixed ideal of moral personality and then go on to ask
what political forms would best support and express the requirements of
people's realizing that ideal. What is radical about politicization is that it
insists that we work in just the reverse. Political liberalism, insofar as it
starts with anything, starts with a very general idea of *society*—something
like the idea of a moral union, or democratic agreement, in the face of
reasonable pluralism. It then asks whether such a society is possible. One
of the conditions of having such a society is that people share certain moral
elements of fellow-treatment. In particular, people in such a society must
share the moral idea that humans are the kinds of beings who are owed
reasons, in terms that they themselves can accept, that justify coercive actions undertaken by the state with respect to them. Political liberalism is
only suited for a social environment in which people do affirm that moral
ideal, so no doubt there are a great many social environments in which
political liberalism can have no place. But the contours of the moral personality that political liberals affirm are always in service to what they make
possible—the conception of society—and not the reverse.[16] The contours
of moral personality requisite for liberal politics are not fixed in advance
philosophically. Political liberalism does not rest ultimately on any theory
of the good for persons. Strictly in terms of its justificatory structure, political liberalism is a radically new liberal view.

However, there is a different way of challenging political liberalism that
I find potentially much more interesting. This is a challenge not about
political liberalism's formal justificatory structure—for example, about
whether political liberalism starts from the same thing or proceeds in the
same way as ethical liberalism. It is a challenge about political liberalism's
practical implications.

This different challenge springs from the worry that political liberalism—even if formally distinct as a justificatory type—in practice *amounts
to* the same thing as ethical liberalism. In terms of the psychic economies
of real citizens' lives, the effects of meeting the "purely political" requirements of the one turn out over time to be indistinguishable from the comprehensive ethical requirements set out by the other. Liberalism has the
same transformative and homogenizing implications as ever before. It just
now brings about those changes in an indirect and long-term way. To some,

political liberalism may even seem to be a kind of fake or fraud: ethical liberalism in stealth mode.

The two directions of criticism I just mentioned—the justification-directed one and the one about sociological effects—are not wholly distinct. One part of the sociological challenge I have in mind can be addressed only by developing more detailed arguments about threshold problems of stability (arguments that are central to the justificatory project as political liberals currently understand it). But there are dimensions of this latter challenge that persist even if, on its own terms, the form of justification sought by political liberals *succeeds*.

These worries about political liberalism's sociological effects are more elusive than the purely justification-directed ones I described a moment ago. They are elusive because they do not emerge directly from the conceptual domain within which analytical philosophers traditionally confine themselves. These worries emerge from the interstices of theory and practice. For this reason, the challenge based on them persists even after the formal, conceptual conditions for the legitimate use of state force have been met. Let us consider this challenge.

Neutrality of Effect

I said earlier that neutrality plays an important part in any liberal conception of justice. One sense of neutrality to which political liberals do see their account of legitimacy committed is neutrality of aim: the liberal state should not to do anything *intended* to favor or promote any particular comprehensive doctrine rather than any other. But there is another dimension of neutrality, neutrality of effect, that political liberals reject as a constraint on their view: the state is not to do anything that makes it *more likely* that individuals accept any particular conception rather than any other. Rawls is adamant about this:

> It is surely impossible for the basic structure of a just constitutional regime not to have important effects and influences as to which comprehensive doctrines endure and gain adherents over time, and it is futile to try to counteract these effects and influences, or even to ascertain for political purposes how deep and pervasive they are. We must accept the facts of commonsense political sociology. . . . Neutrality of effect or influence political liberalism abandons as impracticable.[17]

Political liberals are right to reject neutrality of effect as impracticable. Indeed, it would be difficult to imagine *any* set of norms that succeeded in binding people together into a polity that could be neutral in this sense. Political arrangements intimately affect people's life prospects and thus shape their ethical orientations. These effects typically extend well beyond the formal requirements of citizens' allegiance to the political institutions of their society, influencing the wider culture of the society as a whole.

Let us call the wide social culture generated by any regime's public norms the *ethical background culture* of that regime. An ethical background culture provides a kind of map of meaning to citizens of each regime type. This map influences the personal values, the basic ways of world perception, of the people making their lives there. To abandon neutrality of effect or influence is to affirm that even political liberal regimes unavoidably generate a distinctive ethical background culture. Political norms, even gently and indirectly, cannot help but shape the character of people in their own image. Political institutions have a wider educative function. Society is itself a kind of schoolhouse. This general principle—that every political regime shapes the world outlook of its citizenry—has often been emphasized by historians.

Consider, for example, Gordon Wood's thesis about the radicalism of the American Revolution. According to Wood, the radicalism of the Revolution was not found in the signal it sent about the demise of empire, or in the fact of political secession, or even in the establishment of a new political type. Rather, what was truly radical was the tremendous transformation in *social relations*—the way the Revolution encouraged ordinary people in America think of themselves, and of one another, across the whole of their lives.

Being subject to a king is a political status but it also involves a thick set of social, cultural, and psychological implications. In pre–Revolutionary America, the political order encouraged people to think of themselves as connected vertically to one another. Throughout all aspects of their daily lives, people tended to be more conscious of those immediately above and below them than of those alongside them. Rather than locating themselves in groups, "most people could locate themselves only in superiority or in subordination to someone else."[18] Under the English monarchical system, people did not have class positions or even occupations so much as they had relationships. "Individuals were simultaneously free and subservient, independent and dependent, superior and inferior—depending on the person with whom they were dealing." "Personal relationships of dependence, usually taking the form of those between patrons and clients, constituted the ligaments that held this society together and made it work."[19]

A monarchical society admits no strong separation between subjects' public and nonpublic identities. Indeed, for the British subjects, that psychological distinction would be difficult even to comprehend. This fusing of public and nonpublic identities was basic to the ethical background culture associated with the pre-Revolutionary monarchy in America. But Wood's account goes on to show that even political orders that *do* separate public and private realms likewise have sweeping effects on people's day-to-day moral outlooks. Indeed, in the American case, it was the very act of making that separation that produced these wider effects.

As Wood says of the revolutionaries, "In destroying monarchy and establishing republics they were changing their society as well as their governments." In particular, their "social relationships—the way people were connected to one another—were changed, and decisively so." The idea that effected the broad social revolution in early America was the rights-based idea of equality on which the U.S. Constitution was established. This idea, once politically affirmed, transformed the social relations between American citizens from a vertical to a more horizontal model. Wood, following Tocqueville, describes this idea of equality as the most radical and powerful force let loose in the Revolution. "Its appeal was far more potent than any of the revolutionaries had realized. Once invoked, the idea of equality could not be stopped, and it tore through American society and culture with awesome power." Within just a few decades following the Revolution, the social effect of allegiance to those political principles became clear: "what remained of the traditional social hierarchy virtually collapsed, and in thousands of different ways connections that held people together for centuries were further strained and severed."[20]

But then what of political liberalism? Is there an ethical background culture characteristic of this political form? Neutrality of effect is indeed impracticable. Liberal institutions cannot help but affect the broad ethical orientations of the people living among them. "The institutions of the basic structure have deep and long-term social effects and in fundamental ways shape citizen's character and aims, the kinds of persons they are and aspire to be."[21] This is why it is so important that the basic structure be just. But it also explains why the attainment of justice in that structure tends to generate unintended effects beyond what justice formally requires. Even within a liberal society that seeks to maintain a strong separation between public and nonpublic matters, no group of people can completely insulate themselves from these wider unintended effects of political membership.

But what precisely are these effects? What is the nature of the ethical background culture associated with political liberalism? How does that culture affect the ethical orientations of people living there? What kind of schoolhouse is a political liberal society?

The Ethical Culture of Political Liberalism

I begin by examining a principle that marks out the exact frontier of the psychological commitments political liberalism formally requires. This is a principle, if you like, describing the ethical effects on the citizenry that political liberalism does intend. Unlike ethical liberalism, political liberalism does not seek to cultivate in citizens the distinctive personal virtues of autonomy or individuality. Instead, as Rawls tells us, political liberalism honors the claims of those who reject those traditional liberal values "*provided only that* they [1] acknowledge the principles of the political conception of justice and [2] appreciate its political ideals of person and society."[22] People are free to approach life's problems any way they like, provided only that they satisfy this conjunctive requirement. Call this two-pronged principle the *political liberal proviso*, or the proviso.[23]

To satisfy the first prong of the political liberal proviso, each person must "acknowledge the principles of the political conception of justice." Citizens must know about the conception of justice that regulates their society and so recognize the rights held by all citizens. To do this, all citizens must develop a facility with the principles of public reason. This is a form of reasoning people use to help them identify laws and policies that satisfy the substantive principles of justice. They use public reason to pick out the fundamental rights and duties they have regarding one another.

Of course, public reason is not meant to supplant the other forms of human reasoning that are likely to be found within a free society—the forms of reasoning found within churches, voluntary associations, friendships, and families, for examples. The public principles are meant to serve as guidelines for how the basic institutions in a society are to realize the values of liberty and equality. Still, public reason is an evaluative perspective that people are expected to be capable of entering at any time, not just on those periodic occasions when they are debating particular legislative proposals or constitutional questions or are deciding how to vote. Within the liberal social world, there is no context that is private in the sense that rights protections are not relevant there.[24] At the minimum, the demands of justice pervade everyday life because of the duties citizens have to respect the rights people have as political equals in all that they do. So the first prong of the proviso requires that citizens know the rights they have as citizens. They must have an appreciation of one another's public standing as they participate in even the most intimate realms of interpersonal life.[25]

The second prong of the political liberal proviso requires that each person "appreciate [that conception of justice's] political ideas of person and society." In particular, each must understand that these principles are justified by reference to political ideas rather than to any particular view about human moral nature. Notice that, unlike with the first prong, politicization here brings about a crucial change. Under many versions of ethical liberalism, people who affirm less reflective, "Romantic" comprehensive conceptions may find the traditional justificatory requirement difficult to meet. Such people find themselves subject to philosophical arguments by liberals aimed at convincing them of the falsity of their worldview and of the truth of the individualistic philosophy of mankind on which comprehensive liberalisms are (variously) grounded. By contrast, political liberals allow that people can affirm the principles of justice for political reasons found within their own comprehensive doctrines, whether individualistic or Romantic. Political liberals, as such, do not *intend* to promote the philosophy of individualism as a way of life, any more then they intend public reasoning to condition or supplant the various forms of nonpublic reason that most citizens make the center of their lives.

Political liberals hope—solely on the strength of this difference in justification—that their view will not exert a nonpolitical individualizing influence like that of comprehensive liberalism. As Larmore says, political liberalism "offers those opposed to full-scale individualism the best means for blocking a chief way that ideology [of corrosive individualism] has come to play such a large role in our culture, namely, by riding piggyback on the liberal principle of political neutrality."[26]

Is this hope well founded? Are the unintended effects of a commitment to liberal justice ones about which political liberals, as such, have no need to worry? Liberals have increasingly recognized that liberal institutions unavoidably influence the ethical worldviews of all reasonable citizens. What's more, most liberals now acknowledge that these unintended effects are likely to form a pattern: a distinctively liberal curriculum.

William Galston, for example, describes the ethical culture that is inadvertently associated with liberal politics—political and comprehensive alike—as being like a current in a river.[27] Some strong vessels can overcome the reflective, individualizing effects of the liberal background culture. But that current nonetheless exerts an influence on the course of life taken by each and every citizen.[28] Galston describes a basic fact of liberal sociology: "The greatest threat to children in modern liberal societies is not that they will believe in something too deeply, but that they will believe in nothing very deeply at all." Thus, "liberalism is not equally hospitable to all ways of life or to all subcommunities. Ways of life that require self-restraint, hierarchy, or cultural integrity are likely to find themselves on the defensive, threatened with the loss of both cohesion and authority."[29]

Stephen Macedo also has shown a keen appreciation of the social consequences of liberal politics. "Even a suitably circumscribed political liberalism is not really all that circumscribed: in various ways it will promote a way of life as a whole."[30] The skills of detachment and critical reflection that are required of liberal citizens in their public lives will naturally tend to spill over into other spheres of life. Liberal principles cannot just "stay on the surface" of people's lives. Citizens who do not affirm individualism or autonomy as personal values will be forced to divide their lives in a way that is psychologically demanding. Macedo calls this "a system of unequal psychological taxation," a system that is "sufficient to drive out certain patterns of deeply held belief and practice, not all at once but over the course of generations."[31]

Liberal education theorists have been particularly skeptical of the claim that the move to a political liberal form of justification makes any real psychological difference. Amy Gutmann, for example, argues that the civic educational requirements of the most plausible versions of political and of comprehensive liberalism, even if logically distinct, are in practice convergent: "most (if not all) of the same skills that are necessary and sufficient for educating children for citizenship in a liberal democracy are those that are necessary and sufficient for educating children to deliberate about their way of life, more generally (and less politically) speaking."[32] According to Eamonn Callan, "The political virtues that implement the fair terms of cooperation impose educational requirements that bring autonomy through the backdoor of political liberalism."[33] In the realm of education, the actual effects on children of their meeting the "merely political" requirements of political liberalism, though unintended, are said to be indistinguishable from the demands made on them via the supposedly abandoned ethical liberal view.

We must beware some complications here. I defined a political regime's ethical background culture as the collection of informal social effects characteristically generated by that regime's political values. So characterizing a background culture is in part an empirical matter, sandy ground on which to erect any theoretical structure. Two empirical soft spots are especially worth marking.

First, to gain a precise understanding of the ethical background culture of political liberalism, influences on people's general moral outlook that are said to be generated by the political regime would need to be distinguished from changes brought about by other, causally independent social forces—such as advances in science and technology or broad revolutions in religious belief. Galston would argue that the rise of critical individualism he sees in contemporary liberal societies is not only a result of modernization, but is also traceable directly to liberal political forms. But the exact boundary is difficult to mark.

Second, to gain a precise understanding of the ethical background culture of political liberalism, the broad *unintended* effects of that regime's political forms would need to be distinguished from the transformations in people's worldviews that are strictly *required* by that regime's political forms.[34] Some of the transformations Macedo describes, for example, seem to be formal requirements of a society's moving from injustice to greater justice, while other changes he describes seem to be further, unintended transformations in people's outlooks. That crucial line is also difficult to mark precisely. Both these ambiguities about political liberalism's ethical background culture take us to the interstices of theory and practice, of conceptual and empirical modes of inquiry. On that mixed terrain, imprecisions such as these are ineliminable.

Still, the work of these theorists is enough to raise a new and pressing set of questions. Is political liberalism really as successful as it hopes in avoiding the imposition of a single ethical doctrine on all of society? If liberals cannot prevent the spillover of potentially homogenizing effects of liberal doctrine and practice from public to nonpublic spheres, how accommodating of ethical diversity can a political liberal regime actually be? Can a society whose coercive institutions are founded on a political conception of justice actually be receptive of those citizens with whose views it is logically compatible? To what degree can a political liberal society be *a home* to the people it was formally designed to include?

The most basic motivational commitment of liberals is to respond to concerns that their citizens have. Liberal theorists, in everything they write, can be thought of as providing answers to questions that might reasonably be asked by would-be citizens. In response to their citizens' questions, liberal theorists owe arguments that the citizens themselves can accept. They must answer not in a way that pretends that citizens are all and only logicians. Rather, they must answer in a way that takes citizens as they can reasonably be expected to be.

That in mind, I wish now to begin sharpening these questions about spillovers. I wish to consider how various citizens in a diverse society might respond to the admissions about unintended spillovers that liberals themselves have made. Rather than attempting to dig out a foundation of my own in this sandy, empirical terrain, I shall simply imagine would-be citizens as responding to what liberals have themselves said about the wider, unintended effects of liberal political forms. In keeping with good liberal practice, we will take our instructions from these would-be liberal citizens. Since we are describing a social world in which they are to live, we will allow them to tell us what course of theory construction political liberals are now bound to pursue.

Chapter Two

THE BOUNDARIES OF POLITICAL THEORY

Alphabet People

Let's say that we are setting out to justify the exercise of political coercion within a society with a history of free institutions. As a simplifying device, think of this society as populated by four main groups of adult citizens. I shall assign alphabetical labels to these groups not so much to denote rigidly separate categories but rather as broad markers lying along a kind of continuum. At one end are a range of views held by what I shall call the A-people. The A-people, let's imagine, affirm the values of autonomy and individuality as governing most if not every aspect of their lives. People in this category tend to live highly mobile, experimental, fallibilist, reflective, and self-aware lives. The A-people build the morality of their everyday lives from the ground up, as it were, seeing it as essential that each person decide completely for himself about all the moral dimensions of his life. If any of them chooses (or refuses) to eat red meat, for example, he will stand ready to explain his choice in a detailed manner. When asked at the grocery checkout line to choose "paper or plastic," his reply will be principled and firm. When married, each A-person may assiduously refer to the other as "my spouse" or, better, "my marriage partner." At one pole of this broad category we might find extreme individualists, such as the one-dimensional egoists championed by Ayn Rand or—less exultantly—isolated sufferers of atomistic anomie. But the center of the A-person category, I suppose, could be thought of as embodying the ideal from popular culture of the Eastern intellectual establishment or of a particularly devout secular humanism. The A-people are the kind of people who celebrate the birthdays of John Stuart Mill, Betty Friedan, and Immanuel Kant—not those of Edmund Burke, Jimmy Swaggart, or the Pope.[1]

At the other end of the continuum in this imaginary society are a range of views held by what I shall call the D-people. If we think of the A-people (in their various ways) as affirming liberalism itself as an ethical worldview, the D-people, by contrast, affirm (various) comprehensive doctrines that conflict with even the general values on which political liberalism is founded. This category may include racists or sexists of such a virulent kind that they reject the idea that people should be treated as free and equal even for political purposes. At the extreme, some D-people may advocate a return to the racist principles of the Confederate South or advocate a system of suffrage based oppressively on gender, religion, or class. More typical of this category, though, are religious believers who express their piety by seeking to impose their views on other citizens. For example, people who demand that Creationism be placed at the center of all biology classes in public schools are D-people.[2] So are people who petition for the outlawing of all divorce because they think it sinful. Other D-people express their piety by seeking selectively to withdraw from basic terms of the liberal settlement, for example, by withdrawing their children from the core civics lessons on which social unity depends.

In affirming their (various) antiliberal principles for political purposes, the D-people typically also affirm those same ethical norms as governing their nonpublic lives. So they may affirm various forms of social inegalitarianism in their personal relationships as well—whether religious hierarchism, patriarchism within their families, or even racism against other citizens. But what is distinctive about the D-people for our purposes is that they are willing to trade off other citizens' political autonomy to further other aims they themselves have (e.g., salvation, religious purity, or love of Jesus). In their various ways, D-people deny the political primacy of justice. They allow themselves to be led by imperatives internal to their own doctrines even when those doctrines are in direct conflict with the dictates of public reason.[3]

Next to the D-people on our continuum, but importantly distinct from them, are the C-people. Like the D-people, the C-people may affirm some general ethical doctrine that is based on religious authority—for example, the Church or the Bible. The C-people may affirm traditionalist doctrines that impose social roles on persons or generate moral conclusions regarding them, which turn on people's gender, religious heritage, or sexual orientation. Unlike the D-people, however, the C-people do not demand that those elements of their worldview be enforced coercively against citizens who do not accept the "truth" as they see it. Nor do they seek selectively to deny the primacy of political values whenever those values do not mirror the nonpublic view they affirm.

For example, if C-people affirm a normative system of social roles based on gender, they do so only concerning the nonpublic aspects of their lives, the internal life of their families as well as more voluntary organizations such as clubs and churches.[4] Examples from the American context might include the Amish or the people of Kiryas Joel—though on some issues such groups lie dangerously close to the D-people border of this category. The center of this category, I suppose, is best exemplified by many Fundamentalist Christian groups or by mainstream practicing Catholics in America today.

Regarding the contemporary Catholics, their Catholicity allows them to affirm not only the liberal liberties required by the doctrine of free faith, but also the other core political ideas of the person and society on which political liberalism is founded—in particular, the principle of reciprocity in some form.[5] These citizens, as good Catholics, do not take it upon themselves to reason afresh about all basic moral questions. On many issues they take their ultimate moral guidance as received doctrine from the Church.[6] For example, they accept, indeed insist, that the priesthood must be restricted to males. As Catholics living in a society with diverse others, however, they also affirm as a political matter that economic roles and public offices in their society should be open to men and women without distinction.[7] If C-people affirm a traditional gender hierarchy within their families, it is not that they have reflected on the matter and decided that it is appropriate to oppress women. Rather, as citizens of faith (say Protestant Fundamentalist or traditional Catholic), they accept the religious dictum (whether from the Bible or from the Church fathers) that the secular language of feminism does not speak to them in that sphere.

Larmore's "reasonable Romantics" and Rawls's "citizens of faith" are C-people.[8] The C-people are precisely those kinds of citizens whose worldview liberals have long seen themselves as bound to criticize, but who political liberals mean to include and on whose nonpublic moral views political liberals, as such, insist they "take no view."

Finally, between the A-people and the C-people lie what I take to be the great sweep of citizens: the B-people. Like the A-people and the C-people, the B-people affirm the liberal idea that people should be treated as free and equal for political purposes. The B-people do not affirm doctrines in their nonpublic lives that are fully general or comprehensive. Their world outlook is not organized around some single expansive doctrine such Millian individualism or Roman Catholicism.[9] In their nonpublic lives the B-people muddle along, as it were, with far less certainty or homogeneity in terms of the normative sources they rely upon in making the various decisions that give the life of each its distinctive ethical shape. In some areas of their nonpublic lives, B-people rely on norms of decision making that are highly reflective, fallibilist, and individualistic (in this, like typical A-people). In other morally foundational areas, they are guided by norms to which they feel deeply committed without having reflected on them in any thoroughgoing way (more like the C-people). In terms of the self-understandings and interpersonal relationships that make up the cores of their lives—their deepest friendships, their careers, their marriages, their most significant spiritual and social affiliations—B-people often experience a complex and unsettled mixture of these two different ways of reasoning. Each B-person lives his nonpublic life through a familiar tension: a tension between attitudes of commitment and of detachment, of reflection and of acquiescence, of certainty and of doubt.

Two Kinds of Cultural Defeaters

Can political coercion on behalf of a conception of justice constructed from widely shared political ideas be legitimately exercised in a society that is diverse in this way? Political liberals emphasize that this depends upon whether these citizens can find sufficient moral reasons within their own comprehensive doctrines to enable them to support the candidate conception in a lasting way.[10] What political liberals emphasize less, though, is that this test for "full individual justification" requires not only that people consider how well their own view of the good life might support their commitment to liberal justice. It also involves people thinking carefully about how their own commitment to liberal justice, if once they give it, may tend over time to affect their commitment to whatever view of the good they hold dear. Each must ask, If I do affirm this candidate conception (and thus affirm for myself the requirements of the political liberal proviso), how might that come to affect my own nonpublic life, that is, the particular ways of reasoning and patterns of interpersonal understanding that make up the core of my life?

In light of what liberals have written so far about the ethical background culture of political liberalism, let's consider how our alphabet people might respond to this question. How might they feel about the broad social curriculum that liberal political forms stand poised to deliver?

For the members of the groups on the extremes of our continuum, their responses seem straightforward enough. The A-people affirm liberalism itself as a worldview, so endorsing a liberal outlook on basic political matters comes naturally to them. For the most part the reflective, rights-aware pattern of self-understanding implied by their satisfying the liberal proviso meshes smoothly with the patterns of self-understanding and the norms of living-together that the A-people affirm in their nonpublic lives.[11] The A-people greatly value impartiality and reflective detachment as mainstays of their own (nonpublic) well-being. The norms of self-understanding (and the processes of critical examination) required by their liberal political understandings may thus sharpen or even help buttress the dispositions and habits of thought affirmed by their "liberal" world-outlook. Of course, they must understand that any such sharpening or buttressing is not *intended* by political liberalism, a doctrine that officially takes no view as to the eudaimonistic worth of any one reasonable doctrine compared to any other. But A-people considering the unintended effects of the proviso on their doctrine are free to consider these possibilities. Political liberals have no reason to expect much complaint when they do so.

For the D-people, the effect of yielding to the political liberal proviso will be different indeed. The proviso requires that the D-people affirm ideas—the political equality of citizens, for example—that are in direct conflict with their personal views. Political liberals see political force as justified by reference to widely shared political values—in particular, to the principle that political power can be exercised against people only on the basis of reasons that those subject to that power can themselves accept. Political liberals are not bound to accommodate those who—like the D-people—would see even political values such as that denied or overthrown.

The D-people might object to this. They might say that if their personal views conflict with the norms of political liberalism, that shows that politi-cal liberalism is itself a personal view. As but one view of value among others, political liberalism can have no special place. No one worldview can be used to justify intolerance toward any other competing worldview, including that of the D-people.

But, as I said earlier, political liberalism is not a worldview. It is a view about *political* norms. This is why political liberals, as such, need not mor-ally condemn the worldviews of all D-people in all social circumstances.[12] It is the D-people's rejection of the political norms of mutuality and reciprocity, norms widely accepted by their fellow citizens despite their many diverse viewpoints, that makes the D-people's views intolerable. It is this "unreasonableness" that legitimates the use of coercion against the D-people—that is, against their attempts to impose their own, person-disrespecting values upon others. Liberals will not allow D-people to en-force a sacramental conception of marriage on others, to prevent the teach-ing of evolution in the public schools, or to exempt their children from basic civics lessons. Such policies will have negative effects on the D-peo-ple. These measures will hinder the D-people's attempt to advance their outlook with respect to other citizens and even to transmit their moral outlook from one generation to the next within their own families. These effects are not unintended, and political liberals, as such, have no reason to regret them.[13]

What about the C-people? The C-people affirm views of the good life that may have much the same nonpublic content as those held by the D-people. Thus the C-people affirm traditionalist doctrines, including doc-trines that may see people's place in the social world as importantly deter-mined by religious authority—the Bible or Koran, for example. Yet, unlike the D-people, the C-people affirm their doctrines in a way that is reason-able from a political perspective. Whatever their beliefs about the proper arrangements between people in nonpublic life, the C-people affirm the idea that all people should be treated as free and equal for political pur-poses. C-people can affirm the political liberal proviso without contradict-ing the self-understandings generated by their own worldview.

For example, there is no logical contradiction if traditional Catholics support a male-only priesthood while simultaneously affirming strong gen-der equality for political purposes. Indeed, to endorse those latter political understandings in the way required by political liberalism, the Catholics must rely on other ideas from their own religion to come to an all-things-considered view that it is *morally* wrong for them, or anyone else, to impose their own religion's norms concerning gender on other citizens.[14] They do this while affirming their own religion's doctrine regarding gender-based differential roles in nonpublic settings. Since the two views about gender relations are affirmed within that equilibrium as operating in different spheres—one public, the other nonpublic—there is no logical contradiction in a person's affirming them both at once.

Nonetheless, the C-people are a particularly significant case for us. The views of people such as the C-people, while not forbidden, may well be embattled by the ethical background culture of even a political conception of liberalism. This erosion threatens not because the moral beliefs of the C-people, or their attendant view about the source of reasons, are contradicted by the political norms of public reason. Rather, erosion threatens simply because the ways of world-perception associated with one fit ill with the forms of world-perception needed to sustain the other.

defeaters

There is an analogy in logic. Logicians sometimes distinguish two ways in which accepting new beliefs, in this context called "defeaters," can work to undermine previously held beliefs. New beliefs may operate as rebutting defeaters or as undercutting defeaters. A *rebutting defeater* presents itself as a logically incompatible challenger to the given statement, such that one logically cannot affirm both statements simultaneously. For example, imagine a child raised to believe in the Bible as the literally true word of God. If that child is taught in school that all religion is superstitious hokum, including religions based on the Bible, that lesson would present itself as a rebutting defeater of her original belief about the Bible.

An *undercutting defeater*, by contrast, is logically compatible with the held belief but works to undermine its justificatory base nonetheless. If the same child went to school and was taught instead merely that the fossil record confirms the main lines of evolutionary theory, that lesson might work as an undercutting defeater of her original belief. She could still accept the Bible as the true word of God, but she must now do so as a member of a world that accepts the broad facts of evolution. This new background inevitably transforms, and may well threaten, her original belief in the Bible as true.

The D-people, correctly, will view political liberalism as a rebutting defeater of their worldview. But the rights-based pattern of citizen self-understanding derived from political liberalism may work as an *undercutting* defeater of the self-understandings of the C-people's view, even if it is not a rebutting one. C-people may still affirm their worldview through the Romantic or faith-based way typical of their group. But they must do so now as members of a social world that accepts the political liberal proviso.

The cultural background generated by the proviso inevitably transforms, and may well threaten, their commitment to the view they cherish.

Why might C-people worry that the psychological requirements of even political liberalism might work over time to undermine the politically reasonable worldview they affirm? After all, liberal principles of justice operate to protect people with such views—for example, by setting out rights to religious liberty.[15] Still, there are good grounds for such a concern. For C-people to "acknowledge the principles of the political conception of justice" (the first part of political liberal proviso), they must become aware that they are as individuals empowered, with the full backing of the state's coercive machinery, to act in ways that are in substantive tension with their own group's internal norms. Liberalism, political or ethical, sets out many individual rights (notably, regarding freedoms of speech, association, and exit). These rights coercively sanction forms of behavior that, if embarked upon by their members, might directly undermine the viability of traditionalist groups.

The C-people are politically reasonable, so they do not object to such rights being recognized. Indeed, the C-people affirm such rights on precisely the grounds provided in the second part of the political liberal proviso: they affirm them as C-people, say Catholics, seeking to obtain the moral benefits of social cooperation with diverse others. Yet Catholics may well be concerned, as Catholics, for the way the awareness of those rights will affect the eudaimonistic fabric of their lives over time.

In particular, C-people may worry that the formal requirements of rights-awareness may encourage individualistic, claim-based patterns of thought even in aspects of people's lives where that way of thinking is *not* politically required. Rights protect interests people have. But, as a practical matter, the method by which one comes to pick out what rights one has may influence (or even *become*) the method by which one decides what interests one actually has. The mind-set of liberal public reasoning can come to influence the way people engage in various forms of nonpublic reason. As citizens take their public lessons home with them, those lessons may be subtly twisted as they pass through the door. Insofar as people begin to consider their interests from a more detached, impersonal perspective, they may begin to see their interests differently from the way they would if they were considering them from the embedded, tradition-emphasizing perspective of their group. This informal shift in the ways people identify their interests may in turn affect the decisions individuals make with their formal claims of right, further transforming the group.

None of this is intended by the political liberal account of justice, and certainly these lessons in "liberal" world-perception are not *required* by that political doctrine. Nor is the tendency of public reason to influence or colonize nonpublic reason in this way even shown to be a sociological necessity. There are simply concerns about the ethical culture of liberalism that some citizens might reasonably be expected to express.

What have the founders of political liberalism said about this concern, a concern that citizens of faith and reasonable Romantics might in particular be expected to voice? Beyond a cursory acknowledgment that neutrality of effect is impracticable, the founders of political liberalism have said practically nothing in response to this worry. Perhaps this is because political liberals are simply skeptical of the empirical claim that individualistic erosion tends to occur in societies founded on individual rights. Or perhaps they are convinced—in advance of the fact—by Larmore's idea that no such erosion need occur in a society where liberal rights were justified in a political way rather than in some ethical one.[16] Still, political liberals have not been completely silent on this issue. What little they have said is not encouraging.

Rawls mentions two groups he thinks will lose out in a political liberal society. First, unsurprisingly, are people who affirm doctrines in direct conflict with the principles of justice—for example, people affirming rights-violating views like those of the antebellum South. In our terms, these are D-people. But Rawls then describes a second sort of group that he thinks will also tend to lose out under well-functioning political liberal institutions. These are groups that, while "admissible" within the political liberal settlement, will tend not to gain adherents "under the political and social conditions of a just constitutional regime." The example he gives is of certain religious groups that could survive only by controlling the state machinery and practicing effective intolerance.[17]

Rawls does not say what makes these latter groups admissible. Presumably, they are admissible because—unlike the first sort of group—they are committed to honoring the principles of liberal justice in their dealings with their fellow citizens. Their own religious views include ideas that allow them to recognize their fellow citizens as free and equal for political purposes. They freely eschew even the coercive political measures on which Rawls says the survival of their religious view depends. These religious people might well balk at joining into a liberal settlement justified by reference to some Millian or Kantian view of moral personality, a view that might conflict with their own very different beliefs about value. But these "admissible" citizens of faith presumably have been attracted to a political liberal society in just the way Rawls and the other political liberals hope. In view of political liberalism's more accommodating form of justification, we are asked to imagine, they freely sign on. In our terms, they are C-people. About their predicted demise within the larger ethical schoolhouse of political liberalism, Rawls says merely that some ways of life that lose out may be viable under other social conditions, may be "worthy" in themselves, and that their passing away may even be "regretted."[18]

But why does Rawls think that the group of admissible citizens of faith he describes would freely sign on to political liberalism—especially in light of Rawls's own prediction that liberal institutions will generate effects that lead to the loss of the religious view they hold dear? Is it because these C-people recognize a just political community as a great good? No doubt they do. But religious people also typically regard the preservation of their religious perspective, the long-term transmission of their faith from one generation of believers to the next, as among the highest and most sacred of their personal commitments. Even while affirming the doctrine of free faith, C-people are typically committed as believers to securing conditions conducive to their children and grandchildren finding, and staying with, the path of religious truth. No doubt, liberal institutions affirm rights that formally keep that particular path open to their descendants. But Rawls's own prediction is that the liberal social world is nonetheless not conducive to their keeping with it.[19]

It is crucial to the political liberal project that admissible citizens of faith can be expected freely to sign on. After all, it was the alleged inability of traditional forms of liberalism to win the free assent of citizens such as these that created the crisis in legitimacy from which political liberalism sprang. But on what grounds could we expect these citizens freely to set aside their sacred commitment to their descendants out of concern for the goodness of a just political community?

There is one obvious way to ground that expectation. We might simply say that these citizens' commitment to the doctrine of free faith effectively commits them also to a conception of ethical autonomy such as liberals have traditionally affirmed. In the case of any formally admissible citizen of faith, there is simply no space between the one (affirming the core principles of their religion) and the other (affirming an ethical liberal life view). Whatever the cultural climate or prevalent form of reasoning by which their children and grandchildren come to choose to leave the path of truth, such people have no complaint as believers so long as their children and grandchildren are choosing freely. Deep down, we might say, all C-people affirm a comprehensive liberal life view after all.

However, political liberals have already loudly claimed to have abandoned all such assumptions about the views of the citizens they mean to bring in. The existence of a gap between political autonomy and full-blown ethical autonomy is basic to the political liberal view. If that gap dissolves, political liberalism dissolves with it. So then what grounds can political liberals give for these formally admissible but sociologically doomed citizens of faith to sign on?

Full individual justification, if it is really to be "full," must require that people do more than merely check whether their own comprehensive doctrine can support or is contradicted by political liberalism (the threshold test Rawls and Larmore emphasize). If people's affirmation of liberal principles is truly to be free and thus lasting, they must be modeled as being able to satisfy themselves regarding more nuanced questions—including questions about liberalism's unintended effects and about any distinctive normative tools they might find within liberal societies to help them counteract or absorb those threatened effects. To know whether groups such as the C-people might reasonably be expected to sign on to political liberalism, we need a more *social* account of liberalism. Such an account, if we could find it, would make clear the distinctive ways in which the political norms required by liberalism interface with the various forms of nonpublic reasoning the devotees of which liberals hope will sign on. This would be an account, that is, of liberal *nonpublic* reason.

The development of a detailed social account of interface is a condition of showing the possibility of people holding diverse but politically reasonable views jointly affirming justice in a way that is free. An account of liberal nonpublic reason is a formal requirement of the principle of legitimacy. But there is a further, conceptually separate reason for liberals to venture into these questions of human interpersonal life beyond the domain of public reason. To see it, we must consider our final and ultimately most important case, that of the B-people.

FREE EROSION

The B-people, recall, represent what I take to be the mainstream citizenry of a liberal state characterized by reasonable value pluralism. The typical B-person is neither a straightforward traditionalist nor a pure Millian self-creator. He is a complex and uneven mix of these two extremes. Unlike an A-person, the B-person's world-outlook includes important traditionalist elements—psychological nooks and crannies, some quite central to his character, from which reasons for action emerge potently for him. These secure, authoritarian areas may provide important anchors to his identity, anchors that give him confidence in using the other modes of world-perception that also characterize his view. Unlike a C-person, the B-person is also well versed in the habits of autonomous value formation. It is central to his identity that he wields this "spotlight of reason" with skill and boldness in some ethically foundational areas of his life, seeing himself as fallibly reflective there, and reveling in that.

What concerns might the B-people have about the ethical background culture associated with liberal politics? Unlike the A-person, the B-person will not find the detached, claim-based ways of thinking associated with public reason wholly congenial to the full set of his nonpublic self-understandings, if he were to adopt such manners of thinking there. The B-person values his anchors and would not wish to be cut off from them. For him, being cut adrift like that might make his autonomy seem pointless.[20] Unlike the A-person, the B-person will not likely find that the whole structure of his worldview is buttressed (albeit unintentionally) by the detached, rights-based manner of public thinking required by the proviso.

On the other hand, compared to the C-person, the B-person will be unlikely to find nearly as much tension between his own nonpublic worldview and the sorts of claims and patterns of personal action that become available with the affirmation of liberal justice. The mixed comprehensive doctrine typical of B-people allows them to "acknowledge the principles of the political conception of society" without concern that the bare laying out of the rights this implies will sanction actions that directly damage the eudaimonistic fabric of their lives.

But the B-people may share a different concern with the C-people. This is the concern that, quite unintentionally, the formal requirements of rights-awareness in political matters may tend to encourage autonomous, claim-based ways of thinking (and of interest identification) even in areas of life where that way of evaluating the social possibilities is not politically required. We have seen that the C-people might reasonably worry about facing eudaimonistically unequal pressure from satisfying the political liberal proviso compared to that faced by the A-people. So too within each B-person, the traditionalist C-person-like elements of his worldview may come under a pressure that the reflective A-person-like aspects of his worldview do not. One primary vehicle transporting this worry is the liberal emphasis on rights as foundational arbiters of social disagreement.

There is a long and recurrent tradition of criticizing liberal regimes for generating a culture of individualism, a culture that is corrosive to many valuable forms of interpersonal life. This worry is about the effects of liberal values on the lives of people in the mainstream, not just on those at the cultural margins. A culture of individualism is sometimes traced to the commercial market forces associated with liberalism, but a culture of individualism is often said to be encouraged by the moral ideals of liberalism itself. Historically, this objection is typically presented as an external objection, as a broad moral or social critique of liberalism as a whole. Karl Marx, in his early writings, captured this objection well: "None of the so-called rights of man . . . go beyond egoistic man, beyond man as member of civil society, that is, an individual withdrawn into himself, into the confines of his private interests and private caprice, and separated from the community."[21] That sort of objection challenges the liberal conception of justice itself. The technical, justification-directed writings of Rawls and the other political liberal pioneers could be read as providing a powerful reply.

But we are also familiar with objections to liberal individualism being raised in a more internal way. Michael Sandel, for example, hit a resonant chord when he worried about the way a quasi-legal discourse has come to define the terms of American interpersonal life. "Though most at home in constitutional law, the main motifs of contemporary liberalism—rights as trumps, the neutral state, and the unencumbered self—figure with increasing prominence in our moral and political culture."[22] Sandel apparently finds this justice-based way of thinking worrying both as liberalism *requires* that it be used, as a matter of settling value conflict in public matters, and also as liberalism inadvertently *encourages* it to be used, in the nonpublic areas of citizens' lives.

The first strand of that objection is, again, a matter of justice. It is thus a matter that contemporary liberals do see their arguments as bound to address. But the second strand, concerning the allegedly destructive pattern of rights-awareness in nonpublic realms, is not conceptually traceable to any formal requirement of any liberal model, whether comprehensive or political. Rather, the concern here is with a particular pattern of world-perception and interest identification that is said to be inadvertently encouraged by those formal requirements. Rights-based ways of thinking in pubic matters—as required of citizens by the first part of the proviso, for example——are said to spill over into other nonpublic aspects of people's lives, where those ways of thinking are not required, such as the realms of social reason or domestic reason.

Expressed this way, the worry of the B-people tracks one of the main critical currents in contemporary American society: a worry about the cultural spread of "rights talk." Law professors have been especially sensitive to this concern, which Mary Ann Glendon states powerfully: "Legal discourse has become not only the single most important tributary to political discourse, but has crept into the languages that Americans employ around the kitchen table, in the neighborhood, and in their diverse communities of memory and mutual aid." According to Glendon, rights talk increasingly "lodges in the collective memory, permeates popular discourse, and enters into American habits of mind."[23]

Macedo has done as much as anyone to call our attention to the effects of liberal public values on mainstream American life. In colorful, sometimes explosive language, Macedo emphasizes the regime character of liberal society. "Liberal politics and liberal autonomy are complementary: both converge on an ideal of character that is actively reflective, self-critical, tolerant, reason-giving and reason-demanding, open to change, and respectful of the autonomy of others." Though gently and indirectly, liberalism fosters distinctive forms of personality, culture, and even religious belief: liberal public values "cannot help but shape people's lives broadly, deeply and relentlessly over time." The liberal social world as a whole is tilted in a certain direction, one that increasingly supports the basic principles of justice and liberal democratic civic virtues. Macedo celebrates this as "the radically transformative dimension of liberal constitutionalism." Liberalism, we are told, involves "a certain ordering of the soul." Concerning those who would find their way of life embattled with such a society, Macedo says, "No one has a right to a level playing field."[24]

These are not merely good pyrotechnics. Macedo is entirely right to think liberalism must confront the cultural consequences of its political forms. However, I think the light from the fireworks may obscure an ambiguity that lies at the base of Macedo's view, and perhaps of political liberalism as well. It is worth our while to pause and consider that ambiguity with care.

What kinds of social transformations, exactly, is Macedo inviting us to celebrate? Sometimes, Macedo seems to be endorsing solely the historical role of liberal institutions in the gradual transformation of unreasonable views into reasonable ones. Racists, sexists, religious zealots must over time modify or abandon their views within the liberal social world. For example, Macedo describes a series of papal encyclicals from the early 1800s that called upon the faithful to embrace doctrines in direct contradiction to liberal principles.[25] Macedo explains how liberal institutions, especially the system of common schooling, gradually made Catholicism more liberal, not just in America but in Rome as well.

If this is what Macedo means to be celebrating, he is on very solid ground. People asserting views that directly contradict liberal public values are clearly disadvantaged within the liberal social world.[26] Certainly those kinds of people—our D-people—could not assert a *right* to a level playing field. In the liberal context, that statement is true by tautology.

But if that is really what Macedo means to be celebrating, it is not clear how that squares with other things he says. In the most famous line from *Liberal Virtues*, Macedo proclaims: "Liberalism holds out the promise, or the threat, of making all the world like California."[27] No doubt very great transformations would be required for all groups holding politically unreasonable views to come to hold politically reasonable ones: there is a great distance between the encyclicals of the 1800s and the documents of Vatican II. Still, political liberals surely must hope that American society could become politically reasonable without its citizens all becoming like "Californians," or even anywhere close.

This brings us nearer to the ambiguity I mentioned before. After affirming his recent adoption of political liberalism, Macedo notes that he continues to affirm all his earlier claims about the regime character of liberal states, but would do so now modulo the changes required by an acceptance of political liberalism.[28] So perhaps that famous line about California would get deleted by the modulo. But then what else gets deleted? Perhaps liberal regimes shape people's lives "broadly, deeply and relentlessly over time"—*strictly for political purposes*? Perhaps liberalism now involves "a certain ordering of the soul"—*merely in public affairs*? But those qualifiers are like water: they take the fizzle from the fireworks. In doing so, they would deprive Macedo's work of its ability to take us to a problem at the very base of the political liberal project.

It seems clear that Macedo sometimes means to be venturing an evaluation of the *unintended* effects of liberal constitutionalism, and to be venturing such evaluations *as a political liberal*. Understood that way, what's being celebrated is not merely the gradual but intended transformation of unreasonable views into reasonable ones, but also the gradual but unintended transformation of views *within* the domain of the politically reasonable. So long as this pressure is exerted gently, through structures that encourage autonomous choices by individuals, Macedo affirms this process not just as it transforms hard-line theocrats of the 1800s, but as it affects the general citizenry in America today.

This position would mark a sharp divergence from the political liberal orthodoxy that claims simply to take no view on these unrequired and unintended social effects (beyond acknowledging the "impracticability" of preventing them). But if Macedo does mean to be celebrating transformations of this kind, it is unclear what grounds he has for doing so. There is one set of grounds—a set of grounds to which Macedo at times seems tempted—that has become deeply problematic with the emergence of the political liberal framework. This is the idea that any social transformations inadvertently encouraged by the norms and institutions of liberal public life should be applauded so long as, and precisely because, those transformations occur through the autonomous choices of individual citizens.

There was a time when liberals could have defended any social structure by showing that it arose through the exercise of moral autonomy and individual, self-conscious reflection.[29] But for anyone who truly accepts the politicization of justice, that time has passed away. Political liberals do continue to valorize liberty. Unlike ethical liberals, they can do so now only for political purposes. The great concern political liberals have for individual self-direction must be fully *and exhaustively* expressed in their political conception of justice. Political autonomy is not full-blown ethical autonomy. Political liberals, as such, are committed to guarding the difference. This is a consequence—ethical liberals may call it "the price"—of truly bypassing those old disputes about moral value.

If someone raises a question not about the grounds of coercion but about the *value* of the extrapolitical forms of life and world perception that seem to be the likely (though unintended) effects of people's affirming political liberal justice, it is no good trotting out the ethical value of autonomy or individualism again to defend those effects, whatever they may be. Political liberals, as such, are committed to recognizing that there are many reasonable people who are committed to political freedom and yet for whom ethical autonomy does not settle every issue and justify every social outcome.

Who might come forward with questions about the unintended side effects of liberal politics, and what might those questions be? We have already seen that the C-people might come forward, and that they might request a fuller sociological account of life on the interface of public and nonpublic values as a condition of their freely endorsing the political conception of justice. But the C-people are not the only group that might be expected to come forward; nor is that familiar sort of justice-directed question the only one political liberals should expect to hear. With politicization, political liberals accustomed themselves to recognizing as reasonable certain concerns of people that could not be captured in terms of people's alleged "desire to express their nature as autonomous." So too political liberals must now accustom themselves to recognizing that not all questions of relevance to their view are questions about basic justice or even about the formal grounds of justified coercion. Defenders of liberalism are bound to attempt to answer *whatever* questions about the liberal social world their citizens might reasonably be expected to ask. This is a metatheoretical consequence of the principle of legitimacy that contemporary liberals have yet to absorb.

It is not only the C-people whose view of moral personality political liberals must give up criticizing or wishing in any way to correct or "perfect." The B-people also, stuck as it were halfway toward realizing a moral ideal of autonomy like that which liberals have traditionally espoused, are also now to be left to live their lives in their own mixed and theoretically uneven way. So long as citizens endorse the proviso, they are politically autonomous. Regarding all the other aspects of their lives, a condition of mere "autarchy" must be now officially recognized as no worse (or better) than any condition of fuller moral autonomy.[30] In their various ways, the B-people too affirm an attitude toward life and social experience that was once considered defective by liberals. But, like the C-people, theirs is an approach to life on which political liberals must carefully take no view.

The B-people, no matter how firmly they are committed to political justice, may very well be concerned about the unintended social effects of liberal political norms. They might be concerned not about any pattern of erosion or loss in their worldview that might intentionally be forced on them as a part of the liberal settlement (the concern of the D-people). Rather, like the C-people, the B-people may be concerned about patterns of erosion of their worldview that may occur voluntarily, step by step, *by them* as the critical and rights-aware habits of public reason gradually are unleashed in the realms of social and domestic reason. Like the C-people, the B-people may worry about those unreflective interpersonal anchors that are currently so important to their worldview, and about the way each will gradually come to think of those anchors. Each may be concerned, as a B-person, about the direction of the social current he will find himself caught in as, through a process of autonomous reflection, he pulls those anchors up, one by one. Even while continuing to affirm liberal justice, these B-people may have real questions about what this new political liberal commitment to "taking no view" actually amounts to with respect to the mixed and idiosyncratic life view they affirm.

To be clear, when B-people express this kind of concern, a concern about what I shall call *free erosion*, they are not expressing any formal challenge to the legitimacy of the liberal conception with respect to fundamental political questions. We can say that the B-people "generally endorse [a liberal] conception of justice as giving the content of their political judgments on basic institutions." We can imagine they have successfully determined that this political conception of justice in fact does "not conflict too sharply with their comprehensive views"—even considering the long-term strains that may be generated by various possible unintended effects (the sticking point for the C-people, recall).[31] Still, the B-people might have an important question ask on behalf of the ordinary citizens of a liberal society. They might put it something like this:

> We accept the fundamental importance of justice for political purposes. Further, from the perspective of our own worldview, we affirm all the conditions of the political liberal proviso. But we remain concerned about *the degree to which* we will find this just society a welcoming one in which to live the kind of life we value. No one has shown us that interpersonal relations in liberal societies must always be excessively litigious, nor has anyone proven that the system of unequal psychological taxation that some liberals describe must necessarily lead us down the path of (to us) unattractive free erosion. But neither has anyone given us any reason to hope that a different way of life might be made available to us in a less embattled way within the structure of these same rights-based liberal norms. The more rigidly defenders of political liberalism insist that they "take no view" on such concerns once full individual justification has been achieved, the more we worry about the social adequacy of their view. After all, it is one thing to recognize that complete neutrality of effect is impracticable. But it is quite another to then act as though that admission excuses one from saying anything more about those effects and their consequences for the personal lives of the citizenry. We have yet-unanswered questions about the unintended social effects of liberal justice. For us those questions become more pressing, rather than less so, when we decide to affirm liberal institutions in an enduring, first-personal way. To whom should we address our worries about life within a political liberal society, if not to the theorists who claim to defend the political liberal view?

Liberal Theory and the Doctrine of Double Effect

No version of liberalism can be justified if its account of political coercion is illegitimate. But why think that minimally satisfying the liberal principle of legitimacy exhausts the grounds on which political liberalism might be elaborated and defended?

In the first place, even a legitimate political order can be less or more stable. The threat of spillovers may positively alienate certain groups of citizens, especially otherwise admissible groups on the society's cultural margins. The bare threat of spillover effects—absent any liberal account of how unavoidable spillovers might be counteracted and absorbed—may disaffect people who might otherwise have signed on (some of our C-people, for example). The fewer citizens that can be brought on freely, the larger the class of those labeled "politically unreasonable" and so the less stable the arrangement as a whole. Second, even firmly within the domain of the politically reasonable, the problem of unaddressed spillovers may weaken citizens' allegiance to the regime (as with our B-people, for example). This decreases the depth by which citizens can affirm the regime as their own, as a kind of home for themselves. The result again is instability.

In both kinds of case, the impossibility of achieving complete neutrality of effect sets a kind of floor as to how completely the concerns of citizens about spillovers can be answered. Some reasonable groups will always lose out, and this prospect may always dissuade some from freely entering. The system of cultural taxation will always be to some degree unequal, and this may unavoidably weaken the commitment of some others. Complete neutrality of effect is indeed impracticable.

But that admission does not excuse liberals from seeking out ways to *reduce* the unintended effects of political spillovers howsoever liberal justice allows. Since society is a schoolhouse, is it possible to take control of the informal lessons it cannot help but teach? Might those lessons be turned to the service of the deepest motivational commitment of political liberals: their commitment to answer the fullest possible range of their citizens' questions, a range that includes questions not only about institutional justice but about the nature of liberal social life? For example, might it ever be possible to design public policies in ways that reduce the unintended effects of liberal justice on some citizens *without* violating the rights of others? We cannot know until we recognize the importance of trying.

There are deeper reasons to examine these interface questions as well. As political theorists, liberals should welcome the opportunity to explore, and to expound, every aspect of the social world associated with their view. Liberalism, as much as republicanism, communism, or fascism, begins as a response to one of the most basic questions of human life: how should people live together? Of course, the coercive element of the liberal answer to that question is constrained in ways that the coercive elements in those other views are not.[32] But that does not mean that those questions about human living-together regarding which liberal state-coercion is not permitted somehow just evaporate or cease to exist. Nor does it mean that an account of those domains, and how they are formed by the coercive ones, has no importance to thinkers concerned to elaborate and defend the liberal view.

A liberal society can be shown to have reached the important level of justification conferred by its achievement of institutional legitimacy *without* our having yet shown all the attractions of that society. We advance our exposition of liberalism insofar as we are able to answer ever more questions that the citizenry might reasonably ask about the liberal social settlement, including questions that would not render the state illegitimate if no completely satisfying answers to them could be given. In that latter case, in light of those relevant but poorly answered questions, we would have to think less of liberalism as a social doctrine. We would think less of liberalism in that respect even while *not* thinking that the use of coercive force on behalf of liberal justice was made illegitimate by this defect. In just the same way, we would have given liberalism an even better defense—shown it to be even more attractive as a way of organizing human social life—if we found that we *could* give attractive answers to those questions (even if in doing so we would not have shown that it was any more just).[33]

If we wish genuinely to *understand* liberalism, let alone fully to exposit and defend it, we must not shirk from questions that ask us to venture beyond the familiar domain of public reason—even if those questions do not always reach down to threshold matters of justified coercion. There are vital issues about human living-together under liberal institutions that are not reducible to concerns about justice but instead arise *after* justice has been freely affirmed. To address these issues, liberals must allow themselves to be social philosophers rather than mere technicians of justified coercion.

Interestingly, I know of no liberal who *denies* that such a broader account might be given. That is, no liberal theorist denies that it might be possible to say something systematic about the mechanism by which people in liberal societies might successfully negotiate the interface of the justice-based normative structures associated with the proviso and the various non-justice-based normative structures that liberals deem "admissible." Nor do they deny that policy makers may have some latitude regarding how they discharge their commitment to social justice. What political liberals *do* deny is that it is their business, as political liberals, to provide any such account for reasons not reducible to a concern for the legitimate use of coercion. This latter form of denial is made more striking by *the way* political liberals express it. Rather than confronting these concerns about the need for a theory of the connection of liberal politics and politically reasonable conceptions of human well-being, and saying plainly why it is not the business of liberal theorists to offer it, contemporary liberals do not even feel the need to explain why they do not take up these questions. Their denial is so deep they do not even bother to deny it.

Prominent liberals repeatedly bump up against these interface questions, but they rarely even consider pursuing them themselves. Rawls notes that "citizens individually decide for themselves in what way the public political conception all affirm is related to their own more comprehensive views."[34] But *how* do citizens make such decisions? If people make such decisions "individually," must they endorse a particular (and, by hypothesis, controversial) view of moral personality after all—namely, that of autonomy or individuality? If not, precisely *how not*?

As a consequence of his requirement for full individual justification, Rawls tells us that "the political virtues expected of citizens would not be those of a just and good society, unless they not only permitted but also sustained ways of life fully worthy of citizens' devoted allegiance."[35] He says, "Justice as fairness assumes, as other liberal views do also, that the values of community are not only essential but realizable."[36] But *how* are the values of community—for example, of religious community—realizable over time for various admissible citizens (e.g., our C-people) within the liberal social world?

Likewise, Galston has expressed an appreciation of the impracticability of neutrality of effect even for political liberalism. "To say that the liberal state should refrain from sponsoring the Enlightenment is not to say that it is or can be a neutral state, fully open to every form of life. There is no such state: among other reasons, every political community is a sharing in some conception of justice and the human good, and this sharing will inevitably limit and shape the human possibilities it contains."[37] Those limits, as we have seen, are drawn by the proviso that all citizens think of one another as holders of politically grounded rights. But precisely how does meeting that proviso *shape* the "human possibilities" across the rest of liberal society? Are life's nonpolitical possibilities experienced in a way that is distinctive to liberal societies?[38]

Macedo tells us that a defense of liberal politics "should have something to say about how the interface between political and personal values is negotiated." He continues, "Managing that interface is, in a sense, *the* crucial public issue."[39] But can we give an account of how that interface might be negotiated beyond the threshold of the fit required for purposes of political justification? Can we do so without valorizing any one politically reasonable worldview over any other one? After all, even if it is inevitable that liberal institutions unintentionally exert an unequal psychological tax on the citizenry, shouldn't political liberals search out and advocate every institutional means to *flatten* that tax, so long as those measures are consistent with justice?

Larmore tells us that political liberalism "relies on our being able to abandon 'the cult of wholeness' and to embrace a certain differentiation between our role as citizens, free of status and ascription, and our other roles where we may be engaged with others in the pursuit of substantial ideals of the good life." Because of this need for differentiation, Larmore says, "there is some point to talking of a 'liberal conception of the person.' "[40] But *what is* this hybridized conception of the person, a conception of moral personality broad enough to "embrace" a differentiation between public and nonpublic normative components?[41] And where might this complex "liberal person" be allowed to make an appearance within the conceptual boundaries of liberal theory? Could this normatively mixed creature somehow be the liberal *citizen* after all?

The closer we look, the longer grows the list of questions that a narrow threshold-of-coercion-based account of political liberalism cannot answer. Consider, for example, the way Rawls addresses the problem of what I call free erosion. Rawls acknowledges that some may feel that the political liberals' abandonment of neutrality of effect "may lead to an excessively secular public life and background culture."[42] Requiring people's education to include the rights-based forms of awareness and reflective habits of thinking required by the liberal proviso may in effect, though not by intention, educate them into a comprehensive liberal conception of moral personality. "Doing one may lead to the other, if only because once we know the one, we may of our own accord go on to the other." Rawls grants that this may happen with some and then, strikingly, concludes: "But *the only way* this objection can be answered is to set out carefully the great difference between political and comprehensive liberalism." Thus, "I would hope the exposition of political liberalism in these lectures provides a sufficient reply to the objection."[43]

But Rawls's exposition of political liberalism, far from answering this objection, makes this question difficult for political liberals even to hear. The lectures in *Political Liberalism* are fixed on threshold questions of justified coercion. Rawls's announced aim is to demonstrate how it is possible for there to exist over time a just and stable society of free and equal citizens who remain profoundly divided by reasonable religious, philosophical, and moral doctrines. But many significant questions reasonable citizens might ask about the unintended effects of liberal justice on them are not "objections" to the account of justified coercion Rawls gives.[44] If there is one sure way this concern about free erosion *cannot* be answered, it is by any further lectures about justice or threshold problems of legitimacy. The only way to take this concern seriously is to take up *well-being*-directed interface questions, such as those I have just laid out.[45]

Why haven't political liberals directly confronted these interface questions, questions we might expect even mainstream liberal citizens, the B-people, insistently to ask? I believe the answer is connected to the peculiarly narrow view most liberal theorists take concerning the boundaries of political theory. On this familiar view, for a defender of liberalism to take a social concern seriously means to show how it fits within the domain of public reason. At the extreme, by this view, to recognize the theoretical relevance of concerns that arise outside the realm of public reason would be to take the first step toward abandoning the political primacy of justice, and thus toward abandoning liberalism altogether. The perspective from which questions about these broader eudaimonistic aspects of liberal societies traditionally have been pressed, after all, is not that of that of liberalism's friends but, famously, that of liberalism's *critics*—by Marx or, in our time, by neorepublicans such as Sandel.

Working within this assumption about the boundaries of liberal theory construction, and thus perceiving citizens' questions about personal well-being within the liberal social world as hostile (where not inadmissible, or irrelevant), liberal theorists have actually ducked this whole set of questions their citizens would like to have answered. To their credit, political liberals have found a sophisticated way of ducking these questions: by invoking what might be described as a metapolitical version of the doctrine of double effect. The most familiar application of that doctrine comes from just-war theory. But political theorists have been employing a version of double effect for their own exculpatory purposes too.

In wartime, the business of soldiers, as soldiers, is to kill or neutralize enemy soldiers. Yet sometimes soldiers conduct military operations that threaten the lives not only of enemy soldiers but of noncombatants. The doctrine of double effect is sometimes invoked to defend risky military actions in such situations. If the soldiers undertaking the operations intend only the destruction of enemy soldiers, they are not blameworthy (as soldiers) for the deaths of the noncombatants—even if those deaths were a foreseeable consequence of their operations. On this simple interpretation, the doctrine of double effect provides moral cover for risky military operations by decoupling (1) responsibility for the *intended* consequences of one's actions as a soldier from (2) responsibility for the foreseeable (but unintended) consequences of one's actions as a soldier.

Within just-war theory, the doctrine of double effect (on this simple version, at least) has been widely criticized for providing *too much* moral cover for soldiers.[46] Noncombatants are owed something more: namely, some positive commitment from soldiers to recognize and look out for their interests no matter how urgent, from a military perspective, the objectives of their soldierly operations might be. Soldiers are obliged not merely to show *just enough* concern for the interests of noncombatants that their military actions are all-things-considered justified. Rather, soldiers must do the *most they can* to protect noncombatants from the unintended consequences of their actions, consistent with the primacy they give their military aims.[47]

But then consider the way defenders of political liberalism demarcate the range of social questions which they recognize as relevant to a defense of their view. In political liberal theorizing, the doctrine of double effect is being applied not across different categories of people (combatants *versus* noncombatants), but *within the lives* of the same group of people—namely, reasonable liberal citizens, whose identities have both public and nonpublic aspects. The objectives of the liberal theorists whose theoretical operations are at issue are not military but moral. The business of soldiers, as such, is the successful prosecution of war; the business of liberal theorists, as such, is justified state coercion in the name of justice. Operating on the narrow view of theory construction I described, political liberal theorists have rigidly fixed themselves—like good soldiers—on the project of showing what the most reasonable conception of justice is and the formal conditions under which (enough) people in a diverse society might be able to affirm (rather than reject) that conception in wide-reflective equilibrium. So long as people are freely committed to justice, there is simply no wider question to be asked about the social world as envisaged by liberal theorists.[48]

From this familiar monocular perspective, the pattern of denial that we have charted in this chapter flows naturally. When liberal theorists confront critics who worry about the damage that may be inflicted on the eudaimonistic fabric of citizens' personal lives, liberals seek cover for themselves by decoupling their responsibility for the consequences of the projects they intend as liberals from other foreseeable but unintended consequences of the projects that they as liberals pursue. They take great pains to show how a just and legitimate society is possible, but say precious little in response to their citizens' residual concerns about setting up shop in Macedo's California, taking their meals around Glendon's litigious kitchen table, or spending a lifetime swimming against the current of Galston's river.

This sort of decoupling is precisely what political liberals are up to when they separate neutrality of aim, to which they recognize a positive commitment, from neutrality of effect, which they abandon as "impracticable" and rarely mention again. As political liberals, their concern is with the possibility of legitimate political coercion—full stop. Given the overriding importance of that objective, they cannot be held responsible, as liberals, for unintended though foreseeable consequences of their research program within noncoercive realms. Collateral impact of liberal justice on the personal side of reasonable citizen's lives—whether openly admitted (as with avowedly doomed groups of "admissible" C-people) or merely implied (as with all the B-people)—is not the concern of a theorist sketching the liberal social ideal.

Political liberals can do better than this. Liberals are social philosophers, and they should not conceive of themselves as being bound by politicization to avoid the important responsibilities that attend that role. Of course, political liberals who wish to take up these wider questions must take care to respect the ideals of mutuality and reciprocity that are central to the architecture of public reason. They must not, for example, demand trade-offs between justice and other social goods. But, within this crucial and fully appropriate constraint, liberals can go far toward answering the residual eudaimonistic concerns of their citizenry.

I have been describing the threat of spillover, and the resulting theoretical need for a fuller theory of interface, primarily in terms of *political liberalism*. But unintended spillovers generate theoretical responsibilities for ethical liberals as well. Liberals have long sought to distinguish liberty from mere license, and a culture of narrow individualism—long associated with liberal societies by external critics—can be seen as a real threat to the conceptions of autonomy that ethical liberals hold up as the human ideal. As I mentioned earlier, ethical liberals such as Raz have become increasingly concerned to stress the importance of rootedness and commitment to genuine ethical agency. The more "communitarian" the ethical liberal conception of autonomy becomes, the more concerned about spillovers ethical liberals—by light of their own guiding star—must be. So ethical liberals stand in need of a fuller theory of interface just as political liberals do.[49] I shall now offer such a theory, a theory of liberal social life. By considering how such a theory must be elaborated in a political liberal framework as opposed to an ethical liberal one, we will uncover some dramatic differences between those two rival forms of liberalism.

Chapter Three

LIBERAL NONPUBLIC REASON

THE LIMITS OF JUSTICE

How do people live well within liberal societies? How must they reason and behave if they are to make personal successes of their lives? These are not normative questions in any straightforward sense. They are not, for example, questions asked from the perspective of political perfectionism, where answering would require that we defend some one approach to value as best for all citizens. But neither are these questions purely empirical or sociological—matters of history or simple fact. They are instead questions about how liberal theorists *imagine* people living within the liberal social world. What form of living together, of mortal experience, does liberalism offer to people? What is the *human point* of the liberal settlement?

Defenders of liberalism have been reluctant to answer, or even to recognize, such questions. Liberalism's critics have been much less reticent: liberals, as such, care *only* about justice and the democratic norms of public life. In the 1980s, Michael Sandel leveled this charge in a memorable way.

Sandel asks rhetorically what we would think of a marriage, originally governed by a spirit of generosity and spontaneity, that becomes "liberalized." Spontaneous affection gives way to demands for fairness and the observance of rights, generosity is replaced by "a judicious temper of unexceptionable integrity," and "the good of justice is realized within their household."[1] Sandel calls justice a remedial virtue: "The virtue of justice is measured by the morally diminished conditions which are its prerequisite." The higher the priority of justice, the greater the moral shortcoming of the community. Since liberals give high priority to justice, the social world envisaged by them must be correspondingly lacking from a moral perspective.[2]

Sandel, famously, withdraws this objection immediately after stating it, saying that an empiricist objection such as this would misunderstand the hypothetical nature of Rawls's argument. Yet this objection hit a nerve. Despite Sandel's explicit retraction, liberals have returned again and again to defend themselves from the charge that liberalism valorizes rights-based ways of thinking across the whole of social life.[3] The most striking example of the continuing liberal sensitivity to this charge comes from Rawls himself. In his final major article, Rawls for the first time takes up any of the numerous concerns Sandel has raised about his view. Significantly, the one

Sandelian concern that Rawls feels he must himself rebut is this one about the intended scope of justice.[4]

So Rawls emphasizes that liberal principles of justice are not intended to apply "directly to the internal life" of nonpublic social structures. A commitment to liberal justice does not require that Catholic citizens demand that the governance of their churches be democratic, for example, by insisting that bishops and cardinals be elected by the laity. Similarly, those principles are not intended to apply directly to the internal life of families, for example by requiring family members to satisfy the difference principle with respect to household benefits and chores. There may well be standards of justice relevant to those domains, but here the liberal principles of justice are "out of place."[5]

Still, principles of political justice do impose "essential constraints" on all nonpublic organizations.[6] Churches cannot enforce intolerance, since public law—as the principles of political justice require—does not recognize heresy or apostasy as crimes. Citizens of faith are at liberty to leave their church at any time. Each must be aware that she has a state-protected right of exit. So too the internal life of families is constrained in certain ways. Married women, for example, must understand themselves as entitled to all the same basic rights, liberties, and opportunities as married men. Both spouses must recognize their standing as equal citizens in order for the divisions of labor within their families to be fully voluntary from a political point of view.

Political liberalism in particular aims to maintain a distinction between the point of view of people as citizens and the various ethical points of view people take as members of families and other nonpublic associations. Still, even political liberalism "does not regard the political and the nonpolitical domains as two separate, disconnected spaces, each governed solely by its own distinct principles."[7] Rather, a domain is not a kind of space, but rather is the result or "upshot" of how the principles of the political conception are applied through the various branches of law. While the basic structure is the primary subject of justice, the principles of justice put restrictions on all other aspects of social life. To satisfy the liberal proviso, people living in a liberal society must know that they have rights and must understand that such rights are grounded in purely political ideas of moral personality. Any social effects this recognition of liberal principles may have on secondary subjects—for example, on the forms of reasoning citizens come to employ within the realms of the politically voluntary—are neither required nor intended by political liberalism.

Most liberals think this is an adequate response to the objection sketched by Sandel long ago. No doubt they are correct about that in a sense, since Sandel himself recognizes that liberalism does not *intend* the ways of thinking and of interest identification picked out by public reason to supplant the ways of world-perception citizens employ in the nonpublic domains of reason.[8] But this response does little to address a deeper lingering concern about liberalism, the concern that liberal public norms may unintentionally encourage that process of supplanting to occur. That is the nerve that keeps this doubt about liberalism alive.

To confront this doubt more adequately, liberals need to provide answers to three questions, questions that arise in serial order. First, *how* do they imagine the political conception of justice impacting on its secondary subjects—the domains of associative or familial reason, for example? Second, if there is an unintended pattern of nonpublic impact that is worrying from the perspective of some reasonable citizens, does liberalism contain any resources that might allow them to address citizen concerns of this sort? And third, if we can locate such resources, do those resources have any *institutional* implications—implications that might concretely differentiate the political and ethical liberal responses to the phenomenon of unintended spillovers?

Beyond a cursory admission of the impracticability of neutrality of effect, political liberals take no view on the first of these questions. So it is no surprise that they never even consider answering the second or third one. As long as the conditions of political voluntarism are satisfied, there is no injustice even if an uneven pattern of social outcome happens to emerge over time. If the bare requirement that citizens attain a condition of political voluntarism inadvertently generates special, residual challenges for some reasonable citizens, these are ipso facto not the kinds of citizen concerns that a liberal theorist has any business addressing.

I believe that liberals can confront the lingering Sandelian concern in a more open and convincing way. Of course, in considering any institutional remedies to interface concerns such as these, we must take care always to respect the architecture of public reason. Full political voluntarism cannot be sacrificed or traded off for any other interpersonal value. But there may be a way to address citizens' concerns about spillovers in a direct and active manner and yet fully respect that architecture. This remedy lies within an account of what I shall call liberal nonpublic reason.[9]

The Personal Uses of Public Reason

The value of political autonomy cannot be reduced to its role in securing justice. Public norms, and rights in particular, have a wider social role as well. This is clearest in the case of claim rights. One way a person can exercise such a right is by asserting the claim associated with it. If you loaned me five dollars last Wednesday on the condition that I would repay you when we meet again Saturday, then when you and I meet on Saturday, you have a right-claim against me. You can exercise your right by seeking repayment of the five dollars. How your assertion of your right-claim will affect the harmony of our relationship will depend on a variety of factors, including the manner (gentle or peremptory) in which you assert your claim. However, our shared public recognition of your rights gives you communicative options. Instead of asserting your claim against me, our shared awareness of your possession of that right-claim enables you to exercise your claim by waiving or, as I say, by withholding it. If you and I are friends, and you know that I am perhaps embarrassed by my continuing financial difficulties, when we meet on Saturday you can use your right— especially in the light of my recognition that you do have such a right—to express your concern for me by withholding your claim.[10]

Rights mark lines between people. But by that very fact they set out social markers by which people can recognize when individualistic lines have been benevolently crossed. Rights-awareness always underdetermines action, but not by saying *nothing* whatsoever about nonpolitical life. Rather, rights underdetermine action in a structurally specific way. Whatever choices people make at the point of action are socially understood to operate against the wider egalitarian background that liberal rights denote. Public norms simultaneously underdetermine *and structure* the personal lives of liberal citizens.

Of course, our main concern is with this process as it applies to rights in the broadest political sense. This will include those rights set out in liberal constitutions, concerning freedom of association, of religious practice, of speech, and of movement. It includes also all those claims recognized by family law, the law of torts, and all the branches of public law as worked out in a democratic society by reference to its political conception of justice. The exact reach of those branchings can be expected to be a matter of ongoing dispute and discovery even within a society that is more or less well ordered. Within families especially, the exact reach of political principles of justice is not fixed or given. But the process of exercising claims, as I am describing it, also could be used to describe communicative possibilities made available by less formal "rights"—for example, regarding the division of household chores or the repayment of small debts between friends. Even informal rights-talk of that sort might be absorbed, and turned to positive uses, by the model I am describing.

Liberals say that when members of a society act out of a sense of justice, and observe one another doing so, they may reinforce the motivational assumptions that give rise to the sense of justice in the first place. A sense of justice can thus spread contagiously through a society.[11] Critics evaluate the effects of this hoped-for contagion very differently. As in Sandel's marital example, "When I act out of a sense of justice in inappropriate circumstances, say in circumstances where the virtues of benevolence and fraternity rather than justice are relevantly engaged, my act may contribute to a reorientation of prevailing understandings and motivations. . . . Justice in this case will have been not a virtue but a vice."[12]

But this is not the only possibility. Decisions to withhold right-claims may gain positive appraisals from third-party community members who observe the benefits of rewarding human encounters. Such other-regarding decisions may thus spread contagiously throughout the relevant nonpublic spheres. When persons treat one another generously or show fidelity to a common cause or system of belief, those actions reinforce the motivational assumptions that gave rise to the actions in the first place. Nonpublic dispositional virtues may thus reinforce themselves, gaining a kind of stability. If when a sense of justice spreads in a community it is accompanied by a vivid awareness of the flexibility in the exercise of political autonomy, then—if there is any goodwill at all in the grouping—goodwill has a chance to take root and spread. A public conception of principles of justice that specify individual rights may *strengthen* citizens' nonpolitical attachments to one another.

In a line reminiscent of Marx's early criticisms of liberal justice, Sandel says, "The morality of right . . . speaks to that which distinguishes us, the morality of the good corresponds to the unity of persons and speaks to that which connects us."[13] But liberal theorists need not be concerned only with the domain of the political and the "morality of the right." They can develop a distinctively liberal account of the relation of the good to the right without in any way challenging the architecture of public reason.

Even if people in liberal societies must be capable of bifurcating their lives, of distinguishing their public point of view from their point of view as members of families and other associations, that bifurcation is relevant only to matters of *justification* (whether of the public commitments people share or of the nonpublic worldviews they variously affirm). People living amid liberal political institutions cannot really keep their public perspectives separate from the nonpublic roles they inhabit, nor should they want to. In the social world made possible by liberal politics, nonpublic perspectives always *include* the public perspective as a eudaimonistically constituent part. Principles of political justice are not intended to be applied directly as regulative norms for the internal workings of families and other nonpublic associations. But they inevitably play a role there by the way they structure people's most intimate understandings of interpersonal virtue. Even if rights-talk does spill over, this is not in itself cause for eudaimonistic alarm. As the withholding model suggests, the role liberals affirm for rights need not just be that of imposing "certain essential constraints." Rights can provide the foundation for a certain conception of virtue, the inner mechanism for the successful exercise of liberal nonpublic reason.

It is understandable that liberal theorists have emphasized the public domain within which members of liberal societies are concerned with jus-

eudaimonistic

tice. But why should liberal theorists think they can elaborate and defend their view only with respect to the justification of political coercion? However deep their commitment to social justice, people in liberal societies do not care only about justice and the conditions of its legitimate enforcement. The concerns of people living in a social world that distinguishes public and nonpublic spheres must of necessity be more complex than that. The project of elucidating and defending *liberalism* is wider than the project of showing the legitimacy of some set of coercive principles for the division of basic social burdens and benefits, or of describing the deliberative norms relevant to liberal democratic decision making. Liberal theory construction includes an invitation to us to lay out and examine those aspects of the liberal view that lie beyond even the widest interpretation of liberal public value.[14]

I have so far sketched only the barest outlines of how liberal political values structure the nonpublic forms of human living-together within liberal societies. In providing this sketch, I am seeking to describe merely the *possibilities* for how citizens might put the spillovers of public reason to work for their own various nonpublic purposes. I am not taking up the empirical question of whether or to what degree such virtues do in fact characterize life in actual liberal societies, nor am I yet considering the important question about what—if anything—the designers of liberal institutions might do to encourage citizens to develop such virtues within the constraints of full political voluntarism. For now, I wish merely to describe the eudaimonistic machinery of liberal nonpublic reason. We shall take up the question of how that machinery might be moved soon enough.[15]

Compass concepts

THE MACHINERY OF NONPUBLIC VIRTUE

Within the liberal social world, each citizen's particular understanding about the *meaning* of his public autonomy is conceptually distinct from his simple understanding that he *is* politically autonomous. The latter understanding—about the variety and character of the rights one has—is one that all citizens share. But an awareness of what liberal justice requires, or makes available, cannot by itself inform a citizen of what he should do— let alone *who* he should be. Liberal citizens routinely have need of supplementary concepts of a different sort, dispositional concepts, by which each understands what his political autonomy means to him.

The practice of exercising rights calls our attention to the importance of the intersection of the impartial concerns addressed by public reason and those thicker, more identity-dependent concepts by which individual liberal citizens steer whenever their political autonomy is engaged. I shall call these latter concepts *compass concepts* because of the role they play in orienting citizens with respect to the meaning of their public rights and liberties. I earlier described a society's background culture as a map of meaning, a map that lays out the basic terrain of social possibilities citizens there may encounter, a map generated in large part by that society's political forms. To extend the metaphor, we might think of compass concepts as providing each person with a set of bearings. These bearings help him find his way around the social world. Because people must often exercise the rights they have as liberal citizens, liberal public norms provide a ready framework for diverse systems of ethics, diverse ways of world-perception that different compass concept traditions express. Such nonpublic traditions prescribe substantive ideals to those people, ideals of what kinds of character are worth developing, of what kind of person each at his best might be.[16]

This machinery of exercising rights has two components. There are norms of political autonomy held by all citizens in common, along with the informal background culture associated with that kind of autonomy. And there the various compass concepts that help orient particular citizens with respect to the meaning of their rights. The process of recognition by which one discovers what rights are his is one to which access is in principle shared by every citizen. Rights are the output of public reason. But the dispositional concepts by which individual citizens steer when exercising their claims arise in a way that is much less formal. Compass concepts come out of people's most basic understandings of their lives and their place in the social or spiritual world. Any description of the sources of those very basic forms of self perception and of nonpublic value formation can at best be rough, especially in conditions of reasonable value pluralism. We are speaking, after all, about how humans pursue value over the course of a life. But there is one very general way of describing the sources of compass concepts that may be useful here, in part because of a feature for which it is often criticized: its extreme flexibility. This is the idea of life as a kind of narrative.

Alasdair MacIntyre suggests that most everyone understands his life as an enacted narrative, an ongoing story in which he and the other people closest to his experience play out their special parts. "Moreover, the story of each of our lives is characteristically embedded in the story of one or more larger units." Thus, "I understand the story of my life in such a way that it is part of the history of my family or of this farm or of this university or of this countryside; and I understand the story of the lives of other individuals around me as embedded in the same larger stories, so that I and they share a common stake in the outcome of that story and in what sort of story it both is and is to be: tragic, heroic, comic."[17]

This idea of life as narrative is flexible enough to include a great variety of compass concept types. The idea that a human life requires narrative unity is sometimes used to show the importance of cultural communities. Will Kymlicka, for example, describes how a person's culture provides a person who is deciding how to live his life with a range of options and an evaluative ranking of those options. Culture transmits this information by means of the stories we hear about people's lives, real or imaginary. We can adopt features from those lives as models for our own lives. "From childhood on, we become aware that we are already participants in certain forms of life (familial, religious, sexual, educational, etc.)." Thus, "we decide how to live our lives by situating ourselves in these cultural narratives, by adopting roles that have struck us as worthwhile ones, as ones worth living"[18]

There are many ways of subdividing modern societies into narratively significant traditions: religious and ethnic ways, profession-based ways, geographical ways, just for starters. A Jewish American narrative tradition has importantly different emphases from an Irish American one—as there are different emphases in being Reform or Orthodox in one's Judaism. There is a different vision of excellence of character associated with being a doctor than with being a lawyer—just as aiming for excellence as a general practitioner may require different dispositions from those of a would-be excellent surgeon. Being a "real Brooklyner" is different from being a "Manhattanite"—as the attitude of people who strongly identify with the Upper East side of Manhattan tend to be different from those who identify with the Upper West. All these groupings—some quite determinant, others more diffuse—promote different patterns of excellence among the individuals who identify with the ongoing stories those groupings write.

Within a liberal society, the question of how one should live one's life and the question of how one should exercise one's rights overlap in significant ways. The systems of beliefs about value on which individual citizens rely in answering each of these questions share many of the same narrative roots. Those beliefs are derived, after all, from people's most basic sense of themselves as the particular person each is. Across and within a large liberal polity, a rich variety of communities and traditions encourage different sorts of character. Looked at this way, a "comprehensive grouping" is but a grouping in which a particular set of compass concepts prevails. To affirm a comprehensive doctrine is to share with others a pattern of understanding about what one's rights mean. It is to agree with them about what political autonomy is *for*.

In a diverse liberal society, groups can be expected to vary with respect to how *totalizing* their interpretation of rights-awareness will be. Consider the people of Kiryas Joel, whom I earlier described as an example, albeit somewhat extreme, of our C-people. Membership in that group requires that one affirm a particular understanding about the meaning of one's rights across an expansive range of issues that principles of public reason

might address. For example, the Satmar Hasidim have a gender-differenti-
ated understanding about what clothing their members wear. Through the
status of each as a member of the wider liberal society, each of the Satmar
is in a moral position to wear different (unsanctioned) clothing any day
that she chooses. But they express their membership by wearing the clothing that the group's internal standards prescribe. So too the women members must understand that they have standing as political equals to pursue
a career outside the home—but under the norms of the Satmar Hasidim,
they must not pursue such careers. The compass concept tradition of the
Satmar is so totalizing that even their rights of political participation come
within the purview of the public statuses regarding which their tradition
generates standards of behavior: the Satmar Hasidim are a formidable political force because they can be relied upon as a group to vote on whatever
occasions and for whichever candidate their rebbe instructs.

The Satmar Hasidim are an extreme case not only because of the breadth
of members' life-concerns to which the Satmar compass concept tradition
speaks. I described the Satmar as lying within the C-person category, but
noted that their traditions take them perilously close to the D-person line.
The question of how best to categorize them turns on whether or not all
members who practice the Satmar norms can do so while satisfying the
conditions of full political voluntarism. To satisfy the liberal proviso, the
individual members of the Satmar must to some degree appreciate their
rights as valuable discretionary powers that each is at liberty to exercise
in constructing a good life. But in a cultural setting where massive social
pressures make only one way of exercising one's rights acceptable, there is
real danger that the conditions of full political freedom cannot genuinely
be met.

For this reason, the Satmar way of life might arguably be described not
as a compass concept tradition but as generating something more like
controlling concepts. Whether this is really the most accurate account of
the traditions currently being practiced in the township of Kiryas Joel is
an empirical question I shall leave to others. But a tradition that "gives
direction" to citizens about the meaning of their rights in so controlling a
way might disable those citizens, and disable them in a way recognizable
even from the merely political perspective that political liberals affirm.
Such a tradition would deny not merely the controversial ideal of personal
autonomy affirmed by ethical liberals. That tradition would deny their political autonomy as well. Any system that effectively makes the conditions
of the proviso unrealizable would be unacceptable to political liberals.
So the Satmar Hasidim push the limits of the compass concept pattern I
am describing.

Still, we can see politically acceptable instances of compass concept use
throughout many familiar forms of membership in modern liberal socie-

ties. Allow me to illustrate with a personal example. For over fifty years, my family has lived in a farmhouse across from a large field in northern Vermont. The families who own the fields on either side of us have been there even longer. Starting twenty-five years ago the town has been undergoing rapid development such that for almost a decade ours has been among the last series of open fields in the town. Neither my family nor any of the others is wealthy, and each of us is well aware that we have the right to sell our field, or parts of it, for housing lots. But we love the land. We would as a group be appalled if any of us decided to subdivide his field for housing lots. Through time, and without planning, a strong bond has grown up between our families, a bond based on our shared understanding of what our rights to ownership in that land mean. As each generation receives property rights in that land from the previous one, they use the history of their own family—a history that includes their relationships to the other families—to help orient them with respect to what their ownership rights mean to them. For us, ownership means stewardship, and solidarity, even in the face of economic opportunity. As families, we do not share similar views about the good life. We do not live the same way, dress the same way, nor, certainly, vote the same way. But we share an intense bond. The bond is our shared, mutually reinforcing understanding about what it means to own that land.

Sometimes people exercise their rights in more dramatic, even heroic ways. Just before Christmas of 1995, Malden Mills, the largest employer in the working-class city of Lawrence, Massachusetts, burned to the ground. Fourteen hundred people were thrown out of work, and there was serious concern in Lawrence that the mill might relocate in an area with cheaper labor. But Aaron Feuerstein, a devout Jew and the mill's owner, felt a special obligation to his workers. At considerable risk to his family business, Feuerstein not only to pledged to rebuild in downtown Lawrence but announced that all employees would continue to receive full pay and benefits for three months while the plant was being rebuilt (indeed, Feuerstein gave every worker a $275 Christmas bonus). In taking these measures, Feuerstein described himself as being guided by the compass concept of *tzedakah*—a Jewish norm that can be thought of as merging social justice and charity. Like justice, tzedakah is a form of giving that is based on obligations of respect. But like charity, tzedakah must necessarily be practiced on an individual basis rather than on a governmental one (in part, perhaps, because the tradition of tzedakah was formed by a people historically governed by others). As a businessperson, Feuerstein was well aware of his rights regarding his mill and workers, but as a devout Jew he felt obliged to act the way he did: "Everything I did after the fire was in keeping with the ethical standards I've tried to maintain my entire life."[19]

It is an uncomfortable fact that some compass concept traditions that are most precious to people have their origins in social injustice. While many people in the United States devote considerable time and resources to the personal care of elderly family members, older African Americans are more than twice as likely as whites to receive care from family members when their health declines. The strong tradition of elder care within African American communities—especially in Southern states—is in part a response to experiences of racism that have made many African Americans skeptical of institutional care. The practice is sometimes even traced back to slavery and to the extra value the experience of slavery placed on people's intergenerational ties.

Whatever its roots, this tradition of elder care is today not merely a burden but a powerful source of pride for many African Americans, a distinctive forum for expressing love and understanding. According to Peggye Dilsworth-Anderson, a gerontologist and sociologist at the University of North Carolina at Greensboro, the African American tradition of elder care is often motivated by a combination of racial awareness and religious faith. "You get cultural reinforcement from your neighbors, your friends, from the church." Gloria Robertson, a retired North Carolina accounting clerk, cared for her aged mother at home for five years. Her response to a doctor who encouraged her to put her mother in a nursing home was typical: "We just don't do that," she said. "Not with our people."[20]

Anyone living in a liberal society could easily multiply examples such as these. No liberal citizen is legally tied to a particular profession much less to a particular place of work. The relationships people develop in the workplace—deep and formative as they become for many people—always take place amid the mutual awareness that the members have moral standing to invoke claims of justice and, at the limit, to dissolve the association and to move on and start up again elsewhere. So too within churches—an organization that for many people provides the core of their lives. Liberal freedom of religion means not just that *the state* cannot endorse any particular religion over any other. Just as important, freedom of religion means that in a liberal society religious people can be bound to their religious group, and the activities performed in its name, only in a very particular way. In a liberal society, any church member at any time is free to leave or strategically to opt out of religious activities. That awareness inevitably affects the understanding they all have about what it means to stay and to practice and worship there together at all. So too within the family: divorce is always a possibility, and so is disinheritance of children, and these possibilities exist in the background of even the most stable and successful family groups. All relationships develop and must exist against the background of rights people have as political equals. Relationships depend upon the understandings members share about the meaning of such rights.

Within a diverse liberal polity, groups differentiate themselves largely through the particular patterns by which members go about exercising their political autonomy (for example, by variously asserting and withholding their many types of right-claims, and doing so in a great variety of subtly shaded manners). And within the liberal social world, individuals must differentiate themselves in much the same way. The penalties for persons who ignore or flout the communal norms do not involve formal state power (nor are they sanctioned by a concern for what justice requires). Yet those penalties may loom large in the psychic economies of real citizens' lives. Divergent actions typically levy a eudaimonistic opportunity cost—a cost expressed in terms of the missed opportunity of continued (or strengthened) attachment to the group or tradition with which one has previously identified.

Of course, each person must—as a right-holder—*exercise* the rights he has, and so there is normative underdetermination at this level too. Depending on the way each exercises his political autonomy, individuals must action-by-action contribute to the strengthening or the weakening of the set of compass concepts that prevail in the group. Members of liberal communities share a responsibility for the world-outlook affirmed by the group as a whole. Each bears a responsibility as a creator for the set of compass concepts that their association affirms in the face of changing circumstances. In the fast-paced liberal social world, the characters within these various and overlapping nonpublic stories cannot help but affect the direction of the stories as they are told.

Still, we might imagine some reasonable people—our B-people and C-people, for example—being alarmed by this conception of nonpublic virtue. As I have described the machinery so far, nonpublic virtues—even as ideals—are centered on a conscious reflection by each citizen on his status as politically autonomous. If citizens must constantly reflect on the meaning of their political autonomy throughout every aspect of their lives they will remain too self-conscious about their interpersonal actions. Liberal citizens will be all too "white-knuckled" about the rights that are theirs: even in withholding their claims they will cling to them. The highly reflective conception of interpersonal virtue I have sketched so far might be acceptable to the forms of personal life endorsed by some of our A-people. But this model of virtue itself is incompatible with the less-reflective anchors of the great majority of liberal citizens. C-people, and many B-people, affirm forms of personal life based on spontaneity and nonreflective expressions of trust. Their worldviews would be under constant pressure from an ideal of nonpublic reason that required them constantly to be aware of what rights each holds toward the others.

Yet justice may play its role in nonpublic spheres even without people consciously considering their rights at all. First, people can withhold not only individual rights but also *whole categories* of right-claims. Within the liberal social world, this seems to be a part of the normal process by which people develop deeper commitments with one another. The practice of withholding discrete claims may, if the relationship develops successfully, lead to a situation where the parties of the relationship come to decide, with varying degrees of self-consciousness, to withhold whole categories of claims regarding one another. The parties' mutual recognition that the others are acting in this reciprocal way may serve as a mark by which people sound out the depth their mutual commitment has reached. If the relationship develops, increasingly important categories of rights may come to be exercised in commitment-confirming ways. Parties who share a public conception of principles of justice have available to them, in those shared principles, the means by which to recognize this as well.

The machinery of liberal nonpublic reason does not require that closely connected people stop in each case to calculate about justice and reflect on the standing that might be accorded them by some public standard. Spouses need not withhold their rights to marital separation first thing every morning, nor need Catholics pause each Sunday to ponder anew which religion freely to exercise. The exercise of political autonomy can be understood not just as a highly self-conscious activity, but also as a voluntarily assumed *attitude*, a settled disposition, that persons in liberal societies can take in relation to certain other persons and toward whole systems of belief.

People may exercise their claims of political autonomy even while having in a sense *forgotten* about them. This notion of "forgetting" does not require that one violate, or lapse in one's satisfaction of, the rights-awareness prong of the liberal proviso. People do not necessarily become "controlled" by a tradition they accept uncritically on a day-to-day basis. Even C-persons must retain a capacity to recognize the rights people have as public persons through every realm of, and during every enterprise within, nonpublic reason. Liberal citizens must always retain this capacity—even when their conceptions of personal value may require that such rights not play any role in their occurrent thinking.[21]

The psychological terrain created by the interface of public and nonpublic norms is nuanced and complexly layered. But even this modified requirement limits the forms of personal reasoning that can be practiced within liberal societies. In particular, all conceptions of virtue that depend upon a background of public *inegalitarianism* are straightforwardly ruled out.

Consider a marital relationship where one spouse is utterly deferential to the other. To make the case vivid, imagine a woman who studiously avoids forming interests and ideals of her own, and instead is utterly deferential to her husband's view of the good. She wears the clothing that he prefers, maintains the friendships of which he approves, and spends her days on whatever tasks he thinks appropriate for her. Imagine that, by the light of their patriarchal and traditionalist worldview, both he and she deny that all citizens—men *and women*—are free and equal even for political purposes. Certainly they act that way in their own relationship: their house and all their financial accounts are in his name, he is active in politics while she takes no part at all, and they agree that even their marriage itself is something that only he could ever choose to dissolve. They are D-people.

Both parties of the deferential marriage may be content within the form of life they share. Indeed, they might well defend their relationship on eudaimonistic grounds much like those that Sandel praised in his original marital relationship. After all, even from an assumption of public inegalitarianism people can develop dispositional patterns that express conceptions of many familiar virtues. Given the inegalitarian background this couple affirms, he is "generous" when he takes her out to dinner, buys her jewelry, or orders up a large wedding for their daughter. She shows "solidarity," even a sort of "independence," when she cuts off her relations with politically active women friends. These conceptions of interpersonal virtue may or may not be judged worthy on various nonpublic grounds. But these conceptions of virtue are themselves incompatible with the ideal of a well-ordered liberal society. Conceptions of nonpublic reason that are built from background assumption of inegalitarianism—regardless of the arguments that might be made for them from some purely eudaimonistic perspective—are outside the bounds of the model I have been describing.

The liberal social world is inhospitable to some entire traditions of virtue. Consider the traditional system of caste in India. All citizens there are differentiated into a series of genera, each characterized by its own type of religiously identified substance. Across that system of caste difference is built a complex system of rules for interpersonal conduct, or what we might call social virtues. Prominent among these caste-based codes of conduct, (or *dharma*) is the practice of *dana*: the Indian system of gift-giving. *Dana* in its essence relies upon a shared assumption among participants of the importance of caste difference. *Dana*, in all its complex variations, is a system of virtue by which tribute to the gods is performed through intercaste gift-giving. This whole social system of virtue (as cataloged, for example, in the *Dharmasutra*) has its meaning and motivational force *only* against the public background of the system of inegalitarianism that caste denotes.[22]

So too, with the aspect of European social construction known as *noblesse oblige*. Like *dana*, that is a noncoercive form of social construction that depends essentially on all participants in the practice accepting an inegalitarian background system. Where *dana* depends on a horizontal system of caste, noblesse oblige depends on a more vertical system such as those of monarchical dependencies. The obligations and expectations of noblesse oblige played a role in pre-Revolutionary life in America and continued for a time even after the Revolution, but in an increasingly unstable form. As public egalitarianism took root and spread in America, people became unwilling, indeed incapable, of giving or receiving goods with the attitude the practice of that virtue once required. Indeed, people rejected that form of nonpublic social construction as a kind of *insult*, a false grandeur on the part of people who happened to be rich to people who happened to be poor. In post–Revolutionary America noblesse oblige became an ever more nervous and uncertain virtue, even among those who hoped to lift themselves up by practicing some faded version of it.

The requirements of the liberal proviso rule out all conceptions of social construction that require a public acceptance of an inegalitarian background, whether those conceptions concern relations within families, religious subgroups, or the norms structuring voluntary interactions between strangers. From the wider perspective of human social possibilities, this is a significant constraint. This constraint is distinctively associated with liberalism because of the particular interface liberalism posits between citizens' public and nonpublic self-understandings. Within liberal societies, it is through the machinery of liberal rights-awareness that nonpublic motives to social construction—in all their variety—must always pass.

Political liberals, as I have said, do not talk much about the particular machinery of nonpublic virtue that is implied by their view. Except insofar as nonpublic matters affect the bare possibility of political stability, they see such matters as beyond their theoretical bailiwick. Still, the nonpublic machinery I have described is fully compatible with the legitimacy-directed arguments that political liberals do see themselves as bound to produce. My account is not an objection to any piece of the formal architecture of public reason. I am merely emphasizing a neglected dimension of the liberal view.

An awareness of political rights cannot help but play a role in structuring the self-understandings of liberal citizens throughout their lives. In this sense principles of justice *are* applied directly to the internal life of families and other nonpublic associations. Rights do not simply "impose essential constraints" on such groupings: rights provide the supports across which nonpublic groupings in liberal societies are built. Our point of view as citizens *cannot* be distinguished in any clean way from our point of view as members of families and other nonpublic groups. Rather, our nonpublic points of view always include our shared public point of view as an essential constituent part. And, crucially, a nonpublic domain or space is *not* simply the upshot of how principles of justice are applied through the various branches of law. In a liberal society, every nonpublic domain or space is the upshot of how the claims of right set out by various branches of law are *interpreted and applied* by individuals seeking meaning and value in their lives. Without shared understandings of the meaning of rights, and the will to conduct oneself accordingly, there can be no domains or spaces within the liberal social world—merely a stable arrangement of (empty) claims.

ANSWERING THE UNEASY CITIZENS

This egalitarian model of nonpublic reason points to an important but little recognized dimension of liberal neutrality. While recognizing the foundational importance of justice, liberal state-institutions must adopt all available means to limit the impact of public values on the compass concepts that guide the various kinds of politically reasonable citizens. This ideal of compass concept neutrality is so much with us that its central role in protecting diversity is rarely recognized. Since managing the interface of public and nonpublic self-conceptions is a crucial public issue, compass concept neutrality is a correspondingly significant aspect of political liberal neutrality. A commitment to maximizing compass concept neutrality falls out directly from the political liberal way of drawing the distinction between public and private spheres. That commitment is a natural consequence of the basic liberal ambition: to find a mutually beneficial form of association that respects each as free and equal while not intentionally advancing any one view of the good life over any other politically reasonable one.

People in liberal societies build their lives by the way they exercise their political rights and liberties. Given their commitment to political equality, there is no other way of living open to them. In a free society, it is not just through their duties but through their freedoms that people bind themselves with one another and construct their social world. For a state to be neutral about the meaning and value of life means that the state must seek all available means to neutralize messages it unintentionally sends about the ultimate meaning and proper exercise of people's political autonomy. Liberals must minimize all compass recalibrations beyond those directly required by people's affirming the principles of social justice.

I have so far merely attempted to identify a theoretical commitment that might allow liberals to speak to their citizens' concerns about the threat of spillover. I said earlier that many citizens—the mainstream B-people in particular—would find political liberalism more theoretically adequate if political liberals could show that their theory allows them to care about more than the conditions of social justice and democratic self-governance, impressive as the liberal commitment to securing those conditions may be. But what citizens really want to know is whether political liberals, as such, can *do anything* regarding their non-justice-based concerns.

After all, we might still find many admissible citizens being unsatisfied with the account of nonpublic life I have given so far. In describing the mechanism by which various personal forms of value might be preserved or developed within liberal societies, I might just as well have been describing the mechanism by which certain of those forms of personal value tend to lose out over time. Even with this fuller account of nonpublic life before us, the system of unequal taxation remains fully in effect. Free erosion is as much of a threat as ever.

But there may be something liberals can do here, something dramatic and something essential to the health of any liberal society. Quite aside from their foundational concern with social justice, perhaps liberals can also show a concern with the wider *civic life* of their society. Institutions, laws, and policies that fully satisfy the liberal commitment to neutrality of aim cannot help but play a secondary role in the broader educational life of liberal societies. Liberals, ethical and political alike, must attend to these broader aspects of their formative project. They must consider how the particular policies and programs they pursue square with their deepest motivational commitments. Liberals have civic ambitions that are not fully captured by their devotion to public reason. In attending to the full range of their social commitments, political liberals may discover *institutional* remedies to the problems of spillovers and free erosion.

Of course, anyone hoping to expand the normative domain of political theory in this way must always respect the architecture of public reason. It is their overriding concern about that architecture which has led the early political liberals doggedly to "take no view" on these interface questions. But the architectural imperative of political liberalism constrains us merely to respect the ideals of mutuality and reciprocity that undergird the principle of legitimacy. It does not constrain us from taking up other closely related concerns that reasonable citizens may have about the liberal social world.[23] "Respect the architecture" does not mean "Hang no Sheetrock!" or "Bring in none of the furniture people need to live as well as they might in a building such as this!"

Can we finish the liberal building and make it a more attractive place to *all* formally admissible citizens while respecting the public codes and keeping the deliberative architecture intact? Can we do this not just as a matter of wishing but of institutional design and structure? The answer, if there is one, may lie with a concept that we have so far considered not at all: the idea of the good liberal citizen.

Chapter Four

CITIZENSHIP: JUSTICE OR WELL-BEING?

THE DERIVATIVE IDEAL

The citizen is the foundation of every social world. Every institutional form requires that ordinary people *behave* in certain ways, that they develop certain expectations and satisfy certain responsibilities on a day-to-day basis. To be a "good citizen" means to engage in those socially constructive projects that lead your society to flourish or succeed as whatever sort of society it is. The norms relevant to people as good citizens are not fixed or universal. Different kinds of attitudes and activities are required of people as citizens within different types of regimes. Norms of good citizen conduct vary, for example, across theocratic, fascist, communist, and liberal regimes.[1] But in every case, the norms applicable to people as citizens are given in terms of each regime's underlying ideal of societal success. The definitions of "good citizen" and of "societal success" stand together, hand in hand.

Liberals, famously, give only a formal account of what it means for a society to flourish or succeed as a liberal society. A liberal society realizes its ideal when its basic institutions are stable with respect to whatever conception of justice it is most reasonable for that society to affirm and when state-backed policies and programs are enacted in ways consistent with the demands of democratic self-governance.

For liberal theorists, as for defenders of every other view, the normative domain of good citizen conduct serves as a kind of indicator for where the boundaries of political theory are understood to be drawn. In a liberal society, there is a very great difference between achieving excellence in one's nonpublic roles and in one's public roles. When asked what it means to achieve excellence as a citizen, it is upon people's public roles that most theorists fix.

For this reason, the criteria of good citizen conduct affirmed by liberals are standardly understood to be *derivative* from public values. The result is a justice-directed conception of good citizen conduct that, while familiar and entrenched, is problematic precisely because of what it leaves out.

Consider the United States, the liberal society par excellence. A narrowly derivative interpretation dominates the understanding most people there have of themselves as citizens. Pamela Johnston Conover and a group of colleagues used focus groups to examine the actual attitudes of Americans regarding their self-understandings as citizens. When asked what it means to be an American, the subjects in Conover's focus groups overwhelmingly pointed to the idea of individual freedom. "At the core of our discussants' identities as Americans is a fundamental sense of having important rights that ensure freedom and encourage the development of the individual." When asked what it means to be a citizen, people in Conover's focus groups emphasized that for them citizenship denoted a legal entitlement, a status directly and narrowly derivable from their sense of themselves as holders of rights. "What it means to be a *citizen* in America is simply what it means to be an American: a person with rights."[2]

Of course, to say that many Americans have a derivative understanding of their citizenship does not mean that their citizen self-understandings concern *only* their sense of themselves as holders of rights. Many people's citizen-identity also involves responsibilities. As before, however, most people in Conover's groups understood their responsibilities as citizens as being directly and narrowly derivative from the political values of the liberal society. When describing their responsibilities as citizens, most Americans emphasized their *public* responsibilities: the duty to pay taxes, to defend the country, and to vote. When asked whether they thought other dimensions of human living together should be considered part of their duties as *citizens*—nonpublic dimensions of living together often associated with well-being, such as "voluntary work and other forms of active participation in the community"—many of Conover's subjects strongly objected.[3] Liberal citizenship, properly understood, involves only those attitudes, dispositions, and self-understandings that are directly derivable from the sets of rights and duties set out by one's political community. The studies of the Conover teams suggest that many Americans currently understand citizenship in a narrowly derivative sense.

This popular understanding of citizenship is fully aligned with the ideal of "good citizenship" that has been espoused by public intellectuals in America for generations. At the turn of the century, partly in response to the waves of immigration and the social upheaval of the industrial revolution, there was a great swelling of interest in the idea of "good citizen" conduct. One forum for those discussions was a series of lectures given to graduating classes at Yale. "The Yale Lectures on the Responsibilities of Citizenship" featured many of the most prominent intellectuals, politicians, and judges of the times—Elihu Root, James Bryce, William H. Taft, David Brewer, Samuel McCall, and Felix Frankfurter, among others. What is most striking about the series for our purposes is the assumption that dominates the lectures: the assumption that "good citizenship" in a society founded on liberal principles primarily involves people's attitudes and activities with respect to *government*.

Charged with discussing the ideal of good citizen conduct, most lecturers in the Yale series seized upon questions of the roles and responsibilities people have through their status as political agents.[4] Samuel McCall was typical: "I fancy that the central idea of this course has reference primarily to those duties that we owe each other, not directly as between man and man, but through the State, and which are discharged through the action we seek to have taken through its instrumentality." Those duties "concern the part we should take in the direction of our governmental institutions, the inspiration and control of which devolve upon ourselves."[5]

On this understanding of liberalism, to exhort people to be "good citizens" is to exhort them to vote regularly and conscientiously, to maintain party loyalties without being overwhelmed by them, to obey the rules of commerce even when one is in position to violate them, and generally to recognize and respect one another as equal holders of civil rights. Indeed, later texts on good citizen conduct can be read as catalogs of the normative requirements of citizenship as laid out in the Yale lectures: registering to vote, studying candidates, urging trained personnel to seek public office, performing jury duty, paying taxes, assuming financial obligations, and generally observing the law.[6]

This whole way of thinking about good citizen conduct—as familiar now as then—was pithily captured in an address given by Grover Cleveland to the Commercial Club of Chicago in 1903. After noting the popular phrase "At least I'm not a *politician*," Cleveland replied: "Every citizen should be a politician enough to bring himself within the true meaning of the term, as one who concerns himself with 'the regulation or government of a nation or state for the preservation of its safety, peace and prosperity.' This is politics in its best sense, and this is good citizenship."[7] There could be no better epigram for the derivative understanding of citizenship. To be a good citizen is to be a politician, in Cleveland's sense.

These empirical and historical usages may seem to spring naturally from the deeper foundations of liberal thought as well. After all, liberalism arose as a response to one of the most challenging features of politics in the modern world: the recognition, and moral acceptance, of intrasocietal value pluralism. In the aftermath of the Reformation and the seemingly endless religious wars it unleashed across Europe, liberal thinkers, in their various ways, sought to find a moral basis for social union among a citizenry holding divergent views about the very meaning of life. In such conditions, a liberal rights-based conception of justice has obvious attractions, both pragmatic and moral. Within societies where those attractions came publicly to be understood, it has seemed natural to political theorists to describe liberalism as aspiring only to the spare citizen ideal of the derivative account.

Rawls, for example, describes the norms of good citizen conduct in this narrowly derivative way. For him, the criteria of good citizen conduct are specified precisely by what I have called the political liberal proviso. The virtues of a liberal citizen, as such, *just are* the political virtues—the statuses, dispositions, and habits of thought directly attendant to a liberal system of democratic self-governance and its justificatory groundwork. About these public ideals and virtues, Rawls says: "They characterize the ideal of a good citizen of a democratic state—a role specified by its political institutions."[8]

A prominent group of theorists have seized on this derivative ideal and developed it in a quasi-republican direction. These theorists argue that liberal states—as much as classical republican ones—require that citizens develop a particular set of moral capacities and dispositions upon which the health of those regimes depends. Liberal polities require citizens who have developed a distinctive set of "liberal virtues."

Galston, for example, notes that there are generic citizen virtues—courage, law-abidingness, and loyalty—required by any type of political system. But for a liberal polity to "function successfully" or to be "healthy" as a liberal polity, citizens must also be characterized by five habits of mind that Galston identifies as the liberal virtues. First, liberal states require that (most) citizens have not only the capacity to recognize the rights of others, but the restraint to respect those rights. Second, good liberal citizens are people who have developed the skills and habits needed to critically evaluate candidates for office. Third, liberal citizens must be moderate in the demands they make for public services. Fourth, Galston says that people must learn to engage in public discourse. That is, people must develop their capacity to understand problems and formulate solutions in the distinctive terms of public reason. Finally, good liberal citizens are those who are disposed to see that justice is actually realized in their society. Good citizens have "the disposition to narrow the gap (so far as in one's power) between principles and practices in liberal society."[9]

Macedo offers a similar catalog. A healthy liberal polity requires that citizens develop and exercise three general dispositions that Macedo identifies as the foundational liberal virtues: "a willingness [1] to 'live and let live,' [2] to subordinate personal plans and commitments to impartial rules of law, and [3] to persuade rather than coerce." While liberal justice may be "in force" even in a society where these citizen dispositions are absent, still Macedo says, "The liberal virtues will, nevertheless, distinguish a community flourishing in a distinctively liberal way from a community simply governed by liberal justice."[10]

These so-called virtue liberals recognize that these derivative norms are valuable not strictly in terms of preventing the decay of the state institutions. These dispositions may also have nonpublic value to people, a value in their personal lives, insofar as fairness is important even within families and between friends. But no theorist following this derivative route thinks that the hoped-for liberal virtues describe the attitudes and dispositions people must have if they are to live full and ethically satisfying lives. Good citizenship, as such, is at best a small piece of living well.

Still, this movement from an affirmation of a liberal conception of justice to the acceptance of a derivative understanding of citizenship has disappointed, and disaffected, many others. Liberalism, affirming only a proceduralist account of societal flourishing, has seemed to many to yield an unattractive, or least a highly attenuated, account of good human living-together—insofar as it promises any such thing at all.[11] Sometimes this unease has been expressed by internal critics such as Glendon, who affirm liberal justice but worry nonetheless about unintended human costs collateral to that affirmation. For others, the moral truncation of the liberal social ideal signals the need to abandon liberalism altogether.

With the rebirth of interest in liberal theory, there has been a corresponding rebirth of interest in a more robust, ethically charged ideal of human living together: that symbolized by a supposedly ancient or classical conception of citizenship. There is a longing, present in many recent communitarian or neorepublican writings, for an altogether different, nonliberal way of understanding the point of political union generally and of good citizen conduct in particular. This is a longing for the recovery of a classical citizen ideal.[12] Whether there ever was such a citizen and whether we have any reason to affirm such an ideal for ourselves in present conditions are matters on which I am doubly dubious. Still, there is an idea within these longings worth considering: It may be possible to understand these yearnings for the long-lost classical citizen not as a rejection of the liberal approach to politics, but as a rejection merely of the *derivative interpretation* of liberal citizenship. Looked at this way, republican enthusiasts may have something to teach even the most committed liberals about the possibilities inherent in their own view. To discover that lesson, we must pause to allow ourselves to enter the world of the classical citizen.

FROM CIVIC HUMANISM TO POLITICAL LIBERALISM

We are familiar with the outer aspect of the classical citizen from the red-capped images of the French Revolution. The good citizen there was actively involved in the affairs of the Republic. Those activities engaged his main energies, energies by which he nourished his deepest sense of himself.[13] In the history of political ideas, this conception of citizenship has been associated with Rousseau, Machiavelli, and many others. But the theoretical foundations for this ideal citizen, and the definitions of the concepts that support him, are usually traced to the civic humanism of Aristotle. While this idealized classical citizen turns out to be only loosely

connected to the conception of politics Aristotle himself actually ex-
pounded, this "Aristotelian" citizen ideal is worth a close look.

Aristotle saw the study of ethics and that of political science as continu-
ous with one another. This is why Aristotle begins with questions about
the nature of human beings and the activities normatively most proper
for beings of that sort. For Aristotle, the fundamental question of social
philosophy—How should humans live together?—seemed obviously to include the question How should humans live? When Aristotle defined man
as *kata phusin zoon politikon*, an animal that is by his very nature political,
he meant that humans find and develop their true nature in their relationships with others. Humans do this not regarding any topic or other but
regarding the affairs of the political community. Aristotle's civic humanism,
on this telling of it, relied upon a strict separation between the affairs of
the political community, the *polis*, and those of private life, the household
or *oikos*. The realm of private life lacked any complete moral charge of its
own. It was the realm of a subject class concerned mainly with the provision
of everyday wants and needs, the material base from which citizenship
could be launched.[14]

Aristotle defined politics as the activity of ruling and being ruled in turn,
and thus the class of beings who were by nature suited for political activity
were those capable of so ruling and being ruled. The main subject of those
self-ruling activities were the affairs of the *polis*, not those of the *oikos*, affairs
such as commerce and war with other political communities, and debate
about virtue, emulation, and authority. It was through their participation
in these very activities that citizens realized their ethical natures. It was
there that each could hope to find the greatest measure of happiness. It was
with his role there, we are told, that each most closely identified himself as
the person he was.[15]

On this reading of the classical, civic humanist approach to social philosophy, questions about "justice" are understood to come in last, as it were.
For Aristotle, justice is defined as the virtue of a community that functions
well with respect to the conditions of human well-being, where the conditions of that well-being have antecedently been identified as the political
activities of mutual self-rule. Indeed, in *Politics* 3.9 Aristotle explicitly distinguishes two ways of understanding the role of justice within social theory or, as he puts it, two ways of defining justice. On one definition, what
he calls partial or limited justice, justice assigns to the state merely the role
of protecting economic exchange and preventing crimes. Aristotle rejects
this way of using the term, saying that the assignment of such a role, while
necessary for justice, is by no means sufficient to that concept. To achieve
justice in its proper definition, what he calls complete justice, a state must
aim at something with a greater ethical charge: "the state exists for the sake
of a good life, and not for the sake of life only."[16] Justice is the virtue of a

community so constructed by its constitution that by engaging in its activities citizens discover and activate their true nature: by engaging in the affairs of a state and working toward complete justice, each becomes the being he could at his best be. The practices of citizenship are seen as overlapping in important ways with the practices of human well-being. Justice, on this view, is intimately linked to well-being through the concept "citizenship."[17]

No doubt this familiar account is too simple. Aristotle did not see human fulfillment as being *completed* in citizen activities. For example, Aristotle sometimes speaks of citizenship activities as themselves instrumentally linked to a further activity: namely, the godlike activity of pure contemplation, which Aristotle sometimes describes as the activity to the highest degree pleasant, and self-sufficing, for human beings.[18] Also, Aristotle greatly valued friendship (*filia*) and saw opportunities for friendship in both public and private life, so he did not see private life as completely stripped of ethical charge.[19] Further, he describes the virtues of citizens within specific regimes as varying according to people's social roles, and the virtues of citizens generally as varying from regime to regime: for Aristotle, the definition of the "good man" is fixed at a deeper level than is the definition of the good citizen.[20] Any detailed examination of these themes in the work of other thinkers in this tradition—Rousseau or, perhaps, Machiavelli—would require similar qualifications and others besides.[21]

This classical understanding of citizenship, however qualified, is famously exclusive and exploitative. It might well be argued that—in its Aristotelian formulation at least—this conception of citizenship depended even *as a concept* on its exclusiveness.[22] Still this conception contains within it an exceptionally powerful and attractive idea. That idea is this: for any society to do well or flourish is for the people within it (all of those recognized as citizens at least) to do well or flourish too.

At the core of this tradition is the contention that there should be a strong linkage between the activities described under the heading "citizenship"—the normative requirements of which it is the job of political theorists to describe—and the payout of those activities in terms of human fulfillment or well-being. The forms of social construction people engage in as "citizens" serve as the primary focus for self-identification, the center of each person's self-understanding. One can perhaps depart from that center temporarily to take up other deliberative or affective perspectives as the need arises. But those other identities are partial, incomplete. When one returns home, it is to an understanding of one's responsibilities as a citizen that one returns. For civic humanists, it is through the activities of citizenship that each of those recognized as a citizen in important ways becomes *who* he truly is. Questions citizens ask such as Why should I act as good citizen would? or What is good citizenship good *for*? are questions that are readily answered. The activities involved with citizenship are *for*, and indeed are largely constitutive of, well-being. To ask What should I do as a citizen? means to take up the question How can I do well as the person that I am?[23] A theory of good citizen conduct, on this approach, must of necessity be broad enough to answer the fundamental question of social philosophy: How should people live together? Social philosophy, while necessarily involving discussions of institutions, engages in those discussions with concerns about the eudaimonistic impact of those institutions on the lives of actual citizens utmost in mind.

It is precisely this feature at the core of the civic humanist view—the idea that any adequate account of societal flourishing must include an account of how the humans living there might flourish too—that has seemed to many critics unavailable within the standard philosophical defenses of liberalism. Beyond the important goal of securing the conditions of full political voluntarism, liberals perceive themselves as able to fully do their job without showing any deeper concern for the sorts of lives people actually live— their ground level eudaimonistic prospects—within liberal society. This narrowing of mission is a direct consequence of the very different way liberals think of the concept "justice."

There are as many liberalisms as there are civic humanisms, so generalizations here run the same perils as there. But thinkers in the broad philosophical tradition from Kant to Mill and through to the most recent work by Rawls have affirmed some version or other of the "incomplete" definition of justice that Aristotle rejected. The primary role of the liberal state is to protect interests citizens have as nonpublic persons. Liberals think of justice as the concept that defines the scope and limits of state activity with that aim. As we saw in chapter 1, liberals seek moral foundations for state institutions that are to the greatest degree possible *neutral* regarding which substantive type of human life is best. Social justice is seen more as a framework to support ethical life than as an account or expression of ethical life itself. Unlike the republican separation of oikos and polis, the liberal separation of nonpublic and public actually *amounts to* a significant separation of concerns about human well-being and concerns about political morality.[24] In modern conditions, liberals see political activities and forms of self-understanding as primarily in service to, rather than expressive of, what is highest and most important in human experience. Under liberalism, the justificatory continuum Aristotle saw between the study of ethics and that of politics has been weakened and made less certain.

This broad view about the role of the modern state has important consequences for the liberal conception of good citizen conduct and thus for the boundaries of liberal theorizing—though these are consequences liberals often accept without noticing them. Under liberalism, the social philosopher's question—How should people live together?—is claimed to be readable only as the narrower question of political morality: namely, When is political coercion justified? The virtues and norms requisite to fulfill the liberal social ideal, suddenly, are treated as tracking only the answer liberals give to that narrower question.

In this way, the norms of good citizen conduct are treated as narrowly derivative from the liberal account of justice. Because of the way liberals understand the concept justice, the interpersonal norms that are derived from that concept necessarily leave out much of the thickly eudaimonistic (or well-being based) element of human living-together that were so central to the classical citizen ideal. Typically this is said to happen passively, as in T. H. Marshall's influential account, whereby to be a "liberal citizen" means merely to have been named a holder of rights and immunities that the liberal theory of justice sets out.[25] As we have seen, this derivation of citizenship from justice may also take a somewhat more active form, where the virtues of people as social constructors are found in those practices necessary for the functioning of liberal institutions and the task of liberal public justification.

But whether this derivation occurs actively or passively, when the notion of citizenship gets plugged into the traditional liberal system, the fusing of well-being and justice on which the classical notion of citizenship relied is broken. Under liberalism—on this familiar derivationist view—the norms describing what people are said to owe one another as "good citizens" are only those norms aimed at the support of justice-based institutions and deliberative democratic processes. Citizenship does not include the thicker practices of human interpersonal flourishing. Because of the relatively non-eudaimonistic content of liberal justice (content that helps picks out a theory of justice as *liberal* in the first place), the other substantive features of "citizenship" in its classical sense get truncated or are left out all together. Activities and understandings that people take up as a participants in the liberal project are not claimed to implicate people's highest ethical being, their deepest sense of self-identity. Liberal citizenship, as activities in service to one's political community, may be for the occasional zealot a life project. But most people think of their identities as liberal participants as a "sometimes" identity, an identity one takes up from time to time but in which people have no reason to dwell. Because of the eudaimonistic primacy that liberals accord to nonpublic life, the practice of liberal citizenship is usually thought of as having instrumental rather than operational value. The public activities of the liberal citizen protect people's freedom rather than constitute it.

In this way, the definition of justice favored by liberals threatens the coherence of the very term *citizen*. It does this by revealing the precise point at which citizenship as a concept is most fragile, a point of fragility that was necessarily obscured when we considered that concept in its original setting. Can the norms of "good citizen conduct" be defined as applying only to those interpersonal statuses and definitions that are (1) derivative from the projects and normative ideals of one's state (projects and ideals provided, for liberals, by justice and the deliberative requirements of public reason)? Or must the concept *citizenship*—and the range of socially constructive responsibilities that concept denotes—also refer to those interpersonal statuses and dispositions that are (2) essential to a person's *life*, to whatever activities and projects of human living-together engage and help form a person's deep self-understanding?

Within civic humanism, these two different readings of *citizenship* did not diverge in any radical way. In that idealized world, no gap between political activity and human flourishing could be opened to this degree. The ancients, at least on the popular understanding of them, could easily have allowed the activities of "good citizenship" to be identified as those activities associated with (or derivative from) justice and the projects of the state. For civic humanists, justice was a concept linked straight to human freedom and moral flourishing through the idea of the citizen. So too, from the other side, they could just as well have identified the activities of good citizenship as including those interpersonal activities aimed at actualizing the nature of humans as the kind of animal humans were understood most basically to be. Citizenship, on this idealized classical view, was the very concept through which a strong connection between human flourishing and state-based activity was achieved. But in the modern setting, because of the very different role justice plays in liberal theory, citizenship as a concept seems no longer able to encompass both.

Within the liberal tradition itself, this separating of eudaimonistic questions from political ones reaches a climax only with political liberalism. Indeed, political liberals criticize ethical liberals precisely for *not* breaking the justificatory fusing between ethical arguments and political ones. It is that subterranean fusing that created the crisis in legitimacy from which political liberalism was born. In the social conditions engendered by free institutions, on the political liberal telling, any form of justification for political coercion that relied on a fusion of ethical arguments and political ones would result in a regime unable to act with legitimacy toward many reasonable citizens. Larmore, for example, rejects the traditional understanding of liberalism for just this reason: "For Kant and Mill, *citoyen* and *homme* coincide at heart."[26] Political liberals, by contrast, separate those concepts. With political liberalism, the ancient continuum between the study of ethics and that of politics has at last been cut off and rejected.[27]

I hasten to emphasize that liberals of every stripe have reason to affirm the broad understanding of political life they do and to reject outright any classical or civic humanist one in modern conditions. An acceptance of reasonable value pluralism, and the corresponding drive to recognize all adult people within a society as citizens, morally precludes the coercive imposition of some people's values on other people that the civic humanist conception of justice would require today.[28] There is indeed no road back to the heroic simplicities of the ancient polis. Even in there were, members of diverse modern societies committed to treating one another with mutual respect would have no reason to tread it.

There is a lesson here for liberals nonetheless. Affirming a liberal conception of justice does not commit us to considering only a derivative interpretation of one's responsibilities as a liberal social constructor, any more than affirming the liberal principle of legitimacy constrains us only to theorize about the formal grounds of justified coercion. We can affirm a liberal conception of politics—whether grounded ethically or politically—and yet not think that a concern for public values, though foundational, is *all* that is required of liberal citizens if their society is to succeed or flourish as a liberal society. The boundaries of liberal theorizing can be drawn wider than that by all good liberals, ethical and political alike.

A Different Approach

The criteria of good citizen conduct reside in those activities people must undertake if their society is to realize its ideal—that is, to flourish or succeed as a society of that type. But what if a liberal society, as such, does not automatically realize its ideal when the people in it become freely committed to a liberal conception of social justice? What if the social world as envisaged by liberals flourishes only when people live lives that are as ethically satisfying as possible—each by her own nonpublic lights—given their common commitment to just democratic institutions?[29]

The criteria of good citizen conduct, on this very different approach, are not narrowly derivable from liberal justice or the norms of public reason. Such a derivation would leave out significant elements of the human, well-being-directed component that any ultimate ideal of social flourishing must include. Perhaps the idea of liberal citizenship also implicates us in the question of how well politically reasonable people, from their own various perspectives, negotiate the *interfacing* of the public and the personal normative structures of their world. This would suggest a conception of liberal citizenship and of the liberal virtues that goes well beyond what is required of people as a matter of democratic legitimacy and just constitutional construction. Rather than being simply derivative from the public norms in a liberal society, this is a *substantive* or *eudaimonistically directed* understanding of liberal good citizen conduct.[30]

While this use of the term *liberal citizenship* may fall strangely on the ears of philosophers, this usage is common among people in actual liberal societies. Along with the dominant derivative views, the Conover team found persistent traces of a very different understanding of "good citizen-ship" among contemporary Americans. What understanding do these peo-ple have of the norms relevant to them as citizens? They have the substan-tive one I just described.

In contrast to the majority view, Conover reports, "a minority of our American discussants describe their sense of identity as Americans and their identity as citizens as complementary but not blended, not as one and the same." For these people, "being an American is to be a person with rights. But being a *citizen* in America is to be a person with rights *and* duties."[31]

When asked to describe their distinctive duties of citizenship, these re-spondents, unlike the majority, did not pick out democratic or justice-based duties. Rather, as Conover reports, "The roots of this identity naturally extend below the national level to [personal] experiences within the local communities where people live their daily lives and develop their connec-tions with one another." As Conover says, "The notion of rights, [these respondents] said, 'leaves out the moral issue of citizenship.' " Respondents holding this view fully accept their public responsibilities as an aspect of their duties as citizens. But their conception of themselves as citizens merely *begins* with those derivative concerns.[32]

Americans who accept the derivative understanding described them-selves as "wearing their citizenship lightly." By contrast, those who thought of their citizenship in the substantive way saw their duties of citizenship calling upon them throughout all realms of their lives. On this view, "to be a citizen is . . . to be encumbered, desirably encumbered." As one person said about her activities as a citizen, " 'It's just what I am to be involved in what's going on in my community, in my children's lives, in my family's lives, in my neighbors' lives.' " Questions about their citizenship go to the very heart of how each understands herself, her commitments and projects, and the role those responsibilities play in the unfolding narrative of her life. Conover says, "Citizenship for these discussants is a central aspect of their identities."[33] They think of their citizenship not derivatively but *substantively*—in terms of the thick patterns of interpersonal connections and nonpublic dependencies that define each as the particular person she at her best might be.[34]

The historical roots of this very different way of understanding good citizenship, while not spread as widely as those of the derivative interpreta-tion, run at least equally deep in the American experience. When William Dodge established the Yale lecture series I mentioned before, he described those talks as aiming at "an understanding of the duties of *Christian* citizen-ship." It seemed obvious to Dodge that the duties of citizenship, in a society whose state institutions were limited to the protection of freedom must somehow involve not just the virtues of a politician (Grover Cleveland's ideal, recall) but something deeper—something more like the virtues of a *good soul*. This idea—that liberal citizenship properly involves not only one's responsibilities to protect the outer frame of interpersonal life, but also responsibilities to projects and self-understandings at the very core of nonpublic identity—surfaced from time to time throughout the Yale lecture series. For example, in one passage McCall says, "The term good citizen and good man come near to being synonymous." As if in recognition of the social-constructive power of this rival, substantive interpretation, McCall continued, "A readiness to do unto one's neighbor as one would have his neighbor do unto him would accomplish more in the direction of making a just and beneficent state than all the constitutions and systems of government that were ever devised."[35]

Another speaker in the series, L. P. Jacks of Manchester College, Oxford, described the recognition of liberal rights and political statuses as merely the *first stage* of good citizen conduct. In Jacks's view, "It is through their subsequent transformation into duties that our rights become significant." He described rights that become arrested at the recognition stage as a fruit that never ripened: borrowing from Bunyan, " 'green plums from the garden of Beelzebub.' " Jacks continued, "A community possessed of rights which had failed to grow into duties would be socially imbecile." And thus, "this process of winning our rights, though not complete, has advanced sufficiently far to give us at least a dawning sense of our duties—a phenomenon full of promise for the future of mankind."[36]

In a lecture at Harvard just a few years later, John Hibben argued that citizenship must involve norms beyond those derivable from liberal public values. In a liberal society, the central problem of social order "is not the problem of adjusting [each citizen's] liberty to that of the liberty of another, but it is the problem of *exercising his freedom* so as to make it a contributing factor to the welfare of the whole social mass."[37] According to Hibben, "The growing complexity of our modern life and the multiplicity of relations which bind together more and more intimately the elements of the social mass, increasing the dependence of man upon man in the living organism of society—all this gives to the individual a significant power and influence. His life, his standards of conduct, his character, touch more men and influence them more profoundly, all of his natural powers are intensified and more widely extended."[38]

In such conditions, Hibben claimed, "one who is realizing his responsibilities as a citizen lives for the most part in a sphere quite beyond legal right and wrong." The norms of good citizen conduct come not from the law or from consideration of one's standing in relation to any political institutions, but from what Hibben called "manners"—that is, those diverse sets of self-legislated "moral standards [that one finds] throughout society at large, continuously maintained and realized in customary behavior."[39] It is these norms of civil society that Hibben sees as providing action-guidance to people as citizens.

On this view, to be a good citizen means far more than being merely just, or law-abiding, or consistent in the performance of one's political duties. Liberal citizenship imposes far heavier burdens: citizenship involves the very center of one's life. "As the fundamental basis of citizenship there must be some *philosophy of life*." Hibben himself describes that substantive philosophy in terms of religion: "a fundamental belief in a moral governor of mankind"[40] Of course, no part of the normative framework advocated by political liberals can be justified by reference to a single religion, or to any other single nonpublic outlook affirmed as ethically true. Still, the main thrust of Hibben's account is clear. Even in the heyday of discussions about good citizen conduct, there were persistent reachings toward a broader, more eudaimonistically directed understanding of the burdens of liberal citizenship.[41] People in America have long called on one another *as citizens* to perform responsibilities they have to one another as nonpublic agents.

This dissident understanding of liberal citizenship invites us to recover a feature near the core of the classical citizen ideal. On this reading, the self-understandings required of each person as a "good citizen" and those activities and attitudes required of each as a "good person" are fused once again. This does not mean, à la Hibben, that people must all agree on a single definition of what it means to be a good person. Any such fusing must be achieved in a way compatible with the acceptance of reasonable value pluralism, with the principles of justice and the ideal of reciprocity fully affirmed. In modern conditions, the norms of good citizenship must be substantive *but plural*.

Still, the idea behind these dissident stirrings is that good citizenship must somehow, involve recognizing the ethical claims made by others on one's political freedom. Questions people take up as *citizens* in a free society are questions about the very meaning and purpose of their own lives.[42] These questions center on the complex interface of people's public and nonpublic identities. People in liberal societies have responsibilities to one another as citizens that their common allegiance to public values cannot possibly discharge.

Liberal citizenship is essentially an *activity*. It is by acting on one's justice-based understandings that persons become and remain members of the various socially constructive nonpublic groupings within which each constitutes his identity. One of the field owners in Vermont cannot cut up his field for housing lots and yet retain his status as a member of the group affirming an understanding of property rights in that land in the traditional stewardship sense. So too with the mill owner's decisions with respect to his Jewishness, and with the African Americans with respect to the narrative traditions they affirm. It is only by their activities that people in liberal societies become or remain part of their identity-shaping groups.[43] Persons are free to shift their allegiances, to overlap them in complex ways, and to embark on radically new projects in all the ways that principles of justice protect and make possible.

But within a world structured by liberal institutions, it is by interpreting and acting upon their political autonomy that persons individuate and become the fully dimensioned moral being each has the capacity to be. It is by citizens' skillful use of their various compass concepts that their society as a whole can flourish in a distinctively liberal way. Citizenship requires the skillful exercise of nonpublic reason.

It is only by assuming that "liberalism" is coextensive with "the domain of the political" that we could mistake the derivative aspect of liberal citizenship for the *whole* of liberal citizenship. As we have seen, the normative domain of liberal citizenship inevitably extends *beyond* the domain of public reason. For any self-aware political liberal, any theory of good citizen conduct must include considerations about the way public values impinge on nonpublic spheres, and how those values can be put to personal uses there. Grover Cleveland's "virtues of a politician" cannot alone support a flourishing political liberal society. The real liberal virtues must be more like the ideal William Dodge seems to have had in mind. In a free society, the virtues of good citizens must be the virtues of (diverse) *good souls*.

I believe that we should take seriously these stirrings, however weak and scattered, and reconsider the conception of good citizen conduct most appropriate to liberalism. Our concerns about unintended spillovers and free erosion in mind, I mean to test the idea that what is essential to liberal citizenship are those socially constructive activities that implicate people's deepest ethical natures. Citizenship requires more of us than a freely given commitment to just institutions. To be a good citizen is to be a good *person*.

In this chapter I have merely attempted to gather together these dissident calls about liberal citizenship. I have hoped to show how the vision of citizen excellence they imply contrasts with the dominant derivative view. Of course, people in liberal societies will go on exercising their public claims for nonpublic purposes regardless of whether we think of those activities as ones they perform as "citizens." However, the way we understand what people are doing as they perform those activities becomes a matter of considerable importance when we turn from abstract questions of definition to concrete problems of institutional design and structure. By deciding whether to think of these well-being-directed activities as matters of citizenship—or not—we decide whether concerns people have in the nonpublic realm are matters to which we think political theorists as such must speak—or not. If liberals recognize these concerns as lying within the normative boundaries of their view, this may give them a natural opening by which to counteract any ethical taxes inadvertently levied by liberalism's public values component. The substantive ideal of citizenship may give liberals an opportunity to reduce the threat of free erosion, while fully respecting each person's political autonomy. To see how, we must consider the distinctive social ambitions of political liberalism.

Chapter Five

THE FORMATIVE PROJECT

THE SUBSTANTIVE IDEAL

The arrangement of normative structures within the liberal social world makes available a richly substantive account of good citizen conduct, not just the familiar derivative one. The roots of this substantive ideal run deep in the intellectual soil of the United States. There are persistent stirrings of this ideal among the citizenry today. Still, this rival ideal finds no voice among contemporary political philosophers. On the view that dominates the academy, the uniquely "liberal virtues" are all and only those habits of mind attendant to the public projects of democratic self-rule and liberal constitutionalism. When a citizenry has developed these virtues, along with the more generic citizen virtues, their polity flourishes in a distinctively liberal way.

But can the health of any liberal society—and of a political liberal society in particular—be described in terms derived from liberal justice and the norms of democratic deliberation? As Glendon's concern about the spread of rights-talk suggests, people can recognize that their society is faring poorly—even if no injustice is to be found.

People's encounters with the the ethical background culture of their society must be central to any account of a liberal society's success or good functioning. After all, those encounters shape the very core of people's lives. The concerns of citizens about their society's background culture, if unaddressed, may undermine the ambition political liberals have of showing how a just regime is possible in conditions of reasonable value pluralism. As we saw in chapter 1, the bare threat of spillovers may alienate many "admissible" citizens of faith who might otherwise have signed on—some of our C-people, for example. But, as the questions of our B-people suggest, not all the reasons political liberals have to take up these concerns about spillovers are legitimacy-directed in that formal way. Even regarding the dimensions of citizens' concerns that do not go down to questions of justified coercion, the liberal commitment to answer questions their citizens have as best they are able requires that they do more in this regard. The "liberal virtues," if there are any, cannot simply be attitudes and dispositions that exacerbate (or simply define again) the concerns that admissible citizens have about spillovers. On the contrary: virtues deserving that name must include whatever nonpublic attitudes and dispositions might *mitigate* those serious concerns, by offering themselves as eudaimonistic *remedies* to spillovers. The liberal virtues, properly understood, must be the virtues people have in a liberal polity the social structures of which are as welcoming as possible to the aims and self-understandings of all politically reasonable citizens—A-people, B-people, and C-people alike.

That in mind, I would like to suggest a different view of the liberal virtues. I start from the idea I just mentioned: the most attractive liberal polity is one designed to be as welcoming as possible to all citizens deemed politically reasonable. The most successful political liberal society, as such, is not one that is simply welcoming enough that people will be able to affirm the political conception of justice in an all-things-considered way—this latter being the eudaimonistic threshold test that the Rawlsians call full individual justification. The liberal virtues are the habits of mind citizens need if they are to play their parts in the realization of that former, more ambitious ideal. As before, these liberal virtues are attitudes and dispositions that we cannot require citizens to have—if that were somehow possible. But they are those dispositions that people do require if they are to excel within the form of living-together that political liberalism, by its own motivational ambitions, at its best represents.

We cannot simply assume that the social problem to which liberalism is the answer is one that must be fully solved by the norms of public reason and democratic self-governance. A complete political liberal theory, in particular, needs to do more than affirm some conception of justice as most reasonable and demonstrate the conditions under which it might legitimately be implemented. In light of its own motivational foundations, a complete political liberal theory must also give an account of how a free affirmation of liberal justice affects the diverse sorts of nonpublic social construction in which good citizens, at their best, might engage.

Emphatically, this conception of a successful, well-functioning political liberal society is not one in which people's deeply held beliefs are never challenged. In any liberal society, such challenges can be expected to be thrown up spontaneously and regularly. This is not to say that such challenges are officially endorsed by political liberals (as they might be for some ethical liberals). Rather, the emergence of such challenges is but a predictable consequence of people's exercising their associative and deliberative liberties.[1] Complete neutrality of effect is indeed impracticable. But if certain state policies and programs predictably—albeit unintentionally—have the effect of unsettling the views of some politically reasonable citizens more than those of others, then a different sort of problem arises. Unless justice positively requires it, political liberals have no business endorsing policies the effects of which inadvertently favor some politically reasonable views over other ones.

Political liberalism is not merely a theory about what principles of justice are justified in conditions of diversity. Nor is it merely a view about the standing of those evaluative principles in relation to other normative structures, or about the conditions under which those principles of justice legitimately may be enforced. Political liberalism is a broad theory about social construction. As much as civic humanism, ethical liberalism, or any theory that disallows any clear distinction between public questions and eudaimonistic ones, political liberalism is at base a theory about the norms of human interpersonal life. Like each of the others, it is one answer to an ancient question: how should humans live together? What is distinctive about the political liberal answer is that it includes a nonpublic element that must be worked out *in light of* political liberalisms unique way of drawing the distinction between public and nonpublic realms. Political liberal norms of interpersonal relations—if we could find them—must be norms given within the framework of a conception of justice that itself is constructed as a response to reasonable value pluralism. As such, a liberal theory should tell us what patterns of social construction, of citizen self-understanding, the state should seek to promote so that all people deemed politically admissible have their best chance of living lives they find meaningful over time, given their common commitment to political justice.

Allow me to suggest the following definition of good citizen conduct: the good political liberal citizen is a person who is skillful at the art of exercising her rights. That skill also requires that she has a certain wisdom in her understanding of the political ideas in terms of which her rights are justified. Through the myriad forms of liberal nonpublic reason I described in chapter 3, this person recognizes the flexibility in the exercise of the rights set out for her by principles of justice and the various branches of law. This good citizen reads the impersonal justice-based rules of her society from the perspective of her own commitments and patterns of attachments. Those commitments, what I call compass concepts, do not themselves determine what her conduct should be. Rather, for most people, good citizenship involves the difficult ongoing matter of maintaining an equipoise between one's standing as politically autonomous and the various compass concept traditions with which one identifies. Good citizenship is a matter of finding that equipoise in a way that neither inadvertently severs one from the traditions and ways of reasoning that give one's life moral sustenance nor allows one's personal loyalties to eclipse one's sense of political autonomy (such that one's compass concepts become controlling concepts). The problem of finding that equipoise looms most dramatically for citizens within totalizing compass concept traditions. But it is the central ethical problem faced by every liberal citizen: how to make a success of a life lived on the interface of public and personal identity components.

On this substantive understanding of citizenship, the norms guiding the actions of the good citizen come from her own deepest understanding of who she is and aims to be, an understanding worked out only partially in light of what justice makes possible. The good liberal citizen naturally links the series of questions How should I live? What kind of person should I be? and What do my rights mean to me? The good citizen affirms who she is, and develops herself into the person she will be, through the way she exercises her political autonomy.

The liberal virtues, on this substantive approach, are the dispositions and habits of mind characteristic of the good liberal citizen. The liberal virtues are the virtues of people skillful in the art of exercising their political rights and liberties. In a society marked by the reasonable value pluralism that political liberalism accepts, there will be a great variety of patterns by which that art might meaningfully be developed and perfected. The different forms of that art correspond to the variety of understandings of personal excellence—the politically admissible ways of answering questions such as Who should I be? How should I live? and even By what *mode of reasoning* should I express my concern for others and for myself?

Liberal theorists take reasonable value pluralism as a basic social fact. So their account of citizen virtue, if it is to be a liberal account of citizen virtue, must be importantly plural as well. Out of respect for the ideals of mutuality and reciprocity, these norms of good citizen conduct cannot be rigidly or universally identifiable from some external perspective, as substantive citizen norms might be identified within a civic humanist setting. Rather, the norms of citizenship are immanent in the actions and attitudes of people who live lives of meaning and integrity within a rights-based society. Any account of liberal virtues must be precisely as diverse as the society to which it is meant to be normatively applied.

Earlier in this book, I described a society characterized by alphabet people. Three broad groups in that society affirmed comprehensive doctrines that were compatible with the requirements of liberal public reason. In a society marked by value pluralism of that sort, therefore, the substantive approach would mark out three broad sets of citizen virtue. Each of those sets would consist of the intersection of the universal norms of justice and the more localized norms specific to each group's particular compass concept traditions.

I described the nonpublic forms of reasoning affirmed by the A-people as roughly mirroring the norms of liberal public reason. Like all his fellow citizens, the A-person is a good citizen insofar as he is able to combine his commitment to the justice-based module with his commitment to whatever nonpublic form of reason he affirms, and to do so in a fashion that he finds satisfying in a long-term way. At the point of action, whenever a social situation activates his political autonomy, the A-person typically insists on keeping a critical distance even from commitments and projects that have played an important role in his life thus far. The A-person holds his compass well out before him, in the reflective attitude of the lone orienteer. To be a good citizen, an A-person needs virtues such as an ability to listen to new reasons suggested by others and to create and consider new reasons for himself. He eagerly hones his ability to formulate principles and to act on them in a self-conscious way, and not just in public matters. In his nonpublic life, such a citizen may need the virtues of tenacity and independence, as well as a developed habit of questioning authority. He may also need features of character that enable him to avoid falling into the forms of legal egotism and atomistic anomie that lurk as caricatures of his autonomic view. By developing those virtues, he finds meaning on his own terms within a diverse society committed to justice.

The habits and dispositions needed by the C-people would be quite different. The C-people live comparatively settled nonpublic lives. Their lives are centered more on traditions of authority and less on the ideal of justificatory transparency and the reflective forums of reason-exchanging that attend their society's public institutions. C-people take their direction from compasses that they carry more internally. Citizens of faith need to develop dispositions that enable them to resist the commercial and secular culture of mass society. A central virtue needed by them may be a kind of personal *stasis*—the settled disposition to remain at rest within the roles one finds oneself occupying, a disposition made out in light of one's recognition of one's rights-based sanctions for doing otherwise. The members of Kiryas Joel, for example, need to recognize their rights of individual dissent and even of exit as representing a sort of currency of social communication. Through the way each member of that group, generation to generation, exercises the claims set out by justice, they communicate to each other what norms they as a group think most important as regulators of social action. Insofar at they are politically reasonable, there is no other pattern of piety, of joint "theocratic" commitment, available to them within the liberal social world.

Good citizenship for B-people, representatives of what I take to be the mainstream, involves a richly mixed set of norms containing reason elements from groups on either side. On certain occasions or regarding certain matters, the compass concept traditions of a B-person will require detachment and vigorous reflection from an impersonal evaluative standpoint. At other times and on other matters, he will be called upon to act in ways that show his allegiance to projects that he simply finds himself encumbered with—for example, norms that bear on him simply because he is Catholic, or commitments that are his because of the circumstances of people who are his siblings or parents, or commitments that he freely entered into in the past (e.g., marriage). But to make a success of his life, given who he is, and given his commitment to justice for political purposes, he will need to develop certain habits of mind and manners of perception that are unique to those sharing a worldview such as his.

Of course, even this general way of cataloging the liberal virtues is artificially homogeneous. There may be substantively different visions of personal excellence within each of these three broad categories—categories that primarily mark *styles of reasoning*. Mainstream practicing Catholics in America today may be as equally well categorized C-people as many mainstream Evangelical Protestants, yet the ideals of moral and spiritual excellence characteristic of each are markedly different. A hard-left welfare liberal might be as much an A-person as any devotee of Ayn Rand, even if their visions of interpersonal excellence are near opposites. B-people especially will exhibit so great a range of views that the virtues characteristic of them may stubbornly resist categorization. Even within these subcategories—the extreme individualism of Randians; the authoritarian deference of the Catholics—excellence ultimately must be cashed out in terms of what individual citizens actually do at the point of action, as players within the narratives of their own lives.

Unlike the familiar derivative view, on the substantive approach we do not identify the liberal virtues by making a list only of those virtues whose need happens to be common to all citizens. We proceed in a more foundational way: the liberal virtues are the virtues citizens need if their society is to be healthy or to flourish as a liberal society. Unlike civic humanists, political liberals do not think any single catalog of the virtues of a good human life can be worked out in advance and ascribed to citizens en masse. But, just like for the civic humanists, the social world as envisaged by political liberals ultimately succeeds only to the degree that people living there develop the interpersonal habits and forms of character that a good life (for each citizen) requires.

Given the great elasticity in the range of value traditions that political liberals claim they wish to accommodate, any substantive notion of citizen excellence must allow for a conception of citizen virtue that is at least equally elastic. Such an account is untidy. There is no neat catalog of the liberal virtues that might be printed up and passed around. The liberal virtues, on the substantive interpretation, are highly diverse and variegated, forever emerging in new forms at the moral interstices of real citizens' lives. Compared to the list-based approach of the derivative theorists, the substantive approach offers a markedly more *liberal* conception of the liberal virtues.

Moral Development and Liberal Individuation

The good liberal citizen is a person disposed to use the sanctions justice provides him to engage in ethically meaningful projects of social construction, projects that inevitably extend well beyond the realm of public value. Citizenship involves the desire of people to exercise their rights with art. This is the core challenge that a liberal society puts to each of its members: can you negotiate the interface of public and nonpublic normative structures in your society in a way that you find satisfying over time? Those who succeed are good citizens. When many succeed, their society flourishes in a distinctively liberal way.

However, any political ideal that depends for its realization upon the dispositions and character of its citizenry must provide reasons for us to think that these very dispositions will emerge in a society of that sort. Giving an account of the motivations required of citizens is especially tricky work in the liberal context.

The principle of legitimacy requires that the basic motives required of citizens if the society is to achieve its ideal arise freely. A social ideal does not arise freely if it occurs only as the product of state action.[2] Liberals would reject as illegitimate—indeed monstrous—a society where people followed the rules of liberal justice only through fear of external sanction or punishment, or simply because they had undergone some state-sponsored program of motivational indoctrination. This does not mean that liberals can have no truck with state-mandated programs of civic education. Such programs may be crucial to a well-functioning liberal society, as we shall soon see. But liberals are required to proceed cautiously here. Liberal civic education requires that children arrive at the classrooms *desiring*, at least in some rough sense, to play the socially constructive part the liberal polity requires of them. State-mandated programs of civic education, therefore, must be more a matter of providing information and developing skills than of implanting motives.

Any liberal theory requires an account of free moral development as a motivational base for its account of civic education. The desire to be a good citizen must be shown to be a natural part of each person's good. Rawls, for example, is well aware that questions about free or natural moral development are crucial to the derivative account of good citizen conduct he defends. To prepare the ground for his account of state-sponsored civic education, Rawls offers an account of the stages of moral development as they are likely to emerge naturally in a just society. Rawls's account is developmental. On this approach, originally associated with Piaget, the construction of moral personality proceeds through a definite series of stages. The subsequent stages do not replace the previous stages but compound with them to produce levels of increasing complexity. Rawls describes three such stages, and formulates a psychological law for each.

The first stage, the "morality of authority," is a product of the relationships parents have with their children. This stage explains how a child can begin to care about the well-being of others:

> First law: Given that family institutions are just, and that parents love the child and manifestly express their love by caring for his good, then the child, recognizing their evident love of him, comes to love them.[3]

The morality of association, stage two, is a product of those lessons that both children and adults learn when they participate in shared institutions. Through playing various social roles—within the family, neighborhood, school—and even game playing with peers children develop an ability to recognize perspectives and interests of others that may differ from their own. They develop trust and a sense of reciprocity. Thus:

> Second law: Given that a person's capacity for fellow feeling has been realized by acquiring attachment in accordance with the first law, and given that a social arrangement is just and publicly known by all to be just, then this person develops ties of friendly feeling and trust toward others in the association as they with evident intention comply with their duties and obligations, and live up to the ideals of their station.[4]

The third stage is the morality of principle. Here people become attached to the principles not simply out of particular ties of friendship or out of a desire to win the approval of others. Rather, through seeing the benefits to all of just institutions, people become attached to the principles themselves. They have acquired a sense of justice:

> Third law: Given that a person's capacity for fellow feeling has been realized by his forming attachments in accordance with the first two laws, and given that a society's institutions are just and publicly known to be just, then this person acquires the corresponding sense of justice as he recognizes that he and those for whom he cares are the beneficiaries of these arrangements.[5]

Rawls calls this third stage "the *final* stage" of moral development.[6] Presumably, Rawls means that this is the final stage he thinks relevant to political theory. It is the final stage motivationally relevant to the *citizen*. This idea precisely reflects the derivative paradigm in which Rawls operates. If the normative boundaries of liberal theory construction are assumed to be coextensive with the elucidation and defense of some conception of liberal public principles, then of course an account of the moral motivations necessary for citizenship can be derived directly from those same principles. The motivations necessary for good citizen conduct, insofar as they are necessary for *citizen* conduct, center on "the sense of justice."[7]

The substantive interpretation of liberal citizenship requires a different, more ambitious motivational base (and thus, as we shall see, implies a different, more ambitious account of civic education in schools). Like any defender of the derivative ideal, however, a defender of a substantive ideal must demonstrate the plausibility of the account of moral motivation undergirding his (rival) account of citizenship. If the requisite motives could not be expected to arise freely, then that conception of good citizen conduct would have to rely upon the state to "manufacture" a citizen's motivational commitment to the roles he must play if the system is to function well. That would violate the principle of legitimacy, which any liberal account must satisfy. Can we show that motivations to good citizen conduct—in the substantive sense I have described—might arise in a natural way within a liberal society?

Rawls's developmental account ends with the would-be citizen seeing the social world through the motives that might undergird a sense of justice. This, as I said, is a predictable result within the derivative paradigm. The substantive interpretation of good citizen conduct invites us to see things differently. This approach begins from the observation that from the developmental perspective, the wide perspectivalism and concerns for autonomy on which the sense of justice is based by no means represent the closure or completion of human moral development. Indeed, it is basic to contemporary developmental psychology that one of the most significant stages of personal development—that of individuation—actually *begins* there.

On the main contemporary view, individuality becomes available to a person only after she has achieved the capacity not only for self-reflexivity but for full perspectivalism. At that threshold stage, as is implicit in Rawls's morality of principle stage, the person uses her self-reflexivity to take the viewpoints of persons outside her own group (including, presumably, a political viewpoint like that of public reason). Since a capacity to see the world from many different perspectives leaves the person aware of her freedom to choose among those perspectives for herself, this stage of development has aptly been called "the realization and intoxication of autonomy."[8]

Contemporary developmentalists see that experience of autonomy as merely the doorway toward individuation, the process by which a person employs her autonomy to construct a worldview. Through that activity, she makes her self into a system, a coherent whole. Autonomy, on this view, is not itself a form of individuation but rather a concept or vehicle that underlies two near opposite notions of individuation. One way a person might individuate is in the direction of separation from intense and deeply binding relationships. A person who uses her autonomy to individuate in this direction is what Robert Kegan calls the "atomist" or what Carol Gilligan calls "the lone contemplator": such a person sacrifices relationships and keeps others at a certain distance, typically by relying on abstract principles and impersonal perspectives to make her interpersonal decisions.

But some people who achieve full perspectivalism individuate in the other direction, that in which a worldview is constructed *by means of* one's particular associations and memberships. This form of individuation has been called "interindividuality" or "the collective life" by Gilligan, but perhaps has been labeled best by Jack Crittenden as "compound individuality." As Crittenden describes this schema, "individuality is one stage of selfhood in a hierarchy of such stages and is a compound of all those basic structures that preceded this stage of self and constituted the earlier stages." The complete self-system is thus neither socially imbedded in communal ends that are antecedently given (the view of self, for example, implied by the morality of association) nor impervious to and independent of particular changes in circumstance (the public self implied by the morality of principle). Rather, the individual is "a compound of self and others, an individuality constituted by autonomy and relationship." On this view, one uses one's autonomy to achieve individuality not by separating oneself from particular membership groups. Rather, one exercises one's autonomy to achieve a differentiation within and through the means of one's place in such groups. Autonomy is but the threshold of full individuation—whether the form of that individuation be atomistic or collective.

As we have seen, people's concern about their own rights—long claimed by critics of liberalism to be intrinsically destructive of close personal relations—in fact strongly underdetermines the eudaimonistic outcome of that concern. Whether rights-aware people make successes of their lives and engage in projects and forms of living-together that they find meaningful in lasting ways depends on how each comes to understand the meaning of the rights he has from that stage forward. From a contemporary developmental perspective, the morality-of-principle stage is thus akin to the stage of autonomy. Since the parameters of this form of self-direction are set by people's awareness of the freedoms and liberties they have as political persons only, this is *political* autonomy. Just as liberal rights underdetermine action, so too the morality of principle underdetermines the direction or nature of what I shall call the ethic of individuation.

Because of the flexibility in the exercise of liberal political norms, citizens who recognize their rights have need of a further motivational concept—in my terms, a compass concept—to help them work out or discover what their rights mean to them in various situations. The sources of compass concept norms are less systematic than are the norms of liberal justice—the latter being founded as they are on public values. But it is upon these nonpublic forms of reasoning that people rely when exercising their rights. It is by the way they exercise their rights that people in liberal societies develop themselves, each seeking to make sense of his own identity and experiences in an ongoing way.

As part of compass concept neutrality, no liberal theory can take a position on the question of how people should best answer the question of what their political autonomy means to them. Political liberal theory, at least, cannot even take a position on the degree of self-consciousness, or reflective autonomy, with which all persons ought most appropriately to answer that question (i.e., whether one's own compass should properly be held out at arm's length, or carried inside oneself). People may pass through the stage of political autonomy and individuate in the direction of a life of detachment and principled transparency. The reason-loving people I called the A-people, for example, might be described as having individuated in the direction of atomism. It is the "lone contemplator" standing at the end of the checkout line making the choice between paper and plastic, between bringing her children to the Catholic church in which she was raised or trying out a Unitarian one, between continuing a difficult marriage or seeking a fresh start through divorce.

So too, from the political liberal perspective, fully admissible citizens may use their autonomy to individuate in the direction of strong and thoroughgoing attachment to particular others, even without ground-level reflection on the value of those attachments. Our C-people, for example, might be described as having individuated in the heavily embedded direction of compound individuality. Such people, in my terms, may have "forgotten" their rights for the purposes of their daily interactions with one another, but in doing so they have not totally submerged themselves in the sense of having lost even the capacity to recognize their rights if called upon to do so. Within the liberal social world, politically reasonable citizens of faith cannot renounce their political autonomy—for example, by seeking somehow to return to some earlier associational state. Rather, they must use their political autonomy, as expressed by their awareness of their rights, to firmly bind themselves in traditions they find valuable by the lights of whatever received nonpublic norms they affirm.[9]

In some matters and in some parts of their lives, the B-people routinely invoke abstract norms like those of public reason. On other occasions they act with the spontaneity and lack of critical distancing that characterizes attachments they accept as foundational. The ethic of individuation in a liberal society is strongly plural and unsystematic. It is exactly as plural and unsystematic as the full set of normative structures amid which people in real liberal societies must find their own ethical ways.

All these diverse expressions of individuation are united, however, by their inner psychological mechanism—the mechanism of liberal nonpublic reason. Individuation, in all its varieties, occurs through a stage process in which higher stages do not so much replace as integrate with and incorporate previous stages. The morality of principle does not *merely* underdetermine the ethic of individuation. That stage does so in a way that *structures* the form that any subsequent ethical individuation can take. It is only after recognizing, and internalizing, the pull toward the principles of social construction that are common to all persons in a diverse society that people become politically autonomous. From there they must develop their own interpretations of what their more local and group-specific motives to social construction mean to them. Forms of individuality that are structured this way can exert their influence with great force.

The field owners in Vermont, for example, do not recognize the imperatival force of their stewards' role by somehow losing or abandoning their sense of property ownership in those fields. Rather, they individuate, and become the kinds of persons each of them is (at least in this aspect of their lives), through the collective process of mutual recognition and solidarity. They walk those fields together and enjoy them with one another even on those days when none of them catches a glimpse of any of the others. This has power for them. So too with members of religious groups (whether through memberships like that of the Satmar or simply through one's participation in some nonpublic tradition such as tzedakah), and for many, many other forms of membership group besides.[10] People who make their lives in liberal society naturally acquire a desire to exercise their rights artfully when they have lived among, and benefited from the actions of, other people who are eudaimonistically skillful at that art.

Ethical development, in a flourishing liberal society, is essentially concerned with the drive of people to find personal meaning and value in a life built across the interface of public and nonpublic identity components. It is citizens' freely formed drive toward individuation on those terms that anchors the various liberal virtues and provides motivation to good citizen conduct in what I have called the substantive sense. It is only through the actions and attitudes that people exhibit *after* they have gained a capacity for the full perspectivalism of the morality of principle that persons in liberal societies are in position to complete their self-systems. By doing that within a social system which is known to be just, they fashion for themselves the diverse lives of ethical integrity that are the ultimate mark of a flourishing liberal society. In liberal societies, moral development is essentially the process by which people come to understand the commitments and bonds they have to one another that lie *beyond justice*. It is there, through the natural unfolding of the motives to ethical individuation, that the motivational base for liberal citizenship—substantively understood—is completed.[11]

I said that derivative theorists venture into developmental psychology in order to show how the motives for the virtues on which their conception of citizenship relies might be expected to arise in a natural way in a just society. I have tried to show how the motives for the fuller conception of liberal virtue associated with the substantive understanding of liberal citizenship might freely arise as the natural next step in the account the derivative theorists offer. This has important consequences for the type of civic education political liberals may legitimately pursue through the institutions of the state. For now, allow me to summarize our findings. Rawls ends his own account by formulating three psychological laws, one for each stage of a political liberal citizen's moral development. We can complete our more ambitious account of the citizen's motivational development by adding the natural fourth:

> Fourth Law: Given that a person has developed a sense of justice in accordance with the first three laws, and given that a social arrangement is just and publicly known to be just, and given further that this person observes people around him creating the eudaimonistic fabric of their lives through the way they exercise their political autonomy then this person has reason to develop the art of exercising his political autonomy in a way that he finds fulfilling, since he recognizes that he and those for whom he cares must continually create the eudaimonistic fabric of their lives through the practice of that art.

Rethinking Civic Education

Most debates about the requirements of civic education proceed from the assumption that civic education concerns fitting children for the role they are to play as *public* persons. In particular, liberal civic education is understood to be mainly a matter of legitimately encouraging children in their development of the so-called liberal virtues, attitudes, and dispositions that are understood to be largely derivative from the requirements of the shared public project of pursuing justice. Debates about civic education usually consist of conflicting accounts of what precisely is involved in teaching children about what rights they have and about the moral ideas on which those rights are grounded.

With the terms of debate set up this way, civic education has proven one of the most hotly contested terrains on which proponents of political liberalism have sought to differentiate their view from the various forms of ethical or comprehensive liberalism they seek to displace. Political liberals claim that civic education reveals the great practical divergence between comprehensive and political liberalisms. "The [comprehensive] liberalisms of Kant and Mill may lead to requirements designed to foster the values of autonomy and individuality as ideals to govern much if not all of life." But political liberalism requires merely the skills needed for people to understand and reason about shared political values. Compared to the civic education requirements of comprehensive liberalism, "political liberalism has a different aim and requires far less."[12]

This claim is controversial. As we saw in chapter 1, Amy Gutmann has argued that the civic educational requirements of political liberalism and of comprehensive liberalism—even if logically distinct—converge to a significant degree in practice.

Eamonn Callan draws a more dramatic conclusion from this practical convergence. Among the ideas that a political liberal education must include is a recognition of the "burdens of judgment."[13] But, Callan writes, "The psychological attributes that constitute an active acceptance of the burdens of judgment, such as the capacity and inclination to subject received ethical ideas to critical scrutiny, also constitute a recognizable ideal of ethical autonomy."[14] The requirements of civic education, far from showing how political and comprehensive conceptions of liberalism diverge, reveal that political liberalism is merely a species of comprehensive liberalism. "The partition Rawls labors to erect between ethical and political liberalism has collapsed."[15]

I think Gutmann and Callan have a point. So long as we think of citizenship within the derivative paradigm, the practical implications of political and of comprehensive civic education do show that those two metatheoretical views converge in significant ways.[16] But what if we adopt the substantive paradigm I have been describing? If we think of the requirements of liberal good citizen conduct in that broader way, then civic education may indeed demonstrate the great divergence between comprehensive and political liberalisms after all. This is not because political liberal civic education typically requires less than do forms of ethical liberalism. It is because education for political liberal citizenship requires *far more*.

From the substantive perspective, education for liberal citizenship involves teaching children not merely the skills and attitudes needed for them to grasp the impersonal perspective of justice and its attendant political ideas. Education must also prepare each citizen to play her socially constructive role in making her society flourish as the type of society it is. A liberal society succeeds in that later goal when it is organized in ways that make it maximally worthy of all politically reasonable citizens' long-term devotion. To play their roles well in that project, children need to be taught to appreciate the *fit* between the norms of public reason and whatever politically reasonable views of moral personality they affirm. For this, they must develop skills beyond those needed to see how their nonpublic views support their public ones. They also need to understand how their affirmation of the public norms, if once they give it, can lend support to the particular nonpublic view each holds dear. They need the information and skills required for the art of living their nonpublic lives in a manner each finds rewarding in a long-term way. If they are to succeed in the socially constructive roles they are to play as full citizens, children need to develop the skills and abilities not only of public reason but of liberal nonpublic reason as well.

Political liberals have abandoned the philosophical hope of producing uniformity of opinion about the nature of (nonpublic) moral personality. So the fit political liberals want children to consider is that between public reason and the more local, internal understandings of value particular to the various politically reasonable narrative traditions each citizen will inhabit. Political liberals must do this without assuming that those nonpublic narratives must all be written with the pen of individual autonomy or critical self-reflection. Each person who grows up in a liberal society needs to be taught not merely that she has rights and that those rights are grounded in a political way. Much more, her program of civic education must explicitly invite her to consider the *meaning* of her rights within the context of her own life. She needs to be encouraged to consider those other aspects of her self and her interests that her own politically autonomy—if exercised obtusely or without skill—can gradually erode or corrupt. She needs to be encouraged to consider the meaning of her rights within the story of her life.

What would it mean, in a diverse society, to teach young people to be sensitive about the meaning of their rights? Such a civic education program might begin by telling future citizens that they are entering a highly risky form of human living-together. A liberal society is a place where people are bound together by the way each uses her individual freedoms, not just by her performance of public duties. The success of the liberal social project is measured ultimately through the internal evaluations of each person concerning the quality and value of the life he leads given his commitment to social justice. Those evaluations of quality and value are determined directly by the degree of skill with which each individual person (along with the others around him) manipulates the binding mechanism that liberal societies entrust to each of their members. That binding mechanism—the system of ligaments that holds a liberal society together and allows it to function—is found in the flexibility in the exercise of every right-claim that abstract principles of justice pick out. The norms of political autonomy set out by public reason are not merely protective devices but *communicative* ones. Those norms can be used to communicate goodwill, one's understanding of degrees of commitment so far achieved, and the nature of one's hope for eudaimonistic connections yet to come. In liberal societies, it is through their rights as much or more than through their duties that people build their social worlds. Future citizens need to learn about this distinctively liberal mechanism of social construction. They must be brought to understand that the success of the experiment that a free society represents depends ultimately *on each of them*, and on the attitudes each develops regarding the claims that the political conception of justice sets out.

But civic schooling, from the substantive perspective, requires more than teaching children about the abstract mechanism by which interpersonal virtues are constructed in liberal societies. Young people must also learn why virtues constructed that way are worth having at all. On its most plausible version, the civic education regime of any free society must primarily be a matter of providing information and developing skills by which citizens can best realize the basic motivational norms they have already developed outside the state-schooling system. But just as education into the particular terms and ideals of derivative citizenship can satisfy people's desires to act from their sense of justice, so too the further education into the art of exercising one's rights is aimed at satisfying people's further and equally deep desire toward ethical individuation.

People who grow up in a well-functioning liberal society can be expected to want not merely to be just, foundational as their commitment to that aspect of social construction may be. They also want—and very much so—to make an interpersonal success of their lives on their own terms, just as they have observed other people with whose values they identify doing. Satisfying this desire in a free society requires that children develop the dispositions and habits of mind that enable them to live a life of meaning and integrity, given the public commitments they share. Teaching those virtues necessarily involves discussion in schools about the value of the nonpublic norms by which citizens actually steer when deciding how to exercise their various claims of right. It requires explicit discussion about the complex interface of those nonpublic normative concepts with the norms of public reason. It is along that interface that every citizen must take up the project of constructing a personal life of value and integrity. The political stability of their society depends ultimately on how well they see themselves as equipped to succeed in that project, each by his own politically reasonable light.

Civic education for political liberals must address issues that lie deep in the moral worlds of individual citizens. When we prepare children for citizenship, we immediately find ourselves engaged with questions about the various ways individuals understand themselves, the forms of relation each has to others, and even the various understandings about the sources of reasons held by various formally admissible citizen types. Of course, such education must always take care to respect the architecture of public reason. No liberal program of civic education can mandate determinate *answers* to any of those eudaimonistic questions—whether uniform or global, or even in any highly localized way. But within that constraint, a liberal educational regime must see to it that their citizens are prepared to take up the crucial and unavoidable question of how each of them, as persons who care deeply about justice, can negotiate the interface of public and nonpublic value. The substantive account of liberal civic education requires more than the derivative one because it aims higher. Citizens need to be taught about virtues beyond those needed for the institutions in their society to meet some threshold criteria of legitimacy or justice. They must be supported in developing the traits of character they need if their society—within the important constraints of justice—is to be as much as possible a *home* to people with worldviews such as theirs. Political liberals are committed to the possibility of a distinction between political autonomy and full-blown ethical autonomy. The substantive conception of citizen virtue enables them to stand guard over that difference.

Of course, this is not the political liberal orthodoxy. Like the ethical liberals whose view they seek to displace, most political liberals continue to operate within the familiar derivative paradigm. They thus abdicate responsibility for any and all unintended effects of liberal politics, so long as the burdens caused by those effects do not become so great that they constitute an injustice. After all, such effects are not intended by political liberalism. Even if the prospect of those effects may alienate some otherwise admissible citizens, this is no violation of the liberal commitment to neutrality of aim. Spillovers can never be wholly eliminated, so it is enough simply to acknowledge their possible existence and then leave it at that. But if this denial of theoretical responsibility for unintended effects is plausible anywhere, the state-based education of children is one arena where it clearly is not.

The idea that the liberal commitment to the ideal of mutual respect requires that all nonpublic eudaimonistic discussions be kept out of civics lessons finds an analog in the more familiar (though equally dubious) idea that the American commitment to the First Amendment requires that all religious perspectives be kept out of public school classrooms. Many religious scholars argue that keeping discussion about religion out of the classroom does not necessarily make for classrooms that are more neutral between religions or between religious and secular perspectives. On the contrary, since public schools are committed to providing children with the secular skills and perspectives they need to function in modern society, the concomitant omission of discussion of religious perspectives and attitudes can give children the false impression that religion is dead. Religious ways of thinking—whether concerning the place of mankind in the universe, responses to particular moral dilemmas, or the solution to broad social problems—were something the students' grandparents or parents may have relied upon. But those approaches are insignificant or irrelevant in the world in which the state is now preparing them to play their parts.

Some religious advocates who have this concern make politically controversial demands, such as the inclusion of religious practice within the public schools. But many others simply ask for a more balanced approach, one that does not infringe on the rights of other children but also does not unintentionally send a negative message about religion. *Abington Township School District v. Schempp*, the famous case that disallowed devotional Bible study in public schools, is often misread in this respect. Justice Clark's majority opinion forbade only the advocacy of religion in the schools, not all teaching about it.[17] Warren Nord, for example, uses this reading of *Abington* to argue for a form of liberal education that includes religious and traditionalist elements along with the more familiar secular and critical ones. "Liberal education has both a conservative and a liberating task: it should provide students with a ballast of historical identities and values at the same time that it gives them an understanding of alternatives and provides critical distance on the particularities of their respective inheritances." Nord continues, "The essential tension of a liberal education, properly understood, lies in its commitment to initiating students into the communities of memory which tentatively define them, and, at the same time, nurturing critical reflection by initiating them into an ongoing conversation that enables them to understand and appreciate alternative ways of living and thinking. The error of traditional education was its emphasis on the former; the error of much modern education is its unsystematic and uncritical acceptance of the latter."[18]

The analogous problem with liberal civic education is that by teaching children the detached, rights-based forms of thinking central to public reason, liberal civic education unintentionally encourages those forms of thinking in all domains of reason, including ones where such ways of thinking are transformative beyond what the bare attainment of political autonomy requires. Such lessons may thus unintentionally undercut the nonpublic worldviews that many politically reasonable citizens—and citizens of faith in particular—hold dear. Insofar as citizens perceive this justice-generated cultural current as exerting pressure against their own view, this weakens the commitment that they can give to the political values themselves.

The solution to this problem in the case of general education is to seek out a more balanced approach, one that educates students honestly into the role of religious belief in their society's history and culture and yet does so without falling into proselytization. This is a difficult balancing act, to be sure. But any general education worthy of a free and diverse society must insist upon performing it. Is there an analogous remedy to the problem of spillovers within the sphere of strictly civic education?

Some classic accounts of civic education suggest that there might be. Systems of civic education, along with promoting whatever skills and dispositions citizens there are said positively to need, often include an element designed to counteract the various imperfections each type of regime tends inadvertently to foster. Many types of regime naturally generate a particular set of vices that emerge—unintended and undesired—by the particular political way of life to which each regime is devoted.

Aristotle was a founder of this idea of education relative to the regime. Aristotle was acutely aware that public values live a kind of secondary life as schoolmasters. Political institutions amount to a sort of schoolhouse, not just to children but to adult citizens as well. People are steadily habituated into certain forms of world perception by the political institutions in which they find themselves living. In this way each regime eventually puts its distinctive stamp on all the people there. But Aristotle was also aware that the content of these wider social lessons was not easy to control. Many regimes, quite despite themselves, imprint people with that regime's characteristic vices as much or more than with the dispositions required for the regime to flourish. So Aristotle thought civic education should always include a self-corrective element, one designed to counteract the unintended lessons each regime produced.[19]

There is an insight here for liberal theorists. The rejection of any commitment to neutrality of effect does not excuse theorists from seeking out means of *diminishing* those unintended effects. If a substantive program of civic education can provide political liberal regimes with their own internal corrective, then—so long as the corrective is designed in a way that fully respects the architecture of public reason—political liberals, at least, should enthusiastically affirm such programs. If liberals take this substantive perspective toward civic education, some familiar disputes may come out in unexpected new ways.

Back to Tennessee

Consider the controversy over *Mozert v. Hawkins*, the most highly polished legal touchstone of civic education theory. In this case, a group of Fundamentalist Christians in Tennessee objected to an English textbook mandated by a county school board as part of its civic education requirement. The parents objected to the textbook because it encouraged their children to make critical judgments for themselves in areas where the Bible provides the answer. Thus, complainants objected to a story about a Catholic Indian settlement on grounds that it promoted Catholicism; to biographies extolling the accomplishments of women who pursued careers outside the home (and even to a story of a boy making toast for a girl) on grounds that they denigrated biblical teaching about gender roles; to a science fiction story as advocating the occult; to many passages about the Renaissance, including one describing Leonardo da Vinci as the human with the creative mind that "came closest to the divine touch." Indeed, one of the complainants, Mrs. Vicki Frost, testified that she had spent some two hundred hours studying the mandated civics reader and could distinguish seventeen discrete categories of objectionable materials. In her lengthy testimony, Mrs.

Frost provided the court with numerous examples, many cross-referenced, of each.[20]

Most liberal theorists applaud the Court of Appeals' decision to reject the *Mozert* complainants' plea for exemptions or other special accommodations regarding that text. Deferring to the some demands of the *Mozert* parents, such as classroom exceptions, would effectively mean giving up on civic education beyond teaching literacy and numeracy. Some, such as Gutmann, also draw a metatheoretical lesson from the *Mozert* case.[21] Political liberals claim to advocate a form of civic education that encourages critical and reflective skills only about politically relevant issues, and not as a general world-outlook. But, Gutmann says, because the skills and dispositions conducive to political deliberation cannot help but spill over into nonpublic domains of reason, the form of civic education required by political liberalism does not offer any more accommodation to the kinds of diversity represented by the *Mozert* case than does comprehensive liberalism. "The only discernible difference turns out to be different theoretical rationales for denying the parents' claims." Thus, "comprehensive and political liberalism come down on the same side, once again, in this case."[22]

If Gutmann and the court majority are correct in understanding the uncompromising and politically unreasonable nature of the *Mozert* parents' position, then the conclusion Gutmann draws about the convergence of political and comprehensive responses to the *Mozert* case must also be correct. On that reading, the *Mozert* parents are politically unreasonable. They affirm a religion that requires that they deny even the very general political ideals of reciprocity and equal political respect.[23] Comprehensive and political liberal positions do converge regarding the treatment of such citizens (even though their rationales may differ). However, that is not the only plausible reading of the *Mozert* parents' position.

The case record states clearly that the Tennessee parents did *not* consistently object to the mere exposure of their children to the ideas in the reader. Nor even did the parents consistently object to their children acquiring critical skills such as those needed for political purposes from the reader. Rather, the *Mozert* complainants objected consistently only to the *repetitiveness* and the *depth* of the exposure. They saw the overall effect of the reader, whether intended or not, as denigrating to the faith-based form of reasoning on which their nonpublic worldview depended. For example, the court record indicates that even Vicki Frost was willing to have her child read science fiction, study Renaissance philosophy, and learn about other religious faiths, provided that the presentation was not so "profound" that it "deeply undermined her religious beliefs."[24] Mrs. Frost, on this reading of the case record, produced her long list to the court not so much to show precisely how many discrete objections she had but rather to show the repetitive and unbalanced presentation of the reader as a whole.[25]

What's more, the complainants indicated that—despite even their objections about repetitiveness and depth—they were willing to have their children use the reader, provided that the lessons made explicit and clear to the children that they were not being encouraged to view any of these philosophies or religions as true. Further, the *Mozert* parents only sought measures to protect their own children's faith in their own religion as true: they never sought to use the state apparatus to impose their religion on other people's children.

For all these reasons, it is at least plausible to view the *Mozert* parents not as politically unreasonable outcasts but as exactly those kinds of citizens for the accommodation of whom political liberalism was devised. They are the citizens of faith, the "reasonable Romantics," that ethical forms of liberalism are allegedly too narrow to include.[26] If we think of *Mozert* this way, the case may reveal what is distinctive about political liberal civic education after all.

From the substantive perspective, civic education takes as its task not only preparing students for liberal *politics*, but also for *life* within a society that is bounded by that particular view of politics. Because education for substantive citizenship aims for more in this way, this form of education has not one but two reasons for requiring students to learn about diverse ways of life, such as the stories that the civics reader depicted. First—the point derivative theorists emphasize—political liberals need to teach students about other ways of life because political liberals want them to learn to respect others as political equals. They might thus appreciate why the liberal posture of state neutrality is morally required in a society such as theirs. If they learn to respect others as their equals for political purposes, then they can recognize their own support for state neutrality as the appropriate institutional expression of their (freely formed) desire to act from their sense of justice.

However, the social significance of these lessons in diversity do not stop there. Political liberals must also be concerned that they not send a distorted or misleading message about *nonpublic value* as they go about preparing students for public life. Political liberals are concerned to prepare citizens to play their roles in making their society flourish. A political liberal society flourishes only when it is insofar as possible a home to people who, while politically autonomous, continue to affirm as true a variety of incompatible moral, religious, and philosophical outlooks. The stories about other people are significant not just to teach children equal respect. Those stories also show children how people holding different views of life, and even different views of the nature of reason itself, have found ways to reintegrate their capacity for public reason (and the skills that entails) with the nonpublic commitments that give point to their lives.

On this view, political liberals teach students about their fellow citizens not simply to detach them politically from the traditions of their parents or communities (so that they may come to appreciate the norm of equal respect and achieve political autonomy). Political liberals teach them detailed stories about others in order to show them how people who have attained political autonomy have then gone on to find ways to live lives of meaning and integrity given their own background and set of life experiences. Such stories show how people can achieve a level of individuation that allows them to affirm their own nonpublic view as true. In a well-functioning liberal society, as I have suggested, people can accomplish this integration only by the way they come to understand the particular *meaning* of those public norms and rights to them. They must practice the interpersonal art that their political autonomy makes unavoidable.

Notice that a substantive conception of civic education such as this might in practice generate very different requirements if built atop an ethical rather than a political justificatory foundation—for ethical liberalisms, in their various ways, typically affirm only a narrower view about the forms of human reasoning that are morally (and thus politically) appropriate. Even if ethical liberals affirm the idea that children should be taught to reintegrate their political understanding into their own nonpublic lives for purely eudaimonistic reasons, they typically affirm only some autonomous form of reasoning as appropriate for achieving that reintegration. By contrast, political liberals are committed to affirming as reasonable, and as *equally* reasonable from a political perspective, not only forms of reintegration that match some philosophical ideal of moral autonomy (such as that inspired by the work of Mill or Kant) but also those that come from more embedded, traditionalist ways of understanding reasons for action and attitude (the reasonable Romantics, or citizens of faith).

This has an important consequence. If the *Mozert* parents can plausibly be understood to affirm a doctrine that lies within the boundaries of the politically reasonable, then political liberals—but not most ethical ones—may have reason to *support* some central demands of the Tennessee parents. One way to read the original request of the Fundamentalist parents, after all, was simply that their children's program of civic education include a component concerning how they might *reintegrate* the lessons of public reason into the deep nonpublic self-understandings of their own group. To take one kind of example, before the appellate court decision against the parents the schools had reached an accommodation with the parents of two children (whose parents could not afford private schooling) by "specifically not[ing] on worksheets that the student was not required to believe the stories."[27] This seems to me an eminently political liberal solution. Of course, respect for the architecture of public reason would forbid certain ways of conveying that lesson about nonpublic reintegration and thus certain formulations of riders such as those in the Tennessee case. The reintegrative component could not assert that any one religious view in fact was universally true and that others were universally false—for that would indeed have the state teaching a religion as part of its education of citizens.[28] But the reintegrative component surely could include exercises that encouraged students to consider what attitudes, beliefs, and even *what forms of reasoning* might be most appropriate for them, given their own histories and expectations. Rather than indoctrination, this is merely a matter of calling children's attention to premises from their own lives, premises from which they might draw their own conclusions about what forms of reasoning and ways of assessing value are most significant for them.

This substantive approach would in no way mean denying that children need to gain a "lively" understanding of the burdens of judgment. Nor does it mean denying that children might ipso facto be led to consider how those burdens apply to their own sets of beliefs and traditions (the points Callan emphasizes). Rather, on this reading, people such as the *Mozert* parents are simply asking that the lessons concerning the burdens of judgment be *carried through* in an evenhanded way. To do that, the civics lessons must be carried through in a way consistent with the motivational foundations of political liberalism, and not of some closet preference for the ethical liberal life-view.

It is precisely because of how the burdens of judgment apply to each child's own beliefs—the way the boundaries of the integrity of each are shaped by his particular experiences, the whole story of his life up to now—that each does have reason to give some special weight to the traditions, and to the forms of reasoning, that have already played a prominent role in his life. A political liberal education, from the substantive perspective, should include a broad-minded component that brings that fact to children's attention. Ethical liberal forms of civic education, by contrast, typically are committed to drawing much narrower boundaries about the acceptable forms of reintegrative reason. *Mozert v. Hawkins* demonstrates vividly how the civic educational requirements of ethical and of political liberalism diverge—both in theory and in practice.

Education for citizenship must be concerned about the eventual *ethical situatedness* of developing citizens rather than simply about the *political liberation* of them. Depending on their own backgrounds and the shape of their lives up to then, some reasonable citizens individuate in the direction of highly individualistic, reflective forms of integrative reason liberals have traditionally affirmed. Other politically reasonable citizens, because of their different histories, may individuate toward more embedded forms of integrative reason such as those based on received authority (the Bible,

Koran, or the Church). The form of integration of what I take to be the great sweep of citizens in the mainstream may well involve a complex mixture of reason-elements from each side.

But the only form of liberation that intentionally can be encouraged by the state after the politicization of justice is that of *political* liberation. Of politically acceptable systems of encouraging political autonomy, political liberals are bound to prefer systems with the lesser rather than the greater unintended (nonpublic autonomy-promoting) effects. In a diverse society, there is no other path toward the kind of broad ethical satisfaction of citizens on which the success of that sort of society depends. The challenge for political liberals is to devise reintegrative forms of schooling that prepare students to live lives of integrity affirming their own (diverse and incompatible) doctrines as true, even once recognizing a common moral foundation for the political standing of diverse others.

I am not suggesting that children of Catholics, for example, are to learn to be Catholic in their civics classes. Neither, certainly, am I suggesting that each child is to be assigned to whatever particular ethical orientation it is determined in advance is irrevocably appropriate to him (whether by school authorities, parents, or anyone else). Liberal civic education always centers on the affirmation of strong political freedoms and on discussions about the importance of such freedoms in each person's construction of her or his own life. The concern is not to instill controlling concepts, but rather to include lessons that protect childrens' (politically reasonable) compass concepts.

Since Catholic children are to learn about their rights and about the standing of all citizens as political equals, they must also be brought to understand what it means to be a Catholic within the particular social world they are about to enter. Being a committed Catholic in a world where individual freedoms are strongly protected (for example, a world where no-fault divorce laws, physician-assisted suicide, and wide reproductive rights are politically affirmed) is different from what it would mean to be a committed Catholic in some social world where no such freedoms were recognized (for example, in a world where church and state were merged and thus divorce, euthanasia, contraceptives, and abortion were outlawed).[29] Children need to be taught how it is that the liberal social world makes itself available to people with a worldview such as the one they have so far grown up in—always taking care to avoid proselytization, whether on a general or an individual basis. The emphasis on political freedoms, central to any politically acceptable scheme on the substantive perspective, must be used within classrooms to prevent the fall into proselytizing excesses. Within the classroom, discussions about political freedoms are the balancing weights that make this tightrope walk possible.

A complete schedule of civic education, from this substantive perspective, must address more than young people's latent capacity for a sense of justice. Civic education must also address their freely formed and very deep desire for ethical individuation. This desire for ethical individuation does not spring from nowhere, nor does it emerge with no form. It comes from and is formed by each child's own history, the whole story of her life till now. In a well-ordered liberal society, that story always includes both public and nonpublic normative components—with the child's sense of justice providing a kind of scaffolding for her desire for ethical individuation.

People with an ethical liberal orientation typically argue that parents do not "own" their children, but rather that children own, or at least are on their way toward owning, themselves. While the notion of ownership in this context is famously obscure, such people typically argue for an activist tutorial state, one encouraging students to adopt the thickly autonomous worldview they themselves affirm. But political liberals, by their own view, are required to abandon all such ambitions. The political liberal state cannot aim to promote any particular approach to questions of nonpublic value, whether that of strong individual autonomy, of deference to traditions of authority, or of some complex and uneven mixture of these two extremes. The politicization of justice thus opens a profound reintegrative fissure—a fissure, that is, concerning the form of reasoning by which individual children should most appropriately learn to interpret and exercise their claims of right. Political liberals, but not ethical ones, are bound to defer to the wishes of parents when reintegrative questions arise for developing children. There is no one else, from the political liberal perspective, with the standing to fill that crevasse.

To put the point dramatically, political liberals are committed to a form of "ethical subservience" on the part of the publicly funded school system to children's (politically reasonable) parents when it comes to reintegrative questions.[30] This does not mean denying the state's role in preparing children for full political autonomy, but rather assiduously getting the state out of the business of influencing children—intentionally or not—about the *meaning* and *appropriate use* of the rights citizens have. The alternatives, after all, are either (1) to advocate some ethical ideal of autonomy as a good for all children or (2) simply to tell students about all their rights and their groundings, then halt the lesson and send them out to play. Political liberals, as such, are bound to eschew the first path. But if theorists such as Gutmann and Callan are right, the latter approach unintentionally amounts to sending much the same message as the first one. That approach thus levies a disproportionate psychological tax on certain politically reasonable worldviews. So political liberals are bound to affirm politically acceptable correctives that might save them from pointing all their young citizens down that path too.

What methods are available to political liberals willing to consider a different way? The guiding idea would be to find ways of teaching students about the political norms of their society that did not unintentionally disrupt students from the ethical worldviews they have already formed from their experiences within their families, at least not beyond what an appreciation of their own nascent political autonomy requires (which is already a significant, and politically appropriate, check on the parents). The "subservience" political liberals owe to politically reasonable parents, of course, is owed just as much to people wishing to pass on their autonomous life-ideal as it is to people wishing to transmit their tradition-based one. (From the perspective of the citizens of faith, notice that proponents of wide-ethical autonomy are foisting their own worldview upon their children just as much as is anyone else.) The views of Millian individualists and of Larmore's reasonable Romantics are equally reasonable from the political perspective. The political liberal state, to be true to its own ideals, must be equally solicitous of all politically reasonable parents' concerns about the practical standing of their own reintegrative ideal.[31]

For these reasons, political liberals may have a unique class of reasons, not shared by ethical liberals, for acceding to parental demands for school vouchers and a greater range of school choice. The school system required by political liberalism, after all, must prepare children for the roles they will play in a society where citizens not only respect one another as free and equal but do so *while* continuing to affirm a diverse and irreconcilable range of views—religious, moral and philosophical—as true. Parents may reasonably be concerned about the "substantive civics" lessons their children pick up, not just in their classes but from their wider school environment—lessons about values transmitted by their peers' clothing, manners, and topics of conversation; by their attitudes toward authority figures, athletic events, and voluntary organizations. While a degree of such informal exposure can be crucial to children's learning to respect other children with views unlike their own (A-children as well as C-children), the informal assimilative pressures in large common schools typically go well beyond any such requirement. These concerns, always present, may be exacerbated as political liberals respond to their citizens' reasonable concerns about reintegration.

For example, the measures adopted in response to the reintegrative concerns of reasonable parents, while justified from the political liberal perspective, may *themselves* generate assimilative pressures that would cause additional worries for many parents—especially in schools with large, diverse student bodies. Political liberals who recognize that neutrality of effect is "impracticable" recognize that school classrooms and the wider school environment are always ethically charged, like it or not, and charged in ways that extend far beyond what is politically relevant or required. Because engagement with those reintegrative questions about life and value are unavoidable once the issue of political freedom has been broached, political liberals must seek to level the playing field within the domain of the politically reasonable, however they might.[32] This means allowing *all* reasonable reintegrative ideals a more equitable share of influence in classrooms and hallways and on athletic fields. In a school environment that is ethically charged in this more open and evenhanded way, it would be no surprise to hear parents—Millian and Catholic alike—demanding that their children be given school options that promise a total experience less likely to unsettle their children from the reasonable worldview they themselves hope their children will come to affirm as true.

The political liberal drive toward division and subservience is not unqualified, of course. All students are to be prepared for full political autonomy. Reintegrative ideals that parents hope to encourage in students (whether by informal notes on worksheets or by whole school designs) must always be done in a way compatible with each student's coming to appreciate her or his full range of rights and the political ideas of person and society on which those rights are grounded. The schools owe subservience to parents wishing to protect their children's compass concepts, not to those seeking to enlist the state in the imposition of controlling concepts (in subversion of the liberal proviso). Further, political liberals, while deferring to the demands of all reasonable parents regarding reintegrative questions, must always insist that *all* school environments—public, semipublic, private, and home ones alike—include a mandatory component that ensures that the requirements of the derivative model of civic education are fully met there. Even the most broad-minded political liberal cannot tolerate those whose worldviews lead them to seek to exempt their children from that component of their civic education. Such a demand is a flat denial of the political values on which political liberalism is founded. It is an opting out, a kind of secession from equal political membership, that cannot even masquerade as a form of "reintegration."[33]

The substantive perspective reveals that political liberals must say something positive to young citizens about the task each must take up as a member of the liberal social world. They must say this:

> Become just, but do so in a way that makes sense of the importance that your own particular history up to now has to you. The great good of social justice is not the only good recognizable from a political liberal perspective. For you, citizenship involves not only the performance of public duties but the way you build your life. We encourage you to build that life, not *in spite of* the ethical background culture of your society, but *through your use of* that background culture and the distinctive forms of communication made available there. We must prepare each of you to excel within the particular kind of

social world you are now entering—a world where human lives must be built across the interface of public and nonpublic normative structures. It is as political liberals, therefore, that we respectfully play our part in preparing you all to be good people. For it is in your capacity to live well that the liberal settlement finds its mortal point.

The Tax-Flattening Principle

I have emphasized the importance to liberals of the broad ethical background culture that is ineluctably generated by the political values they affirm. It is futile to try to prevent the generation of such a culture. Attempts to do so would in most cases bring one up immediately against the rights properly held by other citizens. That way is closed to anyone who affirms the primacy of justice—the palladium of any properly liberal view. But, as we have seen, the defense of liberalism need not end there. To meet the challenges posed to the lives of real citizens by the liberal background culture, political liberals must explore and affirm nonpublic ideals that lie within the normative purview of political theory. In particular, the special challenges posed to political liberals by their own ethical background culture might be met by the adoption of a thickly substantive conception of good citizen conduct. Political liberals, as such, should encourage a fundamental shift in their members' understanding of the responsibilities and goals they have as *citizens*. To meet the special challenges of the liberal ethical background culture, liberals should promote this more nuanced and demanding form of citizen self-understanding at every turn. They should promote it through the programs by which they introduce young people to the liberal social world most of all. Even when citizens' concerns about unintended cultural spillover effects do not reach down to matters of justice, still political liberals have reason, and considerable means, to address those concerns.

However, there is an important subset of spillover effects that *do* reach down to matters of justice. Unlike most elements within the ethical background culture, some unintended effects occur as particularly *direct* and *immediate* effects of the liberal commitment to treat all citizens as free and equal. Even laws and policies that are facially neutral can disadvantage citizens affirming worldviews that are formally admissible, eroding the patterns of individuation they value most. Regarding unintended effects that are generated in that specially direct way, liberals may be able to do something special to meet them. Liberals can administer remedies here not only via the broad public philosophy they affirm or through the self-understanding they encourage in their members as citizens. Instead, they can administer their remedies directly *through the concept of justice itself*.

The most reasonable conception of justice is the one that affirms peoples' interest in developing the full set of moral powers they have as citizens. People who satisfy the political liberal proviso must make their lives along the complex interface of their public and nonpublic identity components. To play their parts well in the ongoing drama of a successful liberal society, each must develop not only capacities for a sense of justice and for a conception of the good, but also the distinctive capacity for negotiating the interface of those two in an ethically satisfying way. That is the moral power of ethical individuation, the exercise of which results in the practice of substantive citizenship, in all its diverse forms.

The Rawlsian strategy for thinking about justice is to begin with a very general idea of society and argue from that to a determinate set of principles. The device through which this connection is to be established is called the original position. The original position posits imaginary people, saddled with a carefully wrought set of information constraints, selecting from a list of candidate conceptions of justice. The parties in the original position are fictions, mere gears within a device of representation. But those gears must be cast in a way that reflects a concern for the full range of moral powers people have as citizens. Among those citizen powers—from the substantive perspective—is that of ethical individuation. But for some admissible citizens, this power may be directly and immediately threatened by certain facially neutral laws and policies. Parties in the original position must be modeled as being aware of this fact. This awareness requires that parties have general knowledge of the kinds of social diversity, including knowledge of the various forms of nonpublic reasoning itself, that political liberals hope to bring into their political settlement. Although veiled from knowing whether each might actually turn out to be an A-person, a B-person, or a C-person, for example, the parties must be modeled as considering any candidate conception of justice from the perspective of each one of those politically reasonable possible identities. They must be able to consider the direct (though unintended) effects that each candidate conception of justice might have on them, should they turn out to be members of any of those formally admissible groups.

What candidate conceptions of justice should be included on the list submitted to parties so conceived? Neutrality of effect is impracticable. But the ambition to *minimize* the unintended effects of liberal politics is a recognizably liberal ambition—certainly from the avowedly accommodationist stance claimed by political liberals. The parties in the original position, aware of these direct, non-neutral effects, and not knowing who in particular they will themselves turn out to be, would be drawn to a conception of justice expressing what might be thought of as a metapolitical version of the doctrine of double intention.

We saw in chapter 2 how the doctrine of double effect does not provide adequate moral cover for soldiers conducting military operations that unintentionally risk collateral harm to noncombatants. To discharge their debt to noncombatants, planners of military operations must show a double intention. Soldiers are obliged not merely to show *just enough* concern for the interests of noncombatants that their military actions are all-things-considered justified. Rather, soldiers must do the *most they can* to protect noncombatants from the unintended collateral damage caused by their actions, consistent with the primacy of their military aims.

So too, political liberals, seeking as they are to affirm the moral powers of their citizens, should do the most they can to protect all formally admissible citizens from the direct (though unintended) consequences of policies and laws that are to be enacted pursuant to liberal justice, consistent with their primary commitment to treating all citizens as free and equal.

Along with principles of justice that express concerns for basic rights and liberties and for equality of opportunity, for example, a full conception of justice might include what I shall call the *tax-flattening principle*. Such a principle would be designed to express the double intention I mentioned above. The tax-flattening principle would explicitly state that unintended effects that are directly generated by policies and laws enacted in accordance with the first two principles—that is, so-called direct "psychological taxes"—should be minimized or counteracted whenever possible. Out of respect for the architecture of public reason, this principle would be ordered lexically posterior to the others. Positioned that way, the tax-flattening principle could express this double intention *without* demanding any trade-off of citizens' basic liberties and opportunities for the other important social concerns they may have.

Of course, much would depend on the precise formulation of that third principle and, crucially, on the criteria relied upon to distinguish "direct" from "indirect" unintended effects.[34] Still, even in advance of all that we can see in a general way how the tax-flattening principle might operate.

In our discussion of civic education, for example, I suggested that political liberals have a distinct class of reasons—not shared by most ethical liberals—to accede to some central reintegrative demands made by politically reasonable parents, including, possibly, some of the demands made by the parents in the *Mozert* case. The tax-flattening principle reveals how that claim might be cashed out. On the strongest version, a constitution drawn up with reference to a political conception that included some version of the tax-flattening principle might change what a court hearing a case such as *Mozert* should decide as a matter of constitutional right. Even while denying as unreasonable some of the parents' demands (such as the exemptions from civics lessons altogether), a court might use that third principle to recognize a religious freedom right for the parents in this area of their children's education: something like a right to reintegrative autonomy.

Of course, the tax-flattening principle is ordered lexically posterior to the other principles. It thus might very well not carve out a constitutional right for parents in a case such as *Mozert*, where stakes are so high in terms of securing every citizen's full political autonomy. But even on that weaker reading, this more nuanced conception of justice might provide grounds for determining what the school board should do even if it has the constitutional right to do otherwise. For example, the tax-flattening principle might give reason for arguing strenuously that the Hawkins County School Board ought to seek creative ways to address the concerns of the parents about the direct though unintended effects of facially neutral civics lessons. The school board might allow teachers some discretion to add specially tailored sections to their lesson plans, or even possibly allow carefully formulated notes on some students' papers. They might thus empower teachers to make extra efforts to ensure that the lessons in public reason are not allowed by default to directly erode the religious beliefs of students from families affirming any one formally admissible worldview compared to any other one.

Here again, this more nuanced tripartite conception of justice would require that political liberal societies take up a range of social concerns that do not arise within most ethical liberal schemas. After all, the reintegrative concerns for most ethical liberals, while crucial and regrettably neglected in the recent literature as well, are systematically simpler. The forms of autonomy ethical liberals affirm in the public side of their citizens' lives closely match the forms of autonomy and ways of world perception they encourage in their citizens' nonpublic lives as well, whereas for political liberals those two forms of world perception are admitted often in practice to diverge.

These adjustments in the principles of justice might shape some important public rules and policies affecting adults too. If no-fault divorce laws, for example, were reasonably determined to have the unintended effect of sending a one-sided message about the meaning and value of marriage (as shown, perhaps, by a dramatic rise in the divorce rate in states that enact such legislation), a conception of justice that included the tax-flattening principle might well militate against laws formulated that way.[35] This would not be because political liberals, as opposed to ethical ones, take any particular view about whether long marriages are eudaimonistically better for all citizens than ones ending in quick divorce. Political liberals, as such, take no view on such questions. But a spike in divorce rates might reasonably be claimed to reveal that a no-fault divorce policy sends a direct (albeit unintended) message to citizens about the value of divorce over continued marriage when difficulties arise. Political liberals, at least, are bound to minimize direct messages of that sort whenever they can. They must seek to avoid recalibrating their citizens' personal compasses with respect to the meaning of their political autonomy, consistent with honoring all the basic rights and equality of opportunity.[36]

Would people outside the original position be likely to accept a conception of justice that included the tax-flattening principle?[37] Many reasonable citizens—A-people as well as C-people—affirm strongly perfectionist accounts of nonpublic life. Cosmopolitan militant atheists as well as religious people with a proselytizing agenda, for example, may be deeply concerned to see their view prosper. They may wish to secure conditions that not merely allow their worldview to survive but that encourage the "truth" to spread among the wayward (whether or not that encouragement occurs "intentionally" from a political perspective). The tax-flattening principle that I say would be adopted as a guiding principle behind the veil of ignorance protects ways of life deeply repugnant to them. Why should they—and A-people in particular—endorse that principle?

The very idea of a society founded on a public conception of justice suggests that politically reasonable citizens have reason to endorse a conception of justice that includes some such tax-flattening principle.[38] Citizens in such a society must ask themselves whether they really do want to engage in political association with diverse others on terms that all can accept. They are asked to put aside their own proselytizing beliefs and earnestly do their best to find a political solution that, insofar as is possible, each citizen can endorse as enthusiastically as every other. They must take to heart the idea that within the domain of the politically reasonable, whether one turns out to be a C-person or an A-person is a mere accident of natural fortune. To insist otherwise at the level of selecting principles of coercion would be to violate the principles of reciprocity and mutuality on which liberalism is at the deepest level founded. Fairness requires principles of justice that mitigate such accidents. Citizens have reason to endorse a conception of justice that includes some tax-flattening principle.

Still, the high standards of public reason are fully in effect here. We must proceed cautiously with any of these justice-tracking remedies. No doubt there are some strong versions of this tax-flattening principle that, even if formally just, could not pass the test of legitimacy. There are limits to what state coercion can do with respect to its own unintended effects. Yet again, however, the boundaries of justified state coercion are not the same as the boundaries of liberalism. There remains a further field of response to unintended spillovers, a field that lies beyond the formal grounds of public reason.

Mind the Gap

Once liberals recognize the educative dimensions of all their public rules and institutions, they immediately face a further problem, and with it find a further opportunity. The problem is that there is often a gap between what public reason dictates and the range of institutional options available to decision makers at the policy level. Consider a simple example. Imagine that a liberal conception of justice allows the use of some public monies for purposes of public recreation facilities. Even if justice tells us that the monies may be spent, justice does not give policy makers any further guidance about how to spend it—for example, whether to build tennis courts or dig a public pool. This sort of gap opens before policy makers as they confront many more serious policy questions. Justice may require that civic education include lessons about the rights people have as citizens and about the groundings of those rights. But, as we have seen, that itself does not exhaust the range of normative commitments that must be considered by liberals as they design those lessons.

Regarding the justification of principles of basic justice, political liberals are committed to letting themselves be guided by the high standards of public reason. But when it comes to giving recommendations at the level of actual policy making, public reason runs out—its recommendations are indeterminate among a range of acceptable options. To insist that public reason somehow settle all issues would be recipe for paralysis—there would be neither swimming pools nor tennis courts. Thus, at the level of actual policy making, a gap opens and we face a new question: What liberal norms, if any, should guide policy makers?

When selecting from a range of politically acceptable options, policy makers should be guided by liberalism's broader public purposes, the ambitions for social construction implicit in the ideal of a healthy or flourishing liberal society. So long as policy makers are selecting from among options that are consistent with the formal demands of justice, they should take their guidance from the civic ambitions that are most basic to their society. This gap between theory and practice presents liberals with an opportunity: a chance to harness a fact of commonsense political sociology—that neutrality of effect is impracticable—and drive that fact in service of their own deepest commitment.

But what are these commitments? How can we specify these civic norms, the norms that liberals think should guide policy makers as they attend to the full range of liberal public purposes? This is a difficult question, but two things seem clear. First, this gap, or something like it, is faced equally by theorists working in political or ethical liberal frameworks. Second, and more important, a crucial divergence between political liberals and ethical liberals emerges when it comes time to state the criteria by which the gap is to be filled.

I can specify what that divergence amounts to by proposing a general rule: whatever set of general norms are to guide policy makers when facing the gap, those norms should reflect that society's way of reasoning about basic justice itself. If a theorist accepts a political liberal way of justifying basic rights, for example, then whatever deep concerns led him to accept that form of justification should be reflected somehow in whatever guidelines he recommends at the policy stage. If a theorist accepts some ethical liberal way of justifying basic rights, by contrast, then whatever concerns led him to accept that form of justification should find an echo at the level of actual policy guidance.

What makes some theorists accept ethical liberalism? Roughly, it is their acceptance of some ideal of autonomy or individuality as the true account of moral personality. Such people therefore have a deep view of a well-functioning society that is perfectionist. What makes other people accept political liberalism? Roughly, their acceptance of the fact of reasonable value pluralism. They thus have a deep view of society as a kind of home to diverse citizen types, citizens of faith and autonomous individualists alike. The crucial idea, though, is that whatever deep values led one to the base one accepts, those underlying values should find a distinctive echo when it comes time to instruct policy makers about the full range of liberalism's public purposes.

As we saw in the case of school design, policy-making norms that are specified this way can lead to powerful distinctions between political and ethical liberals. Sharp differences between those two metapolitical views emerge on many other policy questions as well. For example, say that a liberal conception of justice requires that public monies be used provide all citizens with basic food and housing. Legislators and administrators may need to choose between very different ways of effecting those distributions. Political liberals, out of concern for their most basic conception of society and good citizen conduct, may be more likely than ethical liberal to share those monies with civil society organizations—and with churches in particular—as a way of meeting the requirements of social justice, and their broader civic ambitions as well. Ethical liberals may be more likely to employ more uniform, centrally designed distributive means—policies designed with one eye on their distinctively perfectionist goals. Similar opportunities, and so subtle differences between ethical and political liberals, arise with respect to practically every policy decision made within the liberal state.

It is sometimes said that in instructing policy makers about these broader norms of civic construction, liberalism reveals itself to be less wishy-washy about civic virtue than communitarian critics have long claimed. Given the gap between concerns about basic justice and questions of actual policy making, liberals cannot help but play an active role in the formation of their citizenry's character. A liberalism that attends to its full range of public purposes is a "liberalism with spine."[39] This is an important idea. But it seems to me that the crucial idea is the one that comes next. For those who accept political liberalism, whatever spine they show in this area must be flexible in a distinctive way. In general, ethical liberals must attend to the role of policy makers in gently *shaping* diversity toward public ends. Political liberals, by contrast, must be concerned about ways of gently *protecting* diversity from the pursuit of legitimate public ends.[40] Given the divergent commitments at the base of their views, this is the only acceptable way for each sort of liberal to mind the gap.

Chapter Six

HIGH LIBERALISM

The Intuitive Argument

The public philosophy of political liberalism makes central the ideal of an active, engaged citizenry. These citizens see pressing questions of social construction arising in every sphere of their lives rather than in just the public one.[1] They think of themselves as sharing more with one another than the project of mutually providing what is publicly required. Citizens face together a further challenge: the challenge of ethical individuation, each on his own terms, in a society that puts justice first.

Of course, liberals of every sort recognize that people engage in important projects outside the domain of public reason. Theorists who operate within the derivative citizenship paradigm, for example, do not deny that ethical individuation is important to people. What they do deny, though, is that concerns about ethical individuation are relevant to liberal theorizing beyond the formal threshold point that the attainment of legitimacy requires. This causes an unfortunate narrowing of the boundaries of liberal theory construction, as we have seen. But this denial also generates distortions within political constructivism, the process by which liberals assign content to social justice itself. These distortions emerge most dramatically when traditional accounts of liberal justice are cut-and-pasted directly into the context of political liberalism.

The most detailed and powerful comprehensive liberal account of justice is still the one Rawls presented in *A Theory of Justice*. The most famous feature of that account, of course, is the argument from the original position. Yet Rawls also gives a less technical, more intuitive argument in favor of the notoriously expansive, material egalitarian conception of justice he favors. The idea of a genuinely *public* society, as opposed to a private one, implies that every member of society has an equal moral claim on social valuable goods (rights, liberties, etc.). The distribution of such goods should reflect the moral powers that people have in common and not the various contingencies that differentiate them. This suggests a very general formulation of liberal justice:

> First: each person is to have an equal right to the most extensive basic liberty compatible with a similar liberty for others.
>
> Second: social and economic inequalities are to be arranged so that they are both (*a*) reasonably expected to be to everyone's advantage, and (*b*) attached to positions and offices open to all.[2]

This formulation admits of a great many interpretations. The "natural liberty" interpretation is a kind of free-market, libertarian view.[3] Rawls rejects this view. Why do defenders of this view object to legal barriers to positions based on, say, race, gender, or caste? Presumably because they recognize that such personal characteristics are arbitrary from a moral point of view. However, providing formal legal opportunity does not ensure substantive opportunity. Social factors such as one's family background, educational history, or degree of wealth can affect the resulting allocation of goods just as surely as a formal system of legal sanctions. So the system of natural liberty fails on its own terms.[4]

The "liberal equality" interpretation remedies this defect by requiring fair equality of opportunity.[5] Rawls finds the equal liberty view internally inconsistent as well. It is not only one's educational history or financial starting point that are affected by one's social background: one's aspirations, motivations, and realized abilities are affected as well. The system of liberal equality does not fulfill its own ambition to nullify the contingencies of social fortune.

So we are led to the system of democratic equality. Assuming one has institutions guaranteeing equal liberty and fair equality of opportunity, "the higher expectations of those better situated are just if and only if they work as part of a scheme which improves the expectations of the least advantaged members of society."[6]

While Rawls emphasizes that he does not intend this as a formal argument, it is one of the most powerful and influential lines of reasoning in *A Theory of Justice*. The argument derives its power from a plausible core idea: within a public society, justice requires that we seek to nullify the contingencies of natural and social fortune in the distribution of basic goods. Since every view of public society implicitly accepts that core idea,[7] the only question is which view articulates and adheres to that idea view in the fullest and most consistent way. "So however we move away from the system of natural liberty, we cannot be satisfied short of the democratic conception."[8]

But if dropped down onto the terrain of political liberalism, this line of argument turns out not yet to have run its full course. Compared to comprehensive liberalism, political liberalism takes as its starting point a significantly broadened range of moral attitudes as politically reasonable. The tendency of some citizens to rely on traditions of nonpublic authority in response to interpersonal questions is now considered no less "arbitrary from the moral point of view" than those people's race, educational background, or natural endowments. Within the more capacious boundaries of the reasonable that political liberals claim now to accept, one's status as an A-person or a C-person has become one of those social contingencies that our account of justice must seek to counteract.

Of course, it is no more plausible to insist on a conception of justice that completely nullifies this contingency (of being a C-person rather than an A-person) than it would be to insist on one that completely nullifies natural endowments—for example, one's height or native IQ. Yet theorists committed to the idea of a public society clearly are required to *seek* to do so, and to do so in a way that reflects their concern for people's fundamental moral capacities.

This has an important consequence for the material egalitarian dimension of liberal justice. In the conditions of pluralism that political liberalism takes as its starting point, the liberal commitment to nullifying moral contingencies need not generate pressure only in the direction of ever more expansive interpretations of liberal justice. On the contrary, if political liberals are to find a conception of justice that best expresses their commitment to the political nullification of the morally arbitrary, they must begin to ask themselves a new set of difficult but urgent questions: How is each candidate conception of liberal justice likely to impact on the nonpolitical self-understandings of reasonable citizens in a diverse society? How well does each of these conceptions allow various groups of reasonable people to realize their moral capacities, including their capacity for ethical individuation? How much social space does each conception leave for the practice of substantive citizenship, a practice through which individuation is often expressed? Or, to put this new question in the broader terms I prefer, we must begin to ask: Which conception of liberal justice is best suited to play its role *within* an account of liberal society?

I have as yet said nothing about how these questions should be answered. My aim has merely been to introduce them and to show why they arise naturally once one moves to the political liberal framework. We must consider the formal argument from the original position to see whether these considerations affect our understanding of the content of justice. Before doing that, though, I would like to present the same point in a different way. My argument here will be even less formal, but I believe the pause will be worth the pages.

Feudalism or Medievalism?

Political views often define themselves by the manner in which they object to rival views. This is true of Rawlsian liberalism—what Rawls's close followers call "high liberalism." High liberalism defines itself with particular vividness in the way it rejects contemporary libertarianism. I wish now to examine one high liberal argument against libertarianism. My aim is not to defend libertarianism but to highlight a feature of the Rawlsian view I shall discuss below.

According to Rawlsian high liberals the contrast between high liberalism and libertarianism is so great that libertarianism is revealed not even to count as a liberal view.[9] High liberalism, on this view, is understood to be a tradition rooted in the writings of Locke, Kant, and Mill and flowering with Rawls. Central to this tradition is the idea of treating certain rights as basic out of a concern for human autonomy. Mill, for example, expresses this concern for autonomy in his "principle of liberty," a principle that implies a number of rights: (1) liberty of conscience, (2) freedom of thought and discussion, (3) freedom of tastes and the freedom to pursue a plan of life to suit one's character, and (4) freedom of association. Rawls brings this tradition to its peak, expanding this list considerably, to include (5) equal political rights, (6) freedom of occupation and movement, (7) the rights and liberties associated with the rule of law, and (8) the rights and liberties needed to maintain the physical and even psychological integrity of the person.

In contrast to high liberalism, there is libertarianism. Most libertarians anchor their view of justice on the obscure notion of property in oneself. But the very ideas of ownership and property, whether in oneself or in other objects, are complex, socially elaborated notions. Since the notions of ownership and property are parasitic on the elucidation of some system of property rules, self-ownership cannot serve as a fundamental justificatory principle for a theory of politics.

The problem gets even worse, on the high liberal telling, because libertarians typically conjoin their doctrine of self-ownership with the doctrine of full alienability of rights. Libertarian doctrines of self-ownership, unconstrained by any doctrine of inalienability, allow people to treat themselves (and others) as objects, as pieces of property to be bought and sold on the basis of contingent preferences in the libertarian marketplace. The libertarian conception of justice, according to the high liberals, is in the end not rooted in a concern to protect human autonomy but to protect *property*. Libertarianism thus turns out not even to be a liberal view. Indeed, from this perspective, libertarianism greatly resembles a view that liberalism historically defined itself against, the doctrine of private political power that is *feudalism*.[10]

This is not the place for a close examination of libertarianism, nor even of this high liberal argument against it. I have described this high liberal critique only because I wish to point out a feature it shares with Rawls's own positive argument for the democratic equality interpretation. Both arguments, this negative one and Rawls's positive one, have their intuitive force only so long as we assume that the values which are basic to any liberal theory must be fully expressed in that theory's account of justice. This is another manifestation of the assumption I have been questioning throughout this book, the assumption that the normative domain of "liberalism" and that of "justified political coercion" map closely onto each other.

What happens if we free ourselves from this assumption in the context of this dispute between libertarians and high liberals? We might then imagine libertarians rigorously distinguishing their conception of libertarianism from their conception of libertarian justice—with "libertarianism" signifying a broader set of normative grounds that includes a "libertarian conception of justice" as one component. From this perspective, the foundational libertarian concern with freedom and autonomy—hallmarks of any properly *liberal* view—are not claimed to be fully expressed by the libertarian conception of justice. Such libertarians might still claim that their conception of justice is founded on a deeper level, with a concern for freedom and the other moral capacities of persons, but they need not thereby commit themselves to the claim that their concern for freedom and those other capacities is fully expressed in their view of justice.[11] Libertarian justice does not itself fully protect the fundamental human moral powers, they might argue, because those moral powers include elements that by their very nature are not the sort of thing that *justice* could ever protect.

From this perspective, libertarians *can* be fundamentally concerned with securing the social conditions that enable people to develop the full range of their (liberal) moral powers. They merely disagree with the high liberals about the role of the concept justice in doing that. The high liberal argumentative strategy against libertarianism as a doctrine is in fact a nonstarter. The "liberalism" of libertarianism need not be revealed by a narrow inspection of the libertarian conception of justice.[12]

If that sounds strange, it may be because the now-dominant approach to liberal justice—high liberalism—is so very different in this respect. High liberalism is marked, more than anything else, by a tremendously expansive role within the normative domain of liberal theory for the concept justice. We have already noted how high liberalism expands the list of rights affirmed by earlier liberals such as Mill. Justice is now said to be a concept, an obligation-generating form of evaluation, that is relevant not only to matters of conscience and discussion, but to political matters and to matters concerning not only the physical integrity of the person but her psychological integrity as well. The societal consequences of this expansion are shown dramatically in Rawls's sketch of the institutions he thinks would be required by justice in a free society—even after to the shift to political liberalism.

According to Rawls, liberal justice requires full public financing of elections and a public guarantee that information bearing on matters of public policy would be readily available to all citizens. Rawls also thinks justice requires institutions that guarantee fair equality of opportunity, especially in the forms of education and training, which all people are to receive.

Justice requires that income and wealth be distributed in a way that ensures that all citizens have the all-purpose means to freely develop themselves. Justice requires society as an "employer of last resort through general or local government, or other social and economic policies." Justice requires that health care be assured to all citizens. In fact, Rawls thinks liberal justice requires a substantially larger state apparatus than even what is suggested by his own sketch. For example, regarding the requirement of guaranteed income and wealth, Rawls mentions that in his view this requirement involves "far more than provision for food, clothing, and housing, or simply for basic needs." The need for public financing of elections, he explains, "merely hints at" all that would be institutionally required in a society that is just. Of all these institutions, Rawls says that they "do not, of course, fully satisfy the principles of justice as fairness." Rather, institutions such as these would be required merely as "essential prerequisites"—as made obvious by commonsense political sociology—for a society to satisfy the demands of liberal justice.[13]

In a high liberal society, when individuals consider how to respond to questions of fellow-treatment across a great variety of situations, it is *justice* that kicks in, demanding deliberative primacy for itself both institutionally and motivationally. But can justice do this without supplanting the great variety of other ways that well-meaning individuals think or might have come to think of their relations with their fellow citizens—ways of thinking that, for some citizens now recognized as reasonable, may be quite central to their own self-understandings?

If we consider high liberalism simply in terms of the socially constructive work Rawlsians ascribe to it, we see a crucial difference between high liberalism and the modified libertarianism I just described. Unlike libertarianism, high liberalism admits no distinction between itself and its conception of justified coercion. For a high liberal to care about some value *just means* to set out state-backed guarantees concerning that value in terms of justice. It is the expansive reach of high liberal justice that has given the derivative conception of citizenship its plausibility. It is no wonder the substantive interpretation of liberal citizenship has been trivialized, if not stamped out, within today's academy: the high liberal interpretation of social justice leaves it little serious space.

It is from this perspective, one firmly settled in the coextensivity assumption, that high liberals notice that orthodox libertarianism bears its striking and uncomfortable resemblance to feudalism. I think there is something to that charge. But is it worth noting that the high liberalism of the Rawlsians is wide open to a pretty strong tu quoque.

If contemporary libertarianism can be compared to feudalism, high liberalism can be compared to yet another historical epoch that liberalism once defined itself against. I am thinking of Europe not during feudalism but in the period from 1073 to 1300. This is the period that grew out of feudalism; it was not merely the Middle Ages, but the *High* Middle Ages.[14] During that period, the Age of Faith, the Church—especially through the canon law and the internalization of Church-defined causes of guilt—achieved not only a supremacy but an extraordinary pervasiveness in the lives of ordinary Europeans.[15] The Church's objective of unifying the *res publica christiana* forced a holy uniformity on erstwhile diverse communities and provided society with a very medieval stability. In those heady days, formal Church doctrine claimed the authority to fill the social space in which well-meaning individuals (and communities) might otherwise have reflected in their own various ways about these challenges concerning human life and human relations.

High medievalism had the Church, with its octopusal canon law, cashing out all the most interesting questions of life in terms of duties to Christendom or God. High liberalism has *social justice*, with an expansive conception of citizen obligations derived relentlessly from the democratic egalitarian conception of rights. In both societies, high medieval society and high liberal society, a single evaluative perspective, a single socially constructive concept, has been allowed to run amok. And in both cases, as historical conditions force more open-mindedness and a greater acceptance of moral differences as reasonable, a breaking point is eventually reached.

The Idea of Society

On the first page of *Political Liberalism*, Rawls writes: "I begin with a first fundamental question about political justice in a democratic society, namely, what is the most appropriate conception of justice for specifying the fair terms of social cooperation between citizens regarded as free and equal, and as fully cooperating members of society over a complete life, from one generation to the next?"[16]

There is a more fundamental question: What is the role of social justice, as a concept, within the boundaries of liberal theory? Political liberals typically do not ask that question but instead assume an answer to it. An account of liberal justice and its attendant principles of democratic self-rule *just are* an account of liberalism, such that if you have given one you have automatically given the other.

Political liberals assume this coextensivity between the normative domain of liberalism and the liberal public values component because they see the boundary of liberal theorizing as being set by the project of showing the conditions in which the use of state power is legitimate. They are fixed on demonstrating how they can have a moral form of social union that does not illegitimately coerce anyone. This assumption about the coextensivity of liberalism and liberal public values is reflected in the way political liberals describe the most basic idea from which their arguments about the content of liberal justice begins: the idea of society.

For Rawls, "the fundamental organizing idea of justice as fairness, within which the other basic ideas are systematically connected, is that of society as *a fair system of cooperation over time*, from one generation to the next."[17] When the basic institutions of a society are regulated by a public political conception of justice that citizens accept as free and equal, that society is "well ordered."[18]

Yet in the conditions of reasonable value pluralism that political liberalism assumes, a society can be "well ordered" and remain worrying to the citizens themselves. The basic institutions of a just liberal society may systematically—albeit unintentionally—generate an individualistic background culture that makes many admissible citizens ethically uneasy. The ethical unease caused by the prospect of unintended spillovers may positively alienate certain groups of citizens, especially otherwise admissible citizens on the society's cultural margins (certain C-people, for example). But mainstream citizens can also be expected to have residual eudaimonistic concerns about this "well-ordered" society, even if they do affirm justice in an enduring first-personal way.[19]

Our substantive approach to citizenship invites us to think of political constructivism in a different way. On this approach, we begin from the wider conception of "society" also implicit in the background of liberal democracies. Society is a fair system of cooperation in which people live lives that they find valuable from their own perspectives. Such a society does not realize its ideal merely when people have developed their capacity for a sense of justice. Rather, a political liberal society flourishes only when people acquire and exercise a common sense of justice *along with* the diverse, nonpublic norms I call liberal virtues. As much as people in diverse democratic societies care about fairness, fairness is not all they care about, even as a matter of social cooperation. People also care, and very much, that—along with providing the securities of justice—the institutions in their society are arranged such that citizens, insofar as reciprocity allows, are able to navigate the interface of their public and nonpublic lives with integrity and ethical fullness. Such people recognize that the fair terms of social cooperation are not the only terms of social cooperation needed by a liberal polity if it is to flourish as a polity of that kind. They affirm a view of society that squares better with the motivational foundations of political liberalism itself. A successful political liberal society is a fair *and ethically satisfying* system of cooperation over time.

This view of society takes a psychologically realistic approach to persons in a liberal society having a determinate conception of the good. Citizens are not seen as having their public self-understandings in one part of their brains and their nonpublic self-understandings in some different part. Nor are they seen as setting out their public understandings as a kind of corral within which their nonpublic understandings are then free to roam untouched. Instead, a person's response to the challenges raised by interface are *central* to whatever determinate conception each affirms. Certainly, people are affirmed as capable of recognizing the difference between the public and nonpublic norms that apply to them. They know, for example, which norms would have standing before public institutions and which—however urgent from nonpublic perspectives—would not. But they recognize that justice-based forms of evaluation cannot help but seep into and condition even the most intimate of those nonenforceable norms. To have a determinate conception of the good within a liberal society means to have built attachments and loyalties to certain people, and to have become committed to certain projects and ends, *through* one's awareness of one's standing as a political equal—not simply in ways logically consistent with that awareness.

Political theorists must look to the public culture not simply to find materials for building a justifiable account of political coercion—as though providing that account would be to provide an account of liberalism itself. They must look there for the shared materials needed to build an account of political coercion appropriate to play its role *within* a theory of liberal society—because they cannot assume that an account of liberal public values simply amounts to an account of liberalism itself.[20] To assume from the outset that an account of liberalism is simply an account of liberal justice is to risk distorting our view about the content of justice itself. This danger, always present, is magnified with the rise of political liberalism.

The Original Position and Cost-Free Guarantees

Most liberals believe that no major changes in the liberal conception of social justice are required by the adoption of political liberalism.[21] In light of the intuitive concerns I mentioned earlier in the chapter, let us test that belief.

The original position imagines parties behind a veil of ignorance endeavoring to secure the largest possible set of all-purpose goods for those they represent. Since the parties in the original position are selecting principles that will affect their long-term life prospects, they are modeled as employing a conservative decision rule called *maximin*, by which the candidate conception of justice with the best worst outcome is preferred.

In *Theory*, Rawls argues that parties so described would choose democratic egalitarianism (his preferred interpretation of the two principles) over any of the various other candidates, and over utilitarianism in particular. For Utilitarianism may require the sacrifice of some people's most basic liberties in order to produce a larger aggregate utility. The very bad outcomes this makes possible for some people are ruled out by democratic egalitarianism. Parties in the OP are thus modeled as purchasing a form of insurance that provides people with strong downside protection. Whatever policy guarantees the biggest payout if things turn out badly is the rational preference. So democratic egalitarianism is selected.

As we have seen in many contexts, most contemporary liberals focus their arguments narrowly on the domain of the political and the questions of justified coercion that arise there. But in the context of Rawls's description of the reasoning of the parties in the original position, this self-imposed limit has the curious and distorting effect of making the parties' purchase of the insurance that justice provides seem *cost-free to them*. True, parties must compare one insurance policy to another and so can recognize which has greater payout than others (shown, for example, in their preference for the difference principle over strict egalitarianism). But Rawls's argument presents parties as systematically insensitive to the cost of purchasing the insurance—the *guarantee* for delivery—at all. The distortion occurs because Rawls's model asks the parties to assume that they must rely on no other motivational concern except justice to deliver these goods to them. They are thus unable to consider the costs *to those they represent* of choosing a conception of justice that crowds out other motivational delivery mechanisms (including ones by which the delivery, by its very nature, cannot be guaranteed). The difference principle, therefore, will be attractive to maximizing parties in the original position only if they both (1) want to get as high a level of primary goods as possible, the point Rawls emphasizes, *and* (2) are willing to have the delivery of those goods accomplished wholly under the concept justice.

What would it mean to ascribe that additional second motive to the parties in the original position? It does not necessarily require that we describe the parties as willing to have coercive state institutions actually delivering those goods to citizens—like a uniformed delivery service going door-to-door. Nothing in the difference principle favors supply by formal state institutions over supply by the market or other non-state-based agencies. But ascribing that second motive to the parties does require that we conceive of them as willing to think of the supply of those goods as falling under the rubric of justice, a heading that brings with it a distinctive guarantee of delivery. That guarantee implicates the coercive apparatus of the state even if the state apparatus does not itself assume the position of deliverer on a case-by-case basis. Justice casts a distinctive shadow over all voluntary givings done in its name. That shadow falls across the communicative framework in which all citizens are to interact.[22] So to ascribe that second motive to the parties is to claim that the parties are properly modeled as willing to have all their motives concerning the delivery of such goods brought under the shadow of justice. It is to affirm their willingness to have the actions good citizens undertake with respect to one another be thought of in that light.

Is it appropriate to model the parties in this way? Perhaps, if we begin by positing a society in which people uniformly affirm some ideal of ethical autonomy of the sort Rawls himself once ideally assumed.[23] But when considered in the context of a society characterized by the forms of reasonable diversity that political liberalism claims to accept, the modeling of the parties (and so the outcome of their reasoning via maximin) becomes less straightforward.

Among the dimensions of free society's diversity may be a diversity of understandings concerning the ultimate forms of motivation most appropriate to various questions of social construction. The mill owner continues to pay the salaries of his out-of-work employees "because I am a Jew." The field owners in Vermont keep their land open "because this is what our families do." The African Americans contribute their time and resources to elder care "because that is how we treat our people." But these socially constructive activities, along with the substantive citizen identities they support, can be crowded out, or at least undercut, by conceptions of justice that set out guarantees in those same areas—even if those guarantees stand in the background. State-backed employment schemes, aesthetic zoning ordinances, and even an expansive system of medical care all provide a guarantee of something valuable *at the cost of* a different dimension of value to which reasonable citizens are sensitive.

The point here is not that it is unrealistic to expect people sometimes to affirm justice as the guarantor for the delivery of goods on the basis of reasons particular to their own comprehensive conception. That expectation is basic to constructivism, and the substantive perspective of liberal citizenship affirms it entirely. Rather, the point is that—separate from citizens' socially constructive concerns that can, from their own perspectives, be enlisted to support action on behalf of justice—citizens may also reasonably be expected to affirm comprehensive doctrines that include significant elements that *cannot* be so enlisted. For many admissible citizen groups, a crucial link between the activity of providing the good and the identity of the person doing the providing may be severed, or at least twisted, if we insist that the activity be publicly understood to be done under the rubric of even a political conception of justice. There may be such non-justice-reducible motives within reasonable comprehensive doctrines of many kinds, and so some pressures of this sort existed even within the comprehensive liberal framework within which Rawls's famous argument was first devised. But those motives seem most firmly associated with the doctrines that political liberalism claims distinctively to bring in—Larmore's reasonable Romantics, or Rawls's citizens of faith.[24] In the new social context the political liberals assume, these pressures are greatly increased.

Parties making choices among conceptions of justice to regulate the basic structure of their society cannot know whether they will turn out to be C-people, A-people, or the B-people in between. So they must keep in mind something very important: when employing maximin in conditions of reasonable value pluralism, "doing the best they can for those they represent" does *not* necessarily mean choosing the conception with the biggest payout of primary goods via justice. In conditions of reasonable value pluralism, the purchase of social insurance may come at a significant price, a price that must now be tallied in terms of values internal to the choice scenario itself.

That Rawls's original argument for the difference principle misses this point is shown vividly in his discussion of benevolence. In *A Theory of Justice* the aspects of goodwill that are relevant to the securing of primary goods for other people are centrally cashed out in terms of *justice*. "Now the combination of mutual disinterest and the veil of ignorance achieves the same purpose as benevolence." This is because the design of the original position forces each person to take the good of others into account. "In justice as fairness, then, the effects of goodwill are brought about by several conditions working jointly."[25]

On the wider approach to liberal theory construction I am suggesting things have an importantly different emphasis. There will be *elements* of citizens' goodwill that will be cashed out in terms of their sense of justice. But in conditions of reasonable value pluralism, our wider conception of society and person as yet leave it an open question as to how much or what parts of people's goodwill can legitimately be so expressed. The norm of equal respect requires that we seek to make room for reasonable forms of benevolence—for example, elements of the authority-derived doctrines affirmed by certain C-people—that are not reducible to justice in this way.[26] A theoretical process of construction is not freestanding if it covertly relies on the perspective of one group of politically reasonable people (here, the A-people) in devising principles to govern them all. If transplanted directly into the soil of political liberalism, the form of constructivism presented in *A Theory of Justice* would not be freestanding. In that early work the parties in the original position are described in a way that makes them unable to consider the ethical costs of seeking primary goods through the guarantee that justice provides (costs C-people, for example, may feel even if A-people do not). We can deepen this point by considering another argument for democratic egalitarianism: the argument from self-respect.

Rawls treats self-respect as the most basic of all goods. Without self-respect nothing that we do can have meaning for us. The "social bases" of self-respect are those conditions that support self-respect: objective conditions, such as the material circumstances that enable us to develop and pursue our aspirations; subjective conditions, such as our associating with other people in ways that allow us to experience their respect for us. Primary goods provide both subjective and objective bases for self-respect. So we can test whether parties in the original position have chosen the correct conception of justice by asking which conception best provides conditions favorable for self-respect of all reasonable citizens no matter what their position.

Rawls thinks his two principles meet this test. By guaranteeing equal basic liberties to every citizen, the *first principle* provides subjective support for people's self-respect: associative and deliberative liberties allow all people to form associations and life-plans by their own lights. But people's self-respect also depends on the *worth* of their liberties, which Rawls says depends in turn on each person's level of material resources. The difference principle speaks to this by guaranteeing the greatest minimum level of material resources. Together, then, Rawls's two principles provide the maximum worth of liberty. Since this material guarantee is part of the public understanding of the people in such a society as citizens, when citizens affirm these principles as expressive of their understanding of the just terms of social cooperation, they publicly affirm the worth of one another—further strengthening the self-respect of each.[27]

Our wider perspective of liberal society likewise affirms the great importance of self-respect to people, and thus the importance of testing candidate conceptions of justice to see how each affects the social bases of self-respect. This perspective also shows the great value in terms of the subjective bases of self-respect of a principle such as Rawls's first one, which provides a lexical guarantee of equal liberties to all. However, our wider perspective reveals a fact hidden from Rawls's approach: in the conditions of pluralism that political liberals assume, the worth of liberties to people does *not* necessarily increase as a function of justice-guaranteed income and wealth.

The basic elements of self-respect are 1) a person's belief that her aims are worth achieving and (2) the person's reasonable hopes for actually achieving those ends.[28] But among the aims that reasonable persons have in free societies are aims concerning socially constructive projects that are by their very nature not reducible or translatable into justice. These aims diverge from the forms of goodwill that can be reduced to concerns about justice simply because, once provided with deliberative and associational liberties, humans tend to respond in unpredictable and motivationally diverse ways to the challenges and puzzles of social life. Many aspects of reasonable diversity can be captured by a political liberal conception of public reason, with people affirming a common set of public principles each from her own perspective. But people also acknowledge socially constructive reasons for action that cannot be captured in terms of public reason—and yet those reasons may be absolutely central to people's deep self-understandings. This occurs most dramatically perhaps with our C-people, but it is a feature of the social experience of many A-persons as well. It is a common feature of life in a free society.

Even though people do need material goods for self-respect, we cannot treat as a matter of irrelevance the effect that different normative delivery mechanisms for those goods will have on a person's sense of self-worth. People's self-respect is bound up in part with the value they attribute to their own traditional forms of social construction—including those forms which lie outside the parameters of public reason. It *means* something to the African Americans that they are active and responsible in their traditions of elder care. They find value both in their activities being *needed* and in the distinctive form of concern others show them when their needs are so met. So too with the mill owner and his workers, and with many others.[29] They would see it as a kind of Kantian hubris to treat all their various forms of meaning as the generic "grist of benevolence," ready to be poured with all the rest into the philosopher's constructivist machine. For them, the justice of the high liberals is an ethical bully. It is an evaluative perspective that threatens to crowd out the social space in which they once acted and were acted on by one another, activities through with each became and remained the ethically-individuated citizen each by his own lights aimed to be.

In a diverse society, the self-respect of politically reasonable persons may be undercut, rather than supported, by conceptions of justice so wide that they guarantee delivery of material goods in areas where local norms of responsibility and citizen activity might otherwise have operated. In the significantly broadened social conditions that political liberalism assumes, Rawls's self-respect argument is too simple. The worth of liberties to many reasonable persons depends on the material bases of their use *not* being guaranteed to them as a matter of social justice. Because of the link between citizen identity and citizen activity, the minimum position in terms of material bases of self-respect cannot unproblematically be defined as the maximized minimum level of primary goods guaranteed by the concept justice. To define the acceptable minimum that way would be to assume that all reasonable citizens are situated similarly with respect to their willingness to have their forms of goodwill fed into the mill of justice-directed constructivism. But that is to allow a mere moral contingency to have a decisive effect not only on the distribution but *on the moral nature of the distributive mechanism* that characterizes this society.

After all, the C-persons have the same claim to the social bases of self-respect as do the A-persons. Among the social bases on which *their* self-respect relies is that of living is a society where justice has not been allowed to eat up the space of social construction on which their (reasonable) form of social identity depends. So guaranteeing the equal worth of liberties requires recognizing the moral costs (in terms of self respect) of candidate conceptions that seek to maximize the minimum *via justice*. The difference principle, with its simple aim of maximizing the justice-backed delivery of social goods, is blind to those costs. We have no reason to believe that the difference principle maximizes the minimum worth of liberty in conditions of reasonable value pluralism.

Of course, parties employing maximin within the original position must consider the position of all members of society. For example, they must consider people who have fallen on hard times and are not members of any closely knit group who might look after them, or people who have chosen to reject the commitments of such groups. The ideal of a public society almost certainly requires a conception of justice that includes some guaranteed social welfare minimum for such people—at the very least, the sort of "safety net" affirmed by both Friedrich Hayek and Milton Friedman. The ideal of public society may itself require that justice provide material guarantees well beyond that. Still, the point is crucial. The guarantees of delivery that justice provides are never free. In the political liberal context, those guarantees become increasingly costly from an ethical perspective. They are costly in ways that must be tallied internally to the choice the parties are modeled as making. So however theorists who accept liberal constructivism define the guaranteed minimum justice provides, that minimum must be defined as significantly lower after the politicization of justice.

This same worry undermines the other material egalitarian aspects of justice as fairness aside from the difference principle. In *Political Liberalism*, for example, Rawls argues for an interpretation of the first principle that gives a special place to the political liberties. Unless the "fair value" of the political liberties is guaranteed, just background institutions are unlikely to be established or maintained. Unlike the other basic liberties, the political liberties have a distinctive role in determining the laws and policies that regulate the basic structure: all the other basic rights depend on the political liberties. Because of this, Rawls says, the fair value guarantee requires that "the worth of the political liberties to all citizens, whatever their social or economic position, must be approximately equal, . . . in the sense that everyone has a fair opportunity to hold public office and to influence the outcome of political decisions."[30] This argument gets its strong material egalitarian punch from Rawls' claim that people have that fair opportunity only when all citizens have "a full and equally effective voice" in political matters.[31] This will require the public financing of elections, of course. But because of the way people of greater means can band together politically and exclude those with less, even the level of material inequality permitted by the difference principle might be ruled out by the fair value guarantee.[32] So Rawls now argues for an interpretation of the first principle that makes that principle even more materially egalitarian than his second principle.

If one assumes that public forms of reason must do all the socially constructive work required for the society to realize its ideal (for Rawls, the ideal of being "well ordered" in a narrowly justice-based sense), then it is quite natural to guarantee fair value to the political liberties. This is because the political liberties do play a special role in the part of social construction that justice picks out. The political liberties protect the other rights, including those protecting economic concerns, that one takes as basic. Indeed, from *that* perspective—the one that sees justice as the only horse pulling the cart of liberal theory—there is no reason not to give political liberties "fair value." There are no theoretically recognizable concerns that push back against the expansion of state power that the fair value guarantee requires.

From the substantive perspective, however, things have a different look. It is less obvious that giving fair value to political liberties is essential to the protection of basic rights. Social and economic conditions adequate to support a strong and independent judiciary, for example, might adequately protect the basic rights of Rawls's first principle minus the fair value guarantee. In conditions of reasonable value pluralism, the fair value guarantee might not be included as part of one's conception of justice simply because it now less clear that a political liberal conception of justice requires (or even allows) the redistributive measures that Rawls envisages being pursued at the legislative stage (those measures generated by the difference principle, in particular). If justice does not require such measures at the legislative stage, then the value of the political liberties might be secured without engaging in the massive social engineering required to ensure every citizen a "full and effective voice" in legislative matters.

The crucial point, however, is that Rawls's argument for the fair value guarantee, like his argument for the difference principle, is systematically blind to the *costs* of pursuing socially constructive projects through the concept justice.[33] But in conditions of reasonable-value pluralism, those programs may well be costly. Their cost is paid in terms of the vanishing social space in which reasonable people might otherwise have perceived and responded to the challenges of human social existence on their own, eudaimonistically directed terms. Since justice requires a commitment to the ideal of nullifying contingencies, those costs *are* relevant to political liberal constructivism, and so must be considered when we try to decide which conception of justice is most reasonable.

Again, none of the foregoing is intended as a proof that material egalitarian elements have no place in a political liberal conception of justice.[34] Rather, I mean merely to point out that the arguments the Rawlsians give for the egalitarian elements central to high liberalism—the difference principle and the fair value guarantee—are plausible only if we model parties in the original position as being insensitive to ethical costs that *are* relevant from a political liberal perspective. We see those costs when we consider the wider account of society, and of the moral powers of persons, that the substantive view implies.

What might an argument for liberal justice look like that did attempt to recognize those ethical costs that are hidden from Rawls's comprehensive approach? The guiding idea would be that the most reasonable and stable conception of justice for a successful liberal society must be one that is "rooted not in abnegation but in affirmation of our person."[35] The original position must therefore model the ideal of obtaining social conditions that allow the adequate development and exercise of the full range of people's common moral powers: for justice, for goodness, and for what I have called *individuation*.

In a society where people at their best are seen not only as reasonable and rational but also as *responsible*, where citizens are respected not only as free and equal but also as *active*, people will develop their distinctive moral powers not only in one unified way but in a great many ways (some, though not all, irreducible to a concern for social justice). This form of diversity is one of the long-term effects of the deliberative and associative liberties. Benevolence, in a diverse society, will come in many forms, some irreducible to even the most capacious terms of public reason. The moral drive to nullify contingencies must be made sensitive to those contingencies that are generated as an effect of the normal operation of free institutions—for example, the degrees of diversity represented by our reasonable alphabet people. In the face of that diversity, fairness may well require that the concept justice be relied upon to do less of the work of social construction than material egalitarians liberals have long wished.

Part of what it means to make room for people who have a non–Millian/Kantian view of nonpublic reasons is to make room for socially constructive motives of a sort that cannot be reduced into the public reasons on which conceptions of justice feed. Bringing in people with nonliberal views about the sources and authority of nonpublic reasons means being more modest about the range of material egalitarian concerns that liberalism can address through its universalizing, coercion-backed component (justice). High liberalism does not survive the politicization of justice.

LIBERALISM BEYOND JUSTICE

The revised account of justice that political liberalism implies does not deliver precisely the same goods as a conception of justice built for a society where everyone is taken to be an aspiring A-person. The acceptance of reasonable value pluralism requires that liberals now affirm a less materially ambitious and more socially nuanced conception of justice than that of the high liberals. If citizens are to see the attractions of this new conception of justice, they must think seriously about the very idea of a successful liberal society in the wide substantive sense I have described. This is a society that, while founded on a political conception of justice, is also openly, explicitly concerned with the ethical life prospects of all citizens—A-persons, B-persons, and C-persons alike. Citizens must consider how participating in a flourishing liberal society of that sort can be a great good for each of them.

A political conception of justice, suitably retooled, can get us some way toward realizing the social ideal implied by the motivational foundations of political liberalism. This is the ideal of a society that is *genuinely* and not merely formally inclusive. It is the ideal of a society that, beyond being just, is as much as possible *a home* to people affirming diverse but politically reasonable views of value and spirituality. For this reason, this view of society gives a central place to the challenges each citizen faces in negotiating the interface of the public and nonpublic ways of reasoning that beckon him.

A conception of justice that is constructed with an eye toward the importance of that those interface questions is better than one constructed narrowly from the inside. But whether a society sprung from the motivational foundations of political liberalism actually achieves its ideal, of course, will depend in the end on the attitudes of citizens that lie beyond their concern for social justice. It is true that the experiment that a liberal order represents cannot succeed for "a race of devils—if only they are intelligent," as Kant famously claimed it might. But that experiment also cannot succeed even for a race of people who are *just*—no matter how thoroughly they have perfected the dispositions and habits of mind that liberal justice requires.

The success of a liberal society depends on the skill with which individual citizens negotiate the interface of their public and nonpublic identities as they go about building their social worlds. Liberal justice, even on the revised account I am suggesting, can at most play an auxiliary role within a social world that is receptive to the practice of liberal citizenship.

CONCLUSION

ONE OF THE curiosities in the early development of political liberalism is that people attracted to this new view routinely express their attraction by emphasizing *how little changes* if the new view is adopted. This occurs because political liberalism is presented as a change simply in liberalism's *justificatory* strategy. Political liberals think they can move to a broader, more inclusive foundation but make few corresponding adjustments in the design of their existing house. The nature of the liberal virtues and of even the content of justice itself are said to be left largely untouched by the shift from a comprehensive to a political form of justification. Even the requirements of civic education, one place where political liberals claim theoretically to distinguish their view, are widely understood to be left largely unchanged in practice. Beyond the important end of achieving legitimacy, the significance of political liberalism is often seen as confined to metatheoretical matters, for example, its alleged effect of gradually increasing the autonomy of political philosophy from moral philosophy over time.[1]

I have questioned each of these ideas. Because neutrality of effect is impracticable, a just society may fail to be a receptive home even for the groups of citizens it was formally designed to include. A just political liberal society may not be a flourishing political liberal society. For this reason, liberal citizenship requires more than a mutual concern for political freedom or even the most robust commitment to democratic self-governance. The liberal virtues are the dispositions citizens need if they are to negotiate the interface of their public and nonpublic identity components in a way each finds personally satisfying over time. Citizenship is the art by which people exercise their political autonomy to that end.

This more ambitious view of good-citizen conduct suggests a more ambitious account of civic education. To develop the moral capacities people have as citizens, it is not enough that children come to satisfy the liberal proviso—learning narrow lessons about people's rights and the political ideas on which those rights are grounded. Because unintended spillovers are unavoidable within the classroom, lessons about public value must include their own internal corrective. While treating public values as foundational, political liberals are committed to classrooms that genuinely make room for the diverse personal views held by their citizenry. Their schools are vibrant places, full of the color, warmth, and variety found in the society they are to serve.

In early grades, for example, parents should be invited into the schools on a regular basis, to speak to the children about their personal views about work, family, and religion. In later grades, the children themselves should be given opportunities to express the nonpublic views they have come to affirm, whether or not those views happen to be deemed "religious" in an orthodox sense. Thus children in public schools might be allowed to take turns "solemnizing" important moments of the school calendar, by talking about the personal meaning of those events to them: convocation, gradua-tion, the start of classes each day, perhaps even football games and other extracurricular events.[2] After all, while taking no view themselves concern-ing what approach to personal value is best, political liberals recognize that citizens do develop views about personal value. Once the issue of political freedoms is broached, political liberals find themselves unavoidably impli-cated with the central difficulty each of their young members will face as citizens: that of assigning meaning to their political freedoms so that they might live well. They must be careful not to take the lead, even uninten-tionally, as their students set to work on that task.

Regarding the content of justice, political liberals cannot hope to adopt a wholly new motivational base for their view and yet have the content of justice remain exactly the same as before, nor should they wish it to do so. The material egalitarian ambitions of high liberalism are inappropriate within a social world where reasonable Romantics and many other citizens espousing "non-liberal" life views are now recognized as having equal po-litical standing. Politicization requires that space be reserved for the di-verse, socially constructive practices of the world-views liberalism now means to include.

Even in areas where justice sets out certain responsibilities to the needy, for example, political liberals should emphasize that this does not necessar-ily require that governmental agencies provide the services themselves. They may craft their policies in such areas with an eye toward the Roman Catholic doctrine of subsidiarity—the view that social problems are best addressed by institutions closest to those in need—or by other variants on what some call "compassionate conservatism." But, compared to high liberals, people who adopt the political liberal framework must assign less of the socially constructive work done in society to the concept "justice" itself. While insisting on the full political equality of each citizen, their model is one of an active, engaged populace, bonding together creatively, even idiosyncratically, in response to the challenges of social life. For politi-cal liberals, the appropriate ideal of state action is less Lyndon B. Johnson and more Alexis de Tocqueville.

So too, from the other side, the conception of justice that is most reason-able for a political liberal society must include a new element, one not needed by liberals before. This is an element directing social institutions to seek always to minimize their own unintended cultural effects. That element might lend strength to initiatives along the lines of the Religious Freedom Restoration Act in the United States, which sought to impose a high level of scrutiny on government actions that, while neutral in intent, have a substantial external impact on the practice of religion. Taking their cue from environmentalists, political liberals might enlist the best tools of modern social science to study the likely but unintended cultural impact of the various policy options before them, especially in sensitive areas. In the name of political liberalism, such policy makers should forever be searching for creative ways to minimize the unintended impact of what they do, howsoever their commitment to basic justice allows.

Political liberalism does indeed increase the autonomy of political philosophy from moral philosophy in the project of justifying state coercion. But giving a full account of liberalism involves giving more than an account of justified state coercion. Political liberalism—from the broader perspective I have described—depends upon the domains of ethical value and of political value working tightly in conjunction, with interface questions between them being absolutely central to the liberal project.

Political liberalism is not a fraud or trick. It is not ethical liberalism beneath technical camouflage. But neither is political liberalism a kind of tank, a vehicle within which enthusiasts of the high liberal orthodoxy can go on riding safely, undisturbed by, indeed oblivious to, the softer concerns of the citizenry about the interstices of theory and practice. Political liberalism, by its basic design, must be a more flexible, nimble, and *yielding* vehicle. It takes its direction from the social concerns of people deemed politically reasonable, whatever those concerns might be. It should be no surprise to find such a vehicle turning off from the familiar liberal track, and striking out in an unexpected new direction.

NOTES

1. Liberals also disagree about what this involves. Some emphasize the attitudinal component of that formulation—the bit, that is, about the state's authority eliciting citizens' "free assent," no matter why citizens have the positive attitudes they do. Others think the emphasis belongs more on whether citizens have their positive attitudes for "the right reasons"—typically, because those citizens deem the state's actions to be just. A helpful discussion is Simmons 1999.

2. Hume's discussion of the form of scarcity relevant to the circumstances of justice can be found in *A Treatise of Human Nature*, bk. 3, pt. 2, sec. 2, ed. L. A. Selby-Bigge (Oxford: Oxford University Press, 1978).

3. No liberal conception of justice could require (or allow) the state to act so as to instill nonpublic virtues such as the ones I just mentioned (religious piety, personal generosity, etc.). In posing this question, I am not questioning the moral appropriateness of that aspect of liberal justice. I am simply asking you to consider what you would think of a social world where such virtues were absent

CHAPTER ONE
POLITICAL LIBERALISM

1. There are many different explications of this principle. On Waldron's, "A social and political order is illegitimate unless it is rooted in the consent of all those who have to live under it; the consent or agreement of these people is a condition of its being morally permissible to enforce that order against them" (1987, 140). For Rawls, "Our exercise of political power is fully proper only when it is exercised in accordance with a constitution the essentials of which all citizens as free and equal may reasonably be expected to endorse in the light of principles and ideals acceptable to their common human reason. This is the principle of legitimacy" (1993 137; see also 1996, xlvi).

2. See Larmore 1987, 1991, and especially 1996a, 123.

3. Larmore 1996a, 128.

4. Ibid., 129, 130.

5. Ibid., 131. No doubt there is some interesting story to be told about exactly why so many liberal philosophers have come to accept these facts—whether through some perceived intellectual failure internal to the Enlightenment project, through the (to many) surprising resilience of organized religious faith in the face of modern science, or perhaps simply through the greater experience with diverse cultures and life-views that has been brought about by global migration and the new communication technologies. Whatever the cause, the philosophical implications of the acceptance of these "reasonable Romantics" seem profound to many liberals.

6. From the Romantic perspective, it is no surprise that the set of political norms recommended by those foundations—an account of justice that emphasizes individual rights—seems well designed to promote self-understandings on the part of citizens that systematically weaken these other, less-reflective modes of human living together.

7. Rawls 1971, 572.

8. Ibid., 575.

9. Rawls 1996, xlii.

10. The politicization of justice plainly marks a shift from the presentation in *Theory*. "Although the distinction between a political conception of justice and a comprehensive philosophical doctrine is not discussed in *Theory*, once the question is raised, it is clear, I think, that the text regards justice as fairness and utilitarianism as comprehensive, or partially comprehensive, doctrines" (Rawls 1993, xvi). And: "*A Theory of Justice* was a comprehensive doctrine of liberalism" (Rawls 1998, 13).

11. It is not that she must somehow discover that "being a Catholic" is just the same thing as "being a liberal." Rather, the hope is that she can draw on her Catholicity to reach a kind of all-things-considered affirmation of the liberal principles, principles that she affirms in a wide reflective equilibrium peculiar to her group (e.g., Griffin 1997; Daniels 1996, 148–50; Laden 1997).

12. The content of the wide reflective equilibria affirming justice as fairness will mirror the diversity of the society itself. But in every case, to satisfy the requirements of Rawlsian stability persons must affirm the principles not merely as a strategic matter but as a moral one: the Catholic, for example, because she regards those principles as providing the best way for her and others to develop their faith freely, and thus morally.

13. This third level of justification—"public justification by political society"—is meant to show that an internalized sort of justification of a single public conception of principles of justice is possible even in a society marked by reasonable pluralism. At this level, citizens embed the political conception within their various comprehensive doctrines in a way that recognizes that other citizens are engaged in a similar process.

14. The birth of this new view was painful. Some ardent followers of Rawls initially reacted with a great sense of loss to the idea of accepting this "fact of reasonable value pluralism," and to Rawls's concomitant suggestion that they abandon the philosophical project of defending a liberal view of life as true or morally best (see, e.g., Daniels 1996, 151).

15. See the critiques of Raz 1989; Kymlicka 1989; and Callan 1996. I have benefited greatly from an informal study group session on this topic with David Estlund, Erin Kelly, David Stevens, and Allon Hallal in Cambridge, Massachusetts, during February 1999. I also profited from several e-mail exchanges I had at about that time with Callan, Estlund, Amy Gutmann, and, especially, Tony Laden.

16. I owe this point to Tony Laden (personal e-mail correspondence, 1 February 1999).

17. Rawls 1993, 193–94. See also Larmore 1996a 126 n. 6.

18. As Tocqueville wrote, "Aristocracy made a chain of all the members of the community, from the peasant to the king; democracy breaks that chain and severs every link of it" (1996, 508; quoted in Wood 1992, 365).

19. Wood 1992, 24, 63.

20. Ibid., 232, 305.

21. Rawls 1993, 68.

22. Ibid., 200, emphasis and bracketed numbers mine.

23. I note that Rawls himself has recently used the label "the proviso" to refer to a technical refinement in his account of public reason (1997; and 1998, 14). I use the label "proviso" in a different way.

24. Macedo 1998, 70. If Catholics need not ordain women, this is not because they need not recognize women's political equality when they are on church property or making church decisions. Rather, it is because political equality does not include a right that religious organizations be organized as fair systems of cooperation among people with different comprehensive conceptions.

25. E.g., Rawls 1993, 220 n. 7.

26. Larmore 1996a, 151.

27. Galston 1991, 296; 1995b, 530.

28. Galston emphasizes that this current is not completely irresistible, like an undertow. Still, "an activity carried out in the spirit of vigilant resistance is not exactly the same as the formally similar activity conducted in neutral or supportive circumstances. . . . So liberal public principles are pervasive in the sense that they structure a set of influential tendencies in reference to which all activities and choices are compelled to be defined" (1991, 296; see also 1995b, 530).

29. Galston 1991, 255, 293.

30. Macedo 1995b, 477.

31. Macedo 2000, 71–72, 72.

32. Gutmann 1995, 573.

33. Callan 1988, 21.

34. Wood's account of the rights-based social revolution in early America, for example, is a rich mixture of formally required adjustments and wider, unrequired transformations in people's social outlooks (1969, 1992).

CHAPTER TWO
THE BOUNDARIES OF POLITICAL THEORY

1. If they read philosophy, A-people are great admirers of "the old Rawls." On first reading the Dewey Lectures, we can imagine, they wept.

2. This category might include Randall Terry and the members of the Lambs of God, an American group whose members originally opposed abortion not by joining campaigns for anti-abortion legislation but by taking direct actions themselves to forcibly block other citizens from having or performing abortions.

3. As a consequence, as Leslie Griffin says, the doctrines of such citizens may "mandate modifications in politics as power changes hands or as the 'truth' gains supporters" (1997; 306).

4. The boundaries between public and nonpublic are hotly contested even among political liberals. Especially in the case of relations between members of families, the appropriate reach of political justice is not fixed or given. For example, I say that the C-people may be politically reasonable even though they affirm patterns of gender hierarchy within their families (for example, such citizens may take

their guidance on family structures from the Bible or the Church). But precisely what forms of nonpublic hierarchism are permissible in that domain? If substantial revisions within the families of citizens of faith are required by justice, then the political liberal hope of accommodating such citizens is already fragile. (See Okin 1989; Nussbaum 2000) This makes the threat of additional unintended transformations all the more worrying from the political liberal perspective.

5. If they oppose the legality of abortion, for example, they may advance public reason arguments aimed at having abortion criminalized. If they oppose abortion only as a moral choice, they will support efforts within the bounds of the law to encourage pregnant women to "choose life" rather than setting out to prevent others from aborting no matter what the existing political settlement. If the attitude of the D-people to hot-button issues such as abortion is exemplified by the militant Lambs of God, the typical C-person perspective might be found in the attitude toward abortion espoused by Mario Cuomo in a famous speech given at the University of Notre Dame: abortion is morally abhorrent, but should be politically allowed.

6. This does not mean that citizens of faith reject the use of reason in spiritual matters. In the very first sentence of *Fides et Ratio*, Pope John Paul II writes: "Faith and reason are like two wings on which the human spirit rises to the contemplation of truth" (1998). A better characterization of the different attitudes of the C-people and A-people with respect to the use of faith and reason is that it is that A-people who are more likely to fly solo on just one of those two wings (the wing, that is, *without* the prayer).

7. This category may include people who consider divorce a moral disaster, while yet recognizing that all citizens, including people raised in the Church, have rights to seek divorce as a political matter.

8. If we think of the A-people as consistently affirming one of the two interpretations Larmore describes about the source of reasons—the one seeing reasons as properly a matter for persons to decide on their own through a process of individual reflection—the C-people (in this like the D-people) might be thought of as affirming the other interpretation, the one where reasons stem more from some tradition in which a person belongs or a system of authority that one accepts. Rawls says, "Many citizens of faith reject moral autonomy as part of their way of life" (1996, xlv). Note, though, that the increasingly capacious conceptions of autonomy affirmed by ethical liberals allow some of them to endorse the style of reasoning of the C-people. See Callan 1988, at 26 and esp. at 30–31.

9. Rawls says, "Most people's religious, philosophical, and moral doctrines are not seen by them as fully general or comprehensive" (1993, 160). And, "I suppose that we all have a comprehensive view extending well beyond the domain of the political, though it may be partial, and often fragmentary and incomplete" (100).

10. In Rawls-speak, this is the question of whether a society characterized by reasonable value pluralism can satisfy the requirements of second-stage justification, the stage where the conception of justice justified *pro tanto* is freely embedded by citizens in the various comprehensive views they actually affirm.

11. Of course, there is always the danger that some people will slide into the more individualistic extremes within this category.

12. Consider a society characterized not by value pluralism but by value monism: for example, a society in which every citizen is a devout Roman Catholic in an

orthodox sense. All citizens here affirm the principle of legitimacy but also oppose divorce as a moral abomination in all but the most extreme circumstances. Would laws against divorce be illegitimate in a society such as that? (Indeed, from the perspective of political liberalism, would there even be anything "unreasonable" about this value monism?)

13. On reading an early draft of this chapter, Richard Flathman suggested that my argument here looks like a contradiction. Political liberals assert that political coercion can legitimately be applied only on the basis of reasons those subject to that coercion can accept. Yet they advocate the use of force against some people (our D-people) for reasons they admit that those people flatly reject.

The appearance of contradiction here is deceptive, but instructive. Broadly, there are three different positions one might take regarding the legitimate use of state power. One says that force can legitimately be applied even if *no one* subject to it accepts the reasons on which that power is based. The second says force is legitimate only if *everyone*—every single person, no matter what his view—accepts the reasons given for it. The third draws a line between these two extremes and tries to justify it. The first approach is morally bankrupt; the second yields paralysis. Political liberals take a version of the third approach. They use the principle of legitimacy itself as a kind of litmus test to determine which citizens' concerns must be met and which citizens' concerns can be overridden even if unmet. This third approach, by the mere fact that it draws a line, inevitably leaves some people out. There is no contradiction in that—just good moral sense. (I am indebted to Flathman, and especially to David Estlund, who helped deepen my understanding of this point.)

14. I am speaking here of what is owed to adult citizens. The question of what is owed to children raises a different set of questions, on which see chapter 5.

15. Buchanan 1989.

16. No doubt, the requirement that people reflect on their nonpublic practices to see whether they conflict with the requirements of public reason is logically different from requiring them to reflect on those practices to see whether they are valuable at all—a point political liberals rightly stress (e.g., Larmore 1996a, 140). But humans are not all logicians and their minds are not like dresser drawers. Political liberals affirm the idea that arguments should be addressed *to others*—namely, those who are to be coerced. Thus they are *required* to respond to people as they can reasonably be expected to be, not to them just as logicians.

17. Rawls 1993, 196–97.

18. Ibid., 198.

19. Rawls's sociological prediction here, as I understand it, is *not* that religion as a whole will tend to decline within the liberal social world (as marked, for example, by an ever smaller percentage of the population identifying themselves as believers). That would be implausible, as suggested by, for example, the persistence of religious belief in the United States. Rather, Rawls's prediction is merely that some citizens of faith will face special difficulties in transmitting *their particular religious commitments* from one generation to the next within the liberal social world. A balanced and powerful account of how the growth of public institutions has shaped the nature of religious belief in the United States since World War II is Wuthnow 1988.

20. Larmore describes the reasonable Romantics' concern this way, quoting from Wordsworth's *Prelude*: " 'Thus I fared / Dragging all passions, notions, shapes of faith, / Like culprits to the bar; suspiciously / Calling the mind to establish in plain day / Her titles and her honours; now believing, / Now disbelieving; endlessly perplex'd / With impulse, motive, right and wrong, the ground / Of moral obligation, what the rule / And what the sanction; till, demanding *proof*, / And seeking it in everything, I lost / All feeling of conviction, and, in fine, / Sick, wearied out with contrarieties, / Yielded up moral questions in despair' " (1805 version, 10.889–901," in Larmore 1996a, 130–31. A stimulating philosophical exposition of this idea is Susan Wolf 1997.

21. Marx [1844] 1975, 164.

22. Sandel continues: "This is what it means to have become a procedural republic. Assumptions drawn from constitutional discourse increasingly set the terms of moral and political debate in general" (1998a 108).

23. Glendon 1991, 3.

24. Macedo 1990, 251–52; 2000, 30, 137.

25. As Macedo describes them, the encyclicals insisted on close ties between church and state, endorsed censorship, and rejected a variety of basic liberal rights to freedom of conscience and worship (2000, 59–63).

26. As Rawls says about such groups, "In their case the problem is to contain them so that they do not undermine the unity and justice of society" (1993 xvii).

27. Macedo 1990, 278.

28. Macedo 1995a, 477 n. 39.

29. Macedo presented that kind of defense in his earlier book, *Liberal Virtues*. However, after offering a detailed account of the forms of personality and culture that liberal pubic reasonableness encourages, we find Macedo describing life in his liberal society as disorienting to the simple and objectionable to the devout (1990, 260); people's allegiances turn out to be weak and attenuated (267); their personalities, superficial and self-absorbed. Macedo insists the price is worth paying: while the dynamic, fast-paced liberal society will prove inhospitable to some (presumably, reasonable citizens who are traditionalists in our C-person sense), such a society will be a happy environment for many people (at least, for people like our Millian A-people). Macedo eventually signals his own unease with this result: "Liberalism holds out the promise, or the threat, of making all the world like California" (1990, 278). For discussion, see my review in *Ethics* (1991).

30. Stanley Benn distinguishes autarchy—a self-governing condition—both from conditions that fall short of it, what he calls "being impelled," and from a moral ideal that transcends it, namely, autonomy. Benn captures the traditional liberal view, writing: "Autarchy is normal, both in the statistical sense and in the sense that human beings who fail to qualify are held to be in some measure defective as persons" (1976, 113). But the ideal for anyone who attaches importance to his ontological status as a person, according to Benn, is not that of mere choice making. After all, one may choose on the basis of norms and standards taken on unreflectively from others. The fully autonomous person's actions are guided by beliefs and principles not supplied to him ready made by others, but rather *of his own*, "because [they are] the outcome of a still continuing process of criticism and reevaluation"

(124). The autonomous person realizes an ideal which the autarchic person, from this perspective, is said to have merely in potentiality.

31. The quotations are from Rawls 1993, 39, 40.

32. I am not claiming that the coercive elements within liberal regimes are always necessarily *more* constrained than the coercive elements of those others. My point is more simple, and general: in liberal regimes the coercive element is constrained in a way that is different from (each of) the others.

33. We might say then that the fullest possible "justification" of liberalism as a doctrine involves more than settling questions of legitimate state action. I think these further dimensions of justification are available and relevant even if we assume, with the Rawlsians, that our arguments are directed toward people who do not select their state de novo but rather find themselves born into a state in which they can normally be expected to live out their lives. Here, as elsewhere, the boundaries of liberal theorizing are set by whatever questions such citizens might reasonably be expected to ask. Liberal theorists lack the status to tell citizens that the only questions about the liberal social world they may ask are ones directly relevant to the coercive use of state power. To conduct our academic discourse as though citizens were so constrained is in the crudest way to put the cart before the horse.

34. Rawls 1993, 38, also 154.

35. Ibid., 209–10; see also 174.

36. Ibid., 146.

37. Galston 1995b, 527.

38. Galston also says "the state may seek to mitigate the effect of its public current on the navigation of specific vessels whenever the costs of such corrective intervention are not excessive" (1995, 530). I return to this important idea below.

39. Macedo 1990, 62, emphasis in original.

40. Larmore 1996a, 141.

41. Can we develop an ethically coherent account of such a broad hybridized person—one that does not, on the one hand, fall into a kind of "moral multiple personality disorder" or, on the other, allow the public norms steadily to colonize the nonpublic ones? On the threat of moral multiple personality disorder, see Daniels 1996; on colonization, see Laden 1997.

42. Rawls 1993, 194 n. 28.

43. Ibid., 199–200, emphasis mine.

44. As we have seen, the main interface worry of the C-people *can* be expressed as a concern about stability and thus justice. But I assume that even if that concern were met, the C-people would share a residual worry like that of the B-people—a worry that is not justice-reducible.

45. At one place, Rawls notes that the moral powers liberal citizens develop in public life are "also exercised in many other parts of life for many purposes and surely this wider exercise is not just a political good." He then adds simply, "One hopes that the political and nonpolitical sides of life are mutually supporting" (1993, 204–5 n. 36).

46. For example, see Michael Walzer, *Just and Unjust Wars* (1992).

47. In the military case, this typically requires that soldiers take on greater risks to themselves. But this does not mean that the best soldiers *trade off* their tactical obligations: military victory is their uncompromising directive.

48. Again, people count as "freely committed" as soon as a conception of justice has been shown to pass the eudaimonistic threshold test of acceptability at the level of full individual justification. Thus, any residual social concerns citizens may have are matters about which political liberals can stubbornly "take no view."

49. Amy Gutmann, for example, says, "The skills of political reflection cannot be neatly differentiated from the skills of evaluating one's own way of life. That is one reason why civic education is so threatening to some ways of life. It opens the door wider to the possibility of children criticizing their parents' way of life. It also opens the door equally wide to their understanding the virtues of their parents' way of life" (1995, 578). But precisely in what way does an awareness of the equal political status of all citizens "open the door" for children to appreciate their parents' worldview? Can one open that door without altering children's understanding of that worldview in a fundamental way? Without a direct examination of those questions, how can we even begin to evaluate Gutmann's claim that this door opens equally widely in each direction?

Chapter Three
Liberal Nonpublic Reason

1. Sandel 1982, 33.

2. Ibid., 31–32.

3. Among the numerous direct responses to Sandel on this point are: Gutmann 1985; Buchanan 1989; Okin 1989; and Tomasi 1991.

4. Rawls 1997, 789–90 n. 64.

5. Ibid., 789.

6. Ibid.

7. Ibid., 791.

8. Immediately after stating this objection, Sandel withdraws it. In his response to Sandel, Rawls cites only the section in *Liberalism and the Limits of Justice* where Sandel lays out the empiricist objection (citing Sandel 1982, 30–34). Rawls does not include among his citations the passage (at 40–41) where Sandel withdraws it (see Rawls 1997, 790 n. 64).

9. My account of the general structure of nonpublic reasoning is available to theorists working from either an ethical or a political liberal perspective. But, as we shall soon see, it takes on a special significance after politicization.

10. When a right-holder exercises a claim by withholding it, this does nothing to impugn the priority—in the sense of overridingness when it is invoked—of the right. With apologies to Ronald Dworkin, we might imagine a friendly game of cards in which one player—for some nongame reason—decides quietly to discard the trump card she has been dealt (perhaps she is concerned for her fast-going-broke fellow players). Even unplayed, that card—like the withheld right-claim—retains special trumping status (Dworkin 1977). Similarly, even in a situation where a right-holder quietly withholds her claim, justice may still be the first virtue.

11. Rawls 1971, 567–77.

12. Sandel 1982, 34–35.

13. Sandel 1982, 32–33.

14. The aim of liberal theory is to make manifest the full set of grounds for affirming liberalism as the solution to the problem of organizing social life. Because of the liberal separation of public and nonpublic, this requires more than demonstrating why some liberal conception of state coercion is justified.

15. In terms of the ways the exercise of rights relates to the expression of social virtues (and vices), there is a rich spectrum of communicative possibilities here. Regarding claim-rights, for example, there are a great variety of manners in which a right-claim can be asserted or withheld. Proceeding along a kind of continuum, a claim could be asserted angrily, or quietly but firmly, or even apologetically; extending out along the other direction, that same claim could be withheld compassionately, or strategically, even perhaps self-righteously. These attitudes may affect both the moral quality of the right-holder's decision, and the nature of the resulting relationship between duty-ower and right-holder. Matters become complicated—and the expressive possibilities of rights increase—when we recognize that different spectrums of possibilities will be emitted by different kinds of rights in different situations. As a rough approximation, the character of the spectrum of social possibilities produced by the exercise of a person's political autonomy will vary as a function of (at least) both (1) the content of the right (i.e. the nature of whatever it is that the right is a right to) and (2) the norms internal to the grouping(s) in which the right is to be exercised. Individual rights are fundamentally relational concepts, and the various effects of their exercise have extended relational implications: There is art in the exercise of political autonomy.

16. Is it possible to do substantive moral philosophy without political philosophy? I suppose that we can imagine a freestanding system of ethics that by itself sets out more or less fully formed norms of personal excellence in complete abstraction from the political institutions that structure people's world. By contrast, the system of norms I call compass concepts is not freestanding but serves as a *supplement* to people's understanding of themselves as public agents. Compass concepts require some material to work on, so to speak. In the social world produced and sustained by liberalism, public reason provides that material.

17. MacIntyre 1984, 16.

18. Kymlicka takes the unit by which such a narrative-sharing group is identified to be a "societal culture," a group demarked by a shared language, history, and culture (Kymlicka 1989 165; see also 1995, chap. 5). He argues that a concern for autonomy generates a justice-based response to some central problems of cultural pluralism. I suggest a different path of accommodation in Tomasi 1995.

19. Quotation from the *Los Angeles Times*, 19 December 1996. Because of the intense media scrutiny Feuerstein's actions received, a crucial element of tzedakah—anonymity of the giver—is muddied in his case. Other hallmarks of tzedakah were clearly present. For example, tzedakah subscribes to the doctrine of "teaching a man to fish" rather than merely giving support to his immediate needs. Further, true tzedakah must not include any proselytizing element—a condition that a Jew giving Christmas bonuses clearly met. I am indebted to Sara Rosenbaum for research on Feuerstein and the concept of tzedakah.

20. See the fascinating discussion in "Blacks Carry Load of Care for Their Elderly," *New York Times*, 9 March 1998, sec. 1, p. 1.

21. Classicists have squared the deliberation/spontaneity circle in the case of Aristotelian virtue by emphasizing the way agents can adopt policies in advance and thus satisfy the deliberation requirement before the event, as it were. John Cooper says, "Though the virtuous person does not, in general, arrive at his moral policies by any process of deliberation, he must, on demand, be able to defend his acceptance of them, however he may in fact have become committed to them" (1975, 9, 52ff.).

In liberal society, people who have acted virtuously without deliberation must be able, if pressed, to demonstrate their awareness of what the normative situation looked like from the public perspective (and not just from whatever system of non-public norms he may exclusively have had in mind as he acted). If he cannot bring that public perspective forth (or denies it when attributed to him by others), he has fallen afoul of the liberal proviso.

22. Indeed, by Vedic tradition, the coding of each caste's substance essentially includes the coding for the particular forms of intercaste practice appropriate to those characterized by it (see, e.g., Nath 1987). I profited from discussions with Sherally Munshi about caste and the Vedic tradition of virtue.

23. Political liberals cannot, as political liberals, simply take no view on their citizens' residual concerns about spillovers because they cannot know in advance whether taking *that view* saddles political liberalism with greater and more damaging unintended nonpublic effects than might some wider—as yet unconsidered—view of the domain of liberal theory.

CHAPTER FOUR
CITIZENSHIP: JUSTICE OR WELL-BEING?

1. Citizenship is a type of role morality, the criteria of which vary on a number of dimensions. Most obviously, as I've said, those criteria vary from regime type to regime type. But those criteria also vary from particular regime to particular regime, for example, requiring different kinds of behaviors in different kinds of theocracies. They vary also from social role to social role within each particular regime: within theocracies, again, different socially constructive norms apply to priests than to the laity.

2. Conover, Crowe, and Searing 1991, 819–21. See also Oldfield 1990, 178; and King and Waldron 1988.

3. Conover, Crowe, and Searing 1991, 814–15.

4. See, e.g., Brewer 1902; Taft 1906; Root 1907; Bryce 1909; McCall 1915; and Frankfurter 1930.

5. McCall 1915, 8.

6. E.g., Wright and Wright 1938.

7. Cleveland 1908, 28–29.

8. Rawls 1993 194–95; see also, e.g., 84. Further, as Rawls says elsewhere, "The initial focus, then of a political conception of justice is the framework of basic institutions and the principles, standards, and precepts that apply to it, *as well as how these norms are to be expressed in the character and attitudes of the members of the society who realize its ideals*" (1993, 11–12, emphasis mine). Like the mainstream citizens in Conover's study, Rawls urges a sharp distinction between the *political* virtues,

which he sees as the virtues of the liberal citizen, and the wider range of *nonpublic* virtues. Nonpublic virtues include "the virtues that characterize ways of life belonging to comprehensive religious and philosophical doctrines, as well as from the virtues falling under various associational ideals (the ideals of churches and universities, occupations and vocations, clubs and teams) and those appropriate to roles in family life and to the relations between individuals."

9. Galston 1995a 46–48. See also Galston 1991, chap. 10–12.

10. Macedo 1990, 265–66, bracketed numbers mine. See also 1998.

11. "Even if such a society is just," critics complain, "what's the point of such a society? What, in human terms, is a liberal social union *for*?"

12. I am thinking of Pocock 1992; Walzer 1989; and esp. Oldfield 1990.

13. Walzer 1989.

14. Pocock 1992.

15. Walzer 1989.

16. *Politics*, in Aristotle 1984, 1280a32.

17. This reading of Aristotle, and especially of the link between eudaimonia and political activity, seems to me central to the republican longings of Sandel (see esp. 1996, 26, 317–20, 349–51).

18. *Nichomachean Ethics*, in Aristotle 1984, 1177a15–25.

19. E.g., Ibid., 1169b10. None of the ancient Greek city-states (with the possible exception of Sparta) actually embodied this notion of citizenship. It seems more an ideal of ancient philosophers than an account of ancient society (Long 1998).

20. At the minimum, this linkage between citizen activities and human fulfillment can obtain only in a state that is well arranged. In a bad state, as a further consequence of this view, the virtues of the good human being and those of the good citizen will diverge (an implication that motivates Aristotle's famous discussion in *Politics* III).

21. For example, there is an important divergence between Machiavelli's civic republicanism and the civic humanism of Aristotle and Rousseau. Rousseau, like Aristotle, saw politics as the realm of true freedom and human self-actualization: in giving up natural liberty, as Rousseau describes it, the citizen gains not only civil liberty but moral liberty as well, liberty as an internal condition associated with each person's mastery of himself. As citizens gain mutual self-mastery of that sort, each finds that his "faculties are exercised and developed, his ideas are broadened, his feelings are ennobled, his entire soul elevated" (*Social Contract* I.8). For Machiavelli, the link between politics and human fulfillment is less tight. Machiavelli's notion of *virtu* is by no means identical to the Aristotelian notion of virtue—and the roles those concepts play in their respective theories is likewise distinct. In particular, since *virtu* is not offered as a true expression of each citizen's authentic self, the link between (1) the dispositions and attitudes necessary for good citizenship and (2) the dispositions and attitudes attendant to human flourishing has become more tenuous on the civic republican than on the civic humanist tradition. On the civic republican view it is now less clear whether (or to what degree) the life of the successful *citizen* and the life of the successful *human* might diverge (e.g., Taylor 1985, 335). I am indebted to George Kateb and Clifford Orwin for conversation on these issues.

22. Pocock 1992, Okin 1992.

23. It is because of this linkage (between the norms of interpersonal life and the criteria of human eudaimonia) that the activities of citizenship in their classical form are described not just as a means to being free but rather as the way of being free itself. For the ancients, the activities of citizenship are said to provide freedom in its proper definition (a view described critically by Berlin [1969], but with evident approval by Pocock [1992]). Questions about the norms governing politics, on this view, are operationally secondary to questions about the conditions of human fulfillment. Justice is the virtue of a state well functioning in regard to these eudaimonistic requirements.

24. Liberals, like civic humanists, rely on a separation of public and nonpublic realms. But, in a reversal, liberals have long sought to strip substantive conceptions about excellence of character from their arguments for coercive public principles.

25. For Marshall, liberal citizenship primarily involves the political attempt to recognize people as full and equal members of society. From this perspective, it seemed natural to Marshall to rely upon narrowly derivationist terms when describing the historical patterns by which citizenship status was extended within liberal societies. According to Marshall, the status of "citizen" in England was extended from a recognition of civil rights in the eighteenth century to a recognition of political rights in the nineteenth and, finally, to a recognition of social rights in the twentieth. Marshall sees each extension of the purview of liberal justice as identical with an extension of the purview of citizenship. This justice-based holding of status, for Marshall, is liberal citizenship. See Marshall [1949] 1965. A good discussion is Kymlicka and Norman 1994.

26. Larmore 1996a, 128. William Galston makes a similar point about Mill's conception of liberal citizenship: "[Mill] retained a place for the Aristotelian conception of virtue as an intrinsic good but argued that the practice of virtue, so understood, would also be supportive of a liberal polity. In a liberal order, the same virtues are both ends and means: the good human being and the good citizen are identical" (1995a, 40).

27. Enthusiasts of political liberalism, of course, applaud this. Joshua Cohen says of Rawls's *Political Liberalism*: "In due course it will likely change the shape of political philosophy, sharpening political philosophy's autonomy by increasing its distance from moral philosophy, and perhaps will have similarly salutary effects on political argument itself" (1994, 1511). However, one may endorse a political conception of justice and yet, *for that very reason*, insist that something quite like the opposite ought to happen. It is only that part of political liberalism which is picked up by the question of justified coercion whose distance must be increased from the more human, eudaimonistic questions of moral philosophy.

28. The chutzpah some contemporary republicans show in extolling the necessity of "mutilating" modern citizens to fit them for a return to the ancient ideal does not inspire much confidence in their view (the most egregious of these is Oldfield).

29. A diverse liberal society, on that view, would truly succeed as such only when the people living there have achieved, along with their concern public norms, a degree of wisdom about the eudaimonistic value of those norms.

30. Eudaimonia," as I shall be using that term, should not be understood as carrying the essentialist baggage of the Aristotelian worldview. I use the term

broadly to encompass whatever projects and commitments politically reasonable people variously view as most central to their lives. Indeed, I would welcome a more etymological reading of "eu-daimonia": something like, "good soul." Also, when I use terms such as "human well-being" or "ethical satisfaction," I do not mean to be limiting myself to exclusively secular interpretations of human goods and ethical satisfactions, though secular readings are not excluded (religions, for example, are sometimes said to be in tension with, or even in opposition to, certain merely "human goods," including possibly even human ethical goods). Here again, I use such terms nontechnically, as broad markers of whatever attitudes, beliefs, and concerns most centrally animate and provide deepest meaning to people's lives.

31. Conover, Crowe, and Searing 1991 822, emphasis in original.

32. Ibid., 822, 810, 816.

33. Ibid., 1991, 822.

34. The data set collected by the Conover team is small and, arguably, idiosyncratic. Still, these kernels of a neglected form of citizen self-understanding are suggestive: grist for the philosopher's mill.

35. McCall 1915, 8.

36. Jacks 1924, 1–2.

37. Hibben 1927, 5, emphasis mine.

38. Ibid., 5, 10.

39. Ibid., 10, 12–13.

40. Ibid., 19 emphasis mine.

41. There are many other traces as well. For example, the widely read *American Citizen's Handbook* of 1946 included not just exhortations to develop political and judicial dispositions and patterns of self-understanding, but also to personal moral development as part of the duties of citizenship. For example, the *Handbook* included a chapter on moral self-improvement by Benjamin Franklin (Morgan 1946). Even Grover Cleveland in places suggests that citizens, as citizens, must care about more than the interests they have that their rights protect: "Nothing is more unfriendly to the motives that underlie our national edifice than the selfishness and cupidity that look upon freedom and law and order only as so many agencies in aid of their designs" (1908, 21).

42. This approach is akin to the contemporary French understanding of *civisme*, the moral qualities that are considered necessary to the character of the good citizen. *Civisme*, while fully affirming the juridical elements associated with the standard derivative ideal, ultimately gives more importance to social morality than to political morality. As Jean Leca explains this ideal: "Qualities of conformity are considered more central to social morality than the qualities of participation." In contrast to the derivative approach, Leca describes *civisme* as involving a "relative contempt for political virtues." See the discussion in Leca 1992.

43. The field owner who sells her land may by that very act affirm her membership in some other group that is different with respect to its understanding of the meaning of property rights in farmland—for example, the group whose members say it is time to make a change and embrace the suburban realities of twenty-first-century Vermont. But this change requires a shift in the person's own self-understanding and, from that, a shift in the norms of good citizen conduct, the particular ideal of liberal virtues she accepts as binding on her.

CHAPTER FIVE
THE FORMATIVE PROJECT

1. Many citizens' conceptions of the good include a proselytizing element (whether religious or secular), which can put a point on such challenges. I say more about the appropriate response to such citizens in chapter 6.

2. Before school-entering age, children are not old enough to be considered voluntary agents of informed consent. Children's values are never really "freely" developed, but are strongly influenced by one authority or another. After school-entering age, motivational norms are developed simultaneously by parents and school authorities (and, certainly, by peers and other cultural influences). This last point generates important questions about what forms of direct motivational influence may legitimately be exerted by public school programs within liberal societies (e.g., Brighouse 1998). But, like Rawls, I focus my attention on the formation of liberal citizenship's earliest motivational base.

3. Rawls 1971, 490–91.

4. Ibid.

5. Ibid., 490–91.

6. Ibid., 462 n. 8, emphasis mine. When people growing up in a liberal society reach that stage, Rawls tells us, "the complete moral development has now taken place" (474).

7. After linking the morality of principle to what he calls "full autonomy," Rawls writes: "It is the full autonomy of active citizens which expresses the political ideal to be realized in the social world" (1993, 306).

8. Crittenden 1992, 78.

9. Crittenden remarks: "The theory of compound individuality shows that the communitarian reminiscences about the ancients and their way of life are not so much about a lost way of life as about a lost psychological state" (1992, 68).

10. The significance of these "personal uses of pluralism" has been emphasized by my colleague Nancy Rosenblum. The standard hope among liberal theorists for a "congruency" between the values of people's public and nonpublic lives cannot withstand a detailed examination of the forms of membership characteristic of real liberal societies. See Rosenblum's sparkling discussion in *Membership and Morals* (1998).

11. From this perspective, the so-called ethics of care need not appear as a *competitor* to liberalism. From the wider perspective we are considering, the ethic of care becomes a crucial *but non-justice-based* component of a complete liberal theory. For a liberal society fully to realize its ambitions—and thus to flourish as a social union of that type—citizens must engage in acts of social construction both from the norms of public reason common to all *and* from the various traditions of care relevant to each. I develop this point in chapter 6.

12. Rawls 1993, 199.

13. Callan 1996, 10–14. These burdens are the sources of reasonable disagreement—including the ways people's background and experience influence the particular views they hold. To understand these burdens and to accept their consequences for the use of public reason, people must understand these burdens as

applying to the values and convictions that shape the society's background culture, including each person's understanding of the sources of his own view.

14. Callan 1996, 21. The only way to maintain a distinction between the two would be for political liberals to recommend what Callan says would be an integrity-destroying form of compartmentalization (1996, 12–13). One political liberal who grasps this horn is Norman Daniels (1996, 168–74).

15. Callan 1996, 22.

16. I think Callan overstates his case when he calls this a "conceptual" convergence. There is at least a logical difference between recognizing the consequences of the burdens of judgment when applied to one's own doctrine *for political purposes* and recognizing those consequences as part of one's own nonpublic moral evaluation of one's own view. Certainly the distinction may not be hermeneutic: as a practical matter, it may even be *porous*. This practical convergence, it seems to me, generates the most interesting theoretical challenge.

17. Harvey Cox writes, "To teach nothing about religion is, in effect, to teach something wrong about it: that it is unimportant and unworthy of serious study." Cox continues, "This form of exclusion discriminates against those Americans for whom religion has been particularly integral—for example, African-Americans, whose struggle against slavery and segregation was inspired, to a great extent, by their religion, and Catholic immigrants, whose faith helped them survive prejudice." He concludes, "What excluding religion from the classroom produces is simply bad education" (1998, A23).

18. Nord 1995, 202, 203; see also Cox 1998. Nord also finds a place for the idea of narrative teaching as part of this education. Along with equipping us to think critically about the past and the communities of which are part, he says, "a good liberal education should map out the cultural space in which we find ourselves. It should help us fill in our identities, locating us in the stories, the communities of memory, into which we are born. It should root us in the past" (233).

19. As Peter Berkowitz rightly emphasizes, Aristotle saw civic education as concerning "education in virtues that serve as a counterpoise to the characteristic bad habits and reckless tendencies that regimes tend to foster in their citizens" (1999, 11). Berkowitz says: "Education relative to the regime, which Aristotle argued is the preserver of regimes, must in significant measure cut against the dominant tendency of the regime, which is to form citizens with immoderate enthusiasm for it guiding principle. For the guiding principle ceases to become an effective guide if it is allowed to become the regime's sole guide" (176–77).

20. For detail, see *Mozert v. Hawkins County*, 827 F.2nd 1058 (6th Cir. 1987); and especially Bates 1993.

21. See also the discussions in Gutmann and Thompson 1996, 63–69; Callan 1997, 157–61; and Levinson 1999.

22. Gutmann 1995, 573.

23. As Gutmann describes the *Mozert* complainants, "Their religious convictions . . . command them not to expose their children to knowledge about other ways of life unless the exposure is accompanied by a statement that their way of life is true and all the others are false and inferior" (1995, 571).

24. *Mozert* at III.A.[1]; and Bates 1993.

25. For example, an expert witness for the *Mozert* parents in a lower court testified that he found "markedly little reference to religion, particularly Christianity, and also remarkably little to Judaism" in the Holt series (*Mozert* III.A.[1]).

26. The plaintiffs were a diverse group. They had many internal disagreements not only on religious matters but on legal ones, and certainly not all of the demands voiced on their behalf were politically reasonable. Still, even a concurring judge, Judge Boggs, expressed a view of the parents such as the one I have in mind. Boggs writes: "A reasonable reading of the plaintiffs' testimony shows they object to the overall effect of the Holt series, not simply to any exposure to any idea opposing theirs. . . . By focusing narrowly on references that make plaintiffs appear so extreme that they could never be accommodated, the court simply leaves resolution of the underlying issues here to another case, when we have plaintiffs with a more sophisticated understanding of our own and Supreme Court precedent, and a more careful and articulate presentation of their own beliefs." Boggs reported his own profound sense of sadness about this case, quoting hopefully from the poet Edwin Markham: "He drew a circle that shut me out— / Heretic, Rebel, a thing to flout. / But Love and I had the wit to win: / We drew a circle that took him in!" (*Mozert* at Boggs I, II). I believe that political liberals must show that same wit to win— though, as we shall see, many of them may be discomfited by doing so.

27. *Mozert* at [1]I.B.

28. The grounds for this prohibition are especially clear if that reintegrative lesson was to be delivered as the truth to a classroom of children with diverse beliefs. But it would also forbid this sort of conclusory truth-teaching even in private riders to be written only on worksheets by parental request. Calling children's attention to premises from their own lives (from which children might draw their own conclusions about truth) is a different matter entirely. The substantive approach would allow, indeed encourage, that approach both as a general lesson and as part of specific parental request—insofar as the pedagogical and curricular constraints of real public classrooms would allow (and within the constraint of respect for the architecture of public reason).

29. This is much like the way that affirming the Bible as the true word of God must be different in a world where the broad facts of evolutionary theory are scientifically accepted from the way it is affirmed than in a world where those facts are not.

30. Assuming, that is, that the child's parents are politically reasonable and have played a significant role in the story of the child's life up to now.

31. The distinction between curriculum (roughly, course content) and pedagogy (lesson plans and classroom design) opens a whole range of possibilities here. Joseph Coleman, for example, suggests that liberals might employ progressive pedagogies to teach public values, thus allowing them to bypass the familiar debates over curricular content (1998).

32. This is why I say that political liberals must be aggressive *tax flatteners*, even though it is sociologically impracticable for them to be strict flat taxers. (And this remains true even in the case of those citizens who are not owed those flattened taxes as a matter of formal "right.")

33. This political liberal drive toward ethical inclusion and so toward school division would be subject to other constraints as well. Most obviously, political

liberals cannot advocate vouchers or choice under models that result in injustices to other students on other dimensions. For example, they must reject models that leave some classes of student at unjustly poor schools or models that produce so much local homogeneity that in practice they render the teaching of mutual respect a sham.

34. A brilliant argument to this effect is Burleigh Wilkins's "A Third Principle of Justice." I think Wilkins is wrong to think liberals can do nothing to counteract unintended effects from the ethical background culture. I also have reservations about the precise formulation of the third principle Wilkins defends. Still, Wilkins offers by far the most sophisticated defense of a third principle along these lines that I have seen.

35. On the relation between no-fault divorce laws and divorce rates in the United States, as well as the broader social consequences of divorce, see Galston 1996.

36. Even some campaigns undertaken by nonpublic groupings that receive indirect public support—such as some types of proselytizing efforts by religious groups that receive tax exemptions—might receive a heightened degree of scrutiny in light of this third principle. An extreme example of this is Singapore, where religious groups are forbidden from "proselytizing" and limited to merely "bearing witness" to others about their own religious beliefs. The reconfiguring of political liberal justice that I am suggesting would certainly find such a law politically unreasonable (a violation of basic rights). But the reconfiguring I am suggesting would generate pressure in the general direction of increased restraint. I thank John Kekes for suggesting this example to me.

37. That is, in Rawls-speak again, could a candidate conception that included some version of the tax-flattening principle, even if justifiable pro tanto, successfully be embedded by citizens and so become part of the focus of an overlapping consensus?

38. The idea of society can do this without assuming that all such people actually endorse moral pluralism as a metaphysical view—as though political liberalism was suited only to persons, A-persons and C-persons alike, who were closet devotees of Isaiah Berlin's moral doctrine. It is just such controversial assumptions that political liberalism seeks to avoid (I thank Eamonn Callan for calling my attention to the importance of this point).

39. As this book was going to press, I heard Steven Macedo use this expression in a lecture at Harvard sponsored by the Program in Ethics and the Professions, directed by Dennis Thompson. Like me, Macedo advocates a second stage of justification for the policy stage, a stage that he thinks yields a tough-minded, "judgmental liberalism." Like some others in the audience, I worried that Macedo's liberalism is too tough-minded: in my terms, the perfectionist tone of Macedo's advice at the policy stage seems discordant with his political way of justifying his constitutional base. Still, I learned a great deal from the talk and from my exchanges afterward with Arthur Applbaum, Pratap Mehta, Frank Michelman, and, especially, Macedo.

40. Again, the "protection" to be sought for citizens is not protection from the demands of justice, but from the unintended effects attendant to the satisfaction of that demand.

CHAPTER SIX
HIGH LIBERALISM

1. Sandel defines a public philosophy as "the political theory implicit in our practice, the assumptions about citizenship and freedom that inform our public life" (1996, 4).

2. Ibid., 60.

3. On this reading, inequalities are "to everyone's advantage" when they are arranged in a way that is economically efficient. Positions are considered "open to all" when there are no legal barriers preventing people of skill and ability from winning them.

4. Rawls 1971, 65–72.

5. People who are equally endowed and equally motivated ought to have equal chances in life, regardless of the social class of their origin.

6. Rawls 1971, 75. As Joshua Cohen says of democratic equality, "The idea is to carry through on the idea of making outcomes depend on the decisions people make about what to do with their lives, rather than the resources or talents we happen to be born with" (1998, 8).

7. Of course, there are various views of society as *private*—including forms of modus vivendi liberalism—which reject this assumption, but I am still working here within the public schema that Rawls assumes.

8. Rawls 1971, 75.

9. One often hears this line of argument from people who work closely in the Rawlsian framework. By far the most sophisticated version of this argument that I have heard was in a working paper presented by Samuel Freeman at the University Center for Human Values, Princeton University (1994a). I served as respondent to Freeman, with Amy Gutmann, George Kateb, Alan Ryan, Peter Euben, Frances Kamm and Julia Driver participating. My argument here develops the remarks I made that day in response to Freeman.

10. Freeman writes: "By 'feudalism' I mean, not an economic scheme that relies on the institution of serfdom, but a particular way of conceiving of political authority. Under feudalism the elements of political authority are powers that are held by private individuals as their private property. Individuals gradually acquire the power to make, apply, and enforce rules by private contracts . . .; oaths of fealty are sworn in exchange for compensating benefits. Contracting for individual services and the making of individual alliances is the way people protect themselves from one another. There is not a notion of a uniform public law impartially applied to all individuals" (1994a, 23).

11. David Johnston has presented a masterful critique of Nozick's libertarianism—by far the best in the literature (Johnston 1994). I sketch a line of response like the one in the text here in my review of Johnston (Tomasi 1996).

12. Rawls rejects libertarianism as unreasonable: "It lacks the criterion of reciprocity and allows excessive social economic inequalities as judged by that criterion" (1996, lviii). But, from the wider theoretical perspective I am suggesting, libertarianism might well include a criterion of "reciprocity"—it simply refuses to translate its concern for that criterion into coercive terms. Such a view might thus

normatively disallow the inequalities that concern Rawls, even if it does not think it can legitimately guarantee state-backed corrections with respect to them.

13. See Rawls 1996, lvii–lx.

14. The High Middle Ages are usually dated from 1073 because that year marks the start of the papacy of Pope Gregory VII, the famous Clunaic monk Hildegrand. It was Gregory who brought together and systematized the canon law, a project that would provide the legal backbone for the res publica christiana (Berman 1983, 202–18).

15. Bouckaert 1998; Berman 1983.

16. Rawls 1993, 3.

17. Ibid., 15, emphasis mine; see also 303.

18. Ibid. 35, 201–2.

19. Rawls aims to show how an overlapping consensus is possible even in conditions of reasonable value pluralism. For that to be plausible, the full individual justification requirement of political liberalism must be interpreted as presenting a lower eudaimonistic hurdle than did the comprehensive liberal version of the congruency requirement (see chapter 2). Indeed, in *Theory*, Rawls sometimes suggests that a commitment to justice itself delivers the lion's share of a person's good: "It follows that the collective activity of justice is the preeminent form of human flourishing" (1971, 529).

20. Rawls asks: "How is it possible for there to exist over time a just and stable society of free and equal citizens, who remain profoundly divided by reasonable religious, philosophical, and moral doctrines?" (1993, 4). Rawls calls this "the problem of political liberalism" (xxv). But this is only one part of the problem of political liberalism, the part concerning *justice*.

21. When *Political Liberalism* first appeared, there was much discussion about whether the move to political liberalism requires a weakening of the strong economic egalitarianism implied by justice as fairness and by the difference principle in particular. Rawls strenuously denies any such change: "Some think the difference principle is abandoned entirely, others that I no more affirm justice as fairness than any other political conception of justice. And they do so despite the fact that early on [in *Political Liberalism*] I say that justice as fairness is held intact (modulo the account of stability) and affirmed as much as before in TJ. . . . If I had dropped something as central as the difference principle, I like to think I would have said so (1995b, 2, n.1, quoted in Daniels 1996, 153–54; see also Rawls 1993, 6–7, and the superb account in Estlund 1996). So Rawls clearly does not intend the adoption of political liberalism to have the effects on High Liberalism I describe.

22. I am not claiming that actions undertaken under the rubric of justice lose all their social loveliness. There is plainly something lovely about citizens giving one another justice, which is a great expression of mutual concern. But to assume that a system guaranteeing ever-greater deliveries by justice is always *more* lovely is no more plausible than the assumption that a system guaranteeing deliveries by justice is always *less* lovely. There is an ethical advantage and an ethical price for bringing interpersonal concerns under the rubric of social justice. In assembling the device of representation from which justice is to be constructed, to neglect either ethical value would be perilous.

23. Though even people committed to an ethical ideal of autonomy as a basis for liberal politics may object to this (see Tibor Machan 1998).

24. Commentators have long pointed to the danger to the fabric of traditional membership groupings posed by an expansive system of state-backed guarantees. As Tocqueville wrote: "The more [the state] stands in the place of associations, the more will individuals, losing the notion of combining together, require its assistance: these are causes and effects that unceasingly create each other" (515).

25. Rawls 1971, 148. According to Rawls, there may be aspects of goodwill that are not relevant to securing primary goods, but these concern not the sense of justice but rather a general "love of mankind"—the norms of which are always supererogatory (192).

26. Rawls expresses the basic idea underlying his reductive approach in *Theory* in a rare passage of eloquence: "Benevolence is at sea so long as its many loves are in opposition in the person of its many objects" (1971, 190). Rawls's reductionism explains why nothing would be gained for him by attributing benevolence to parties in the OP: "a love of mankind that wishes to preserve the distinction of persons . . . will use the two principles to determine its aims when the many goods it cherishes are in opposition . . . Love is guided by what individuals themselves would consent to in a fair initial situation which gives them equal representation as moral persons" (191). When motives of goodwill are in *opposition*, such a reduction has power, and no doubt a principle like that securing equal basic liberties would follow quite naturally from a device of representation in which that reduction is expressed.

27. Rawls 1971, 179.

28. Ibid. 440.

29. Again, and emphatically, I am not suggesting that government action in the name of social justice has no role in crises such as befell the Massachusetts mill workers or in difficulties such as those facing many African American families as they seek to care for their sick and elderly. My point is merely that there is ethical pressure not only in the direction ever-expanding the role of justice with respect to such problems but also ethical pressures pushing back against that expansion. This is a point to which anyone working within the political liberal framework must be especially sensitive.

30. Rawls 1993, 327.

31. Ibid., 361.

32. Ibid., 356.

33. Of course, Rawls is sensitive to kinds of costs that can be tallied within his own narrowly *justice-based* ideal. Rawls often tallies those sorts of cost, for example, when explaining why the fair value guarantee is not extended to all the other basic liberties in the first principle as well (1993, 329).

34. Nor, obviously, do I offer this as a full defense of some new version of libertarianism—a political libertarianism, for example. The question of whether politicization drives us toward libertarian conceptions of justice is an interesting, but complex, one. I do not take up that question here.

35. Rawls 1993, 317.

Conclusion

1. A view defended by Joshua Cohen 1994.

2. As this book went to press, the Supreme Court handed down its decision in *Santa Fe Independent School District v. Doe*, in which the Court held that a school policy allowing student-led, student-initiated prayer at football games violates the Establishment Clause. From the perspective of political liberalism, this is a worrying decision. I apply the argument presented here to the *Santa Fe* case in my article "Civic Education and Ethical Subservience: From *Mozert* to *Santa Fe* and Beyond."

BIBLIOGRAPHY

Abbott, S.J., Walter M., ed. 1966. *The Documents of Vatican II.* New York: Corpus Books.

Ackerman, B. 1980. *Social Justice in the Liberal State.* New Haven: Yale University Press.

Allen, Anita L., and Milton C. Regan, Jr., eds. 1998. *Debating Democracy's Discontent: Essays on American Politics, Law, and Public Philosophy.* New York: Oxford University Press.

Aristotle, 1984. *Politics.* Translated by Benjamin Jowett. In *The Complete Works of Aristotle,* vol. 2, ed. Jonathan Barnes. Princeton: Princeton University Press.

Audi, Robert. 1989. "The Separation of Church and State and the Obligation of Citizenship." *Philosophy and Public Affairs* 18, no. 3 (Summer): 259–96.

Avineri, Shlomo, and Avner De Shalit, eds. 1992. *Communitarianism and Individualism.* Oxford: Oxford University Press.

Bader, V. 1995. "Citizenship and Exclusion: Radical Democracy, Community, and Justice; or, What Is Wrong with Communitarianism?" *Political Theory* 23:211–46.

Bates, Stephen. 1993. *Battleground: One Mother's Crusade, the Religious Right, and the Struggle for Control of Our Classrooms.* New York: Poseidon Press.

Beiner, R. 1992. *What's the Matter with Liberalism?* Berkeley and Los Angeles: University of California Press.

———, ed. 1995a. *Theorizing Citizenship.* Albany: State University of New York Press.

———. 1995b. "Why Citizenship Constitutes a Theoretical Problem in the Last Decade of the Twentieth Century." In Beiner 1995a.

Benn, S. I. 1976. "Freedom, Autonomy, and the Concept of a Person." *Proceedings of the Aristotelian Society* 76.

———. 1983. "Individuality, Autonomy, and Community." In Kamenka 1983.

Berkowitz, Peter. 1996. "The Decent Society." *New Republic* 25 (November).

———. 1999. *Virtue and the Making of Modern Liberalism.* Princeton: Princeton University Press.

Berlin, I. 1969. *Four Essays on Liberty.* New York: Oxford University Press.

———. 1991. "Two Concepts of Nationalism." *New York Review of Books* 38:19–23.

Berman, Harold. 1983. *Law and Revolution: The Formation of the Western Legal Tradition.* Cambridge: Harvard University Press.

Birnbaum, P. 1996. "From Multiculturalism to Nationalism." *Political Theory* 24:33–45.

Bouckaert, Boudewijn. 1998. "On the Rise of Civil Society in the Medieval West." Paper presented at "Liberty and Civil Society," conference of the Institute for Civil Society, Arlington, VA, 28–31 May.

Brewer, David. 1902. *American Citizenship: Yale's Lectures.* New York: Scribner's Sons.

Brighouse, Harry. 1998. "Civic Education and Liberal Legitimacy." *Ethics* 108, no. 4: 719–45.

Bryce, James. 1909. *The Hindrances of Good Citizenship*. New Yaven: Yale University Press.

Buchanan, Allen. 1989. "Assessing the Communitarian Critique of Liberalism." *Ethics* 99, no. 4: 852–82.

Callan, Eamonn. 1988. *Autonomy and Schooling*. Kingston, ON: McGill–Queen's University Press.

———. 1996. "Political Liberalism and Political Education." *Review of Politics*.

———. 1997. *Creating Citizens: Political Education and Liberal Democracy*. New York: Clarendon Press.

Cleveland, Grover. 1908. *Good Citizenship*. Philadelphia: Henry Altemus.

Cohen, G. A. 1997. "Where the Action Is: On the Site of Distributive Justice." *Philosophy and Public Affairs* 26:3–30.

Cohen, Joshua. 1994. "A More Democratic Liberalism." *Michigan Law Review* 92, no. 6: 1503–46.

———. 1998. "Reconciling Liberty and Equality: Justice as Fairness." Lecture available on MIT Website.

Coleman, Joseph. 1998. "Civic Pedagogies and Liberal Democratic Curricula." *Ethics* 108, no. 4: 746–61.

Conover, P. J. 1995. "Citizen Identities and Conceptions of the Self." *Journal of Political Philosophy* 3:133–65.

Conover, P., I. Crowe, and D. Searing. 1991. "The Nature of Citizenship in the United States and Great Britain: Empirical Comments on Theoretical Themes." *Journal of Politics* 53:801–32.

Cooper, John M. 1975. *Reason and Human Good in Aristotle*. Cambridge: Harvard University Press.

Cox, Harvey. 1998. "Three R's, Plus One." *New York Times*, 5 June, A23.

Crittenden, Jack. 1992. *Beyond Individualism: Reconstituting the Liberal Self*. New York: Oxford University Press.

Dagger, Richard. 1992. *Civic Virtues: Rights, Citizenship, and Republican Liberalism*. New York: Oxford University Press.

Damro, Alfonse, ed. 1986. *Liberals on Liberalism*. Totawa, NJ: Rowman and Littlefield.

Daniels, Norman. 1996. *Justice and Justification: Reflective Equilibrium in Theory and Practice*. New York: Cambridge University Press.

DeLue, Steven. 1980. "Aristotle, Kant, and Rawls on Moral Motivation in a Just Society." *American Political Science Review* 74, no. 1: 385–93.

———. 1986. "The Idea of a Duty to Justice in Ideal Liberal Theory." In Damro 1986, 95–110.

Dworkin, Ronald. 1977. *Taking Rights Seriously*. Cambridge: Harvard University Press.

———. 1986. *Law's Empire*. Cambridge: Harvard University Press, Belknap Press.

———. 1993. *Life's Dominion: An Argument about Abortion, Euthanasia, and Individual Freedom*. New York: Knopf.

Espada, Joao Carlos. 1996. *Social Citizenship Rights*. London: Macmillan in association with St. Anthony's College, Oxford.

Estlund, David. 1996. "The Survival of Egalitarian Justice in John Rawls' Political Liberalism." *Journal of Political Philosophy* 4, no. 1: 68–78.

Etzioni, Amitai. 1996. *The New Golden Rule: Community and Morality in a Democratic Society.* New York: Basic Books.

Feinberg, J., ed. 1969. *Moral Concepts.* New York: Oxford University Press.

Flathman, Richard. 1995. "Citizenship and Authority: A Chastened View of Citizenship." In Beiner 1995a.

———. 1998. " 'It All Depends . . . on How One Understands Liberalism': A Brief Response to Stephen Macedo." *Political Theory* 26, no. 1: 81–84.

Foucault, Michel. 1979. *Discipline and Punish: The Birth of the Prison.* New York: Vintage Books.

Fowler, Robert, et al. 1999. *Religion and Politics in America: Faith, Culture, and Strategic Choices.* Boulder, CO: Westview Press.

Frankfurter, Felix. 1930. *The Public and Its Government: Yale Lectures on the Responsibilities of Citizenship.* New Haven: Yale University Press.

Freeman, Samuel. 1994a. "The Illiberalism of Libertarianism: Why Libertarianism Is Not a Liberal View." Paper presented at the Princeton University Center for Human Values.

———. 1994b. "Political Liberalism and the Possibility of Just Democratic Constitution." *University of Chicago Law Review* 69, no. 3: 619–68.

Galston, Miriam. 1994. "Rawlsian Dualism and the Autonomy of Political Thought." *Columbia Law Review* 94.

Galston, William. 1980. *Justice and the Human Good.* Chicago: University of Chicago Press.

———. 1982. "Defending Liberalism." *American Political Science Review* 76, no. 3 (September): 621–29.

———. 1989. "Civic Education in the Liberal State." In Rosenblum 1989.

———. 1991. *Liberal Purposes: Goods, Virtues, and Duties in the Liberal State.* Cambridge: Cambridge University Press.

———. 1992. "Comments on Tomasi." Paper delivered at the Institute for Humane Studies, Fairfax, VA.

———. 1995a. "Liberal Virtues and the Formation of a Civic Character." In Glendon 1995.

———. 1995b. "Two Concepts of Liberalism." *Ethics* 105:516–34.

———. 1996. "Divorce American Style." *Public Interest* (Summer): 12–26.

Glendon, Mary Ann. 1991. *Rights Talk: The Impoverishment of Political Discourse.* New York: Free Press.

Glendon, Mary Ann, and David Blankenhorn, eds. 1995. *Seedbeds of Virtue: Sources of Competence, Character, and Citizenship in American Society.* Lanham, MD: Madison Books.

Gray, John. 1993a. *Post-Liberalism: Studies in Political Thought.* New York: Routledge.

———. 1993b. "Review of *Political Liberalism,* by John Rawls." *New York Times Book Review,* 16 May, 35.

———. 1997. *Endgames: Questions in Late Modern Political Thought* Cambridge: Polity Press.

Greenawalt, Kent. 1988. *Religious Convictions and Political Choice.* New York: Oxford University Press.

Greenawalt, Kent. 1995. *Private Consciousness and Public Reasons*. New York: Oxford University Press.

Griffin, Leslie. 1997. "Good Catholics Should Be Rawlsian Liberals." *Southern California Interdisciplinary Law Journal* 5, no. 3.

Gutmann, Amy. 1980. "Children, Paternalism, and Education: A Liberal Argument." *Philosophy and Public Affairs*, 9, no. 4 (Summer): 338–58.

———. 1980. *Liberal Equality*. Cambridge: Cambridge University Press.

———. 1985. "Communitarian Critics of Liberalism." *Philosophy and Public Affairs* 14, no. 3 (Summer): 308–22.

———. 1987. *Democratic Education*. Princeton: Princeton University Press.

———. 1989. "Undemocratic Education." In Rosenblum 1989.

———. 1990. "Democratic Education in Difficult Times." *Teacher's College Record* 92:7–20.

———. 1993. "The Challenge of Multiculturalism in Political Ethics." *Philosophy and Public Affairs* 22, no. 3 (Summer): 171–206.

———. 1995. "Civic Education and Social Diversity." *Ethics* 105, no. 3: 557–79.

———. 1996. *Democracy and Disagreement*. Cambridge: Harvard University Press, Belknap Press.

———, ed. 1998 *Freedom of Association*. Princeton: Princeton University Press.

Harrington, M. 1982. "Loyalties: Dual and Divided." In Thernstrom 1982.

Herzog, Don. 1986. "Some Questions for Republicans." *Political Theory* 14:473–93.

Hibben, John Grier. 1927. *Self-Legislated Obligations*. Cambridge: Harvard University Press.

Honig, Bonnie. 1993. *Political Theory and the Displacement of Politics*. Ithaca: Cornell University Press.

Hursthouse, R. 1991. "After Hume's Justice." *Proceedings of the Aristotelian Society* 16:229–45.

Ignatieff, M. 1989. "Citizenship and Moral Narcissism." *Political Quarterly* 60:63–74.

———. 1995. "The Myth of Citizenship." In Beiner 1995a.

Jacks, L. P. 1924. *Responsibility and Culture*. New Haven: Yale University Press.

John Paul II. 1998. "On the Relationship between Faith and Reason." In *Fides et Ratio*, Encyclical Letter to the Bishops of the Catholic Church, publication no. 5–302, United States Catholic Conference, Washington, DC.

Johnston, D. 1994. *The Idea of a Liberal Theory: A Critique and Reconstruction*. Princeton: Princeton University Press.

Kamenka, E., ed. 1983. *Community as a Social Ideal*. New York: St. Martin's Press.

Kateb, George. 1992. *The Inner Ocean: Individualism and Democratic Culture*. Ithaca: Cornell University Press.

Kelley, G. 1995. "Who Needs a Theory of Citizenship?" In Beiner 1995a.

Kekes, John. 1993. *The Morality of Pluralism*. Princeton: Princeton University Press.

———. 1997. *Against Liberalism* Ithaca: Cornell University Press.

King, D., and J. Waldron. "Citizenship, Social Citizenship, and the Defense of Welfare Provision." *Journal of Political Science* 18:415–43.

Kymlicka, Will. 1989. *Liberalism, Community, and Culture*. Oxford: Clarendon Press.

———. 1992. "Comments on Tomasi, 'Virtue Federalism.' " Paper delivered at the Institute for Humane Studies, Fairfax, VA.

———. 1995. *Multicultural Citizenship*. New York: Oxford University Press.

———. 1998. "Liberal Egalitarianism and Civic Republicanism: Friends or Enemies?" In Allen and Regan 1998.

Kymlicka, Will, and Wayne Norman. 1994. "The Return of the Citizen: A Survey of Recent Work on Citizenship Theory." *Ethics* 104, no. 1: 352–81.

Laden, Anthony. 1997. "Constructing Shared Wills." Ph.D. dissertation, Department of Philosophy, Harvard University.

Larmore, Charles. 1987. *Patterns of Moral Complexity*. New York: Cambridge University Press.

———. 1991. "Political Liberalism." *Political Theory* 18, no. 4.

———. 1996a. *The Morals of Modernity*. New York: Cambridge University Press.

———. 1996b. *The Romantic Legacy*. New York: Columbia University Press.

———. "Comments on Tomasi." Paper delivered at the Institute of Humane Studies, Fairfax, VA.

Leca, J. 1992. "Questions of Citizenship." In Mouffe 1992.

Levinson, Meira. 1999. *The Demands of Liberal Education*. New York: Oxford University Press.

Long, Roderick T. 1998. "Civil Society in Ancient Greece: The Case of Athens." Paper presented at "Liberty and Civil Society," conference by the Institute for Civil Society, Arlington, VA, 28–31 May.

Macedo, Stephen. 1987. *The New Right v. the Constitution*. Washington, DC: Cato Institute.

———. 1990. *Liberal Virtues: Citizenship, Virtue, and Community*. Oxford: Oxford University Press.

———. 1995a. "Liberal Civic Education and Religious Fundamentalism: The Case of God vs. John Rawls." *Ethics* 105, no. 3: 468–96.

———. 1995b. "Multiculturalism for the Religious Right? Defending Liberal Civic Education." *Journal of the Philosophy of Education* 29:225.

———. 1998. "Transformative Constitutionalism and the Case of Religion." *Political Theory* 26, no. 1: 56–80.

———. 2000. *Diversity and Distrust: Public Schooling, Civic Education, and American Liberalism*. New York: Harvard University Press.

Machan, Tibor. 1998. *Generosity: Virtue in Civil Society*. Washington, DC: Cato Institute.

MacIntyre, Alasdair. 1971. *Against the Self-images of the Age; Essays on Ideology and Philosophy*. New York: Schocken Books.

———. 1984. *After Virtue: A Study in Moral Theory*. 2d ed. Notre Dame, IN: University of Notre Dame Press.

———. 1988. *Whose Justice? Which Rationality?* Notre Dame, IN: University of Notre Dame Press.

———. 1999. *Dependent Rational Animals: Why Human Beings Need the Virtues*. Chicago: Open Court.

Mansbridge, Jane. 1990. *Beyond Self-Interest*. Chicago: University of Chicago Press.

Marshall, T. H. [1949] 1965. *Class, Citizenship, and Social Development*. New York: Anchor.

Marx, Karl. 1975. "On the Jewish Question." In *Karl Marx: Collected Works*, vol. 3. Moscow: Progress Publishers.

McCall, Samuel Walker. 1915. *The Liberty of Citizenship*. New Haven: Yale University Press.

McDowell, John. 1979. "Virtue and Reason." *Monist* 62, no. 3: 331–50.

Moon, J. Donald. 1994. *Constructing Community: Moral Pluralism and Tragic Conflicts*. Princeton: Princeton University Press.

Mouffe, Chantal, ed. 1992. *Dimensions of Radical Democracy: Pluralism, Citizenship, and Community*. London: Routledge.

Morgan, Joy Elmer. 1946. *The American Citizen's Handbook*. Washington, DC: The National Education Association of the United States.

Nath, Vijay. 1987. *Dana: Gift System in Ancient India*. New Delhi: Munshiram Manoharlal Publishers.

Nord, Warren. 1995. *Religion and American Education: Rethinking an American Dilemma*. Chapel Hill: University of North Carolina Press.

Nozick, R. 1974. *Anarchy, State, and Utopia*. Oxford: Basil Blackwell.

Nussbaum, Martha. 2000. *Women and Human Development: The Capabilities Approach*. Cambridge: Cambridge University Press.

Okin, Susan 1984. "Taking the Bishops Seriously." *World Politics* 36, no. 4: 527–54

———. 1987. "Justice and Gender." *Philosophy and Public Affairs* 16, no. 1 (Winter 1987): 42–72.

———. 1989. *Justice, Gender, and the Family*. New York: Basic Books.

———. 1992. "Women, Equality, and Citizenship." *Queen's Quarterly* 99:1.

———. 1997. "Review of Michael Sandel's *Democracy's Discontent*." *American Political Science Review* 91, no. 2: 440–42.

Oldfield, A. 1990. "Citizenship: An Unnatural Practice?" *Political Quarterly* 61:177–87.

Pocock, J. G. A. 1992. "The Ideal of Citizenship since Classical Times." *Queen's Quarterly* 99:33–55.

Rasmussen, Douglas. 1990. "Liberalism and Natural End Ethics." *American Philosophical Quarterly* 27:153–61.

Rawls, J. 1969. "The Sense of Justice." In Feinberg 1969.

———. 1971. *A Theory of Justice*. Cambridge: Harvard University Press, Belknap Press.

———. 1980. "Kantian Constructivism in Moral Theory." *Journal of Philosophy* 77:515–72.

———. 1993. *Political Liberalism*. New York: Columbia University Press.

———. 1995a. "Reply to Habermas." *Journal of Philosophy* 92, no. 3: 132–80.

———. 1995b "*A Theory of Justice* and *Political Liberalism* and Other Pieces: How Related?" Draft (6 May) of comments to be presented at October 1995 Santa Clara Conference on Rawls's work.

———. 1996. "Introduction to the Paperback Edition." In *Political Liberalism*. New York: Columbia University Press.

———. 1997. "The Idea of Public Reason Revisited." *University of Chicago Law Review* 64, no. 3: 765–807.

———. 1998. "Politics, Religion, and the Public Good." Interview conducted by Bernard Prusak. *Commonweal*, 25 Sept.

Raz, Joseph. 1986. *The Morality of Freedom.* Oxford: Clarendon Press.

———. 1990. "Facing Diversity: The Case of Epistemic Abstinence." *Philosophy and Public Affairs* 19, no. 1: 3–46.

———. 1994. *Ethics in the Public Domain: Essays on the Morality of Law and Politics.* New York: Oxford University Press.

Reed, Donald R. C. 1997. *Following Kohlberg: Liberalism and the Practice of Democratic Community.* Notre Dame, IN: University of Notre Dame Press.

Riesenberg, P. 1992. *Citizenship in the Western Tradition: Plato to Rousseau.* Chapel Hill: University of North Carolina Press.

Roof, Wade. 1993. *A Generation of Seekers: The Spiritual Journeys of the Baby Boom Generation.* New York: HarperCollins.

Root, Elihu. 1907. *The Citizen's Part in Government: Yale Lectures on the Responsibilities of Citizenship.* New York: Scribner's Sons.

Rorty, Richard. 1988. "The Priority of Democracy to Philosophy." In *The Virginia Statute for Religious Freedom*, ed. Merrill D. Peterson and Robert C. Vaughan. New York: Cambridge University Press.

Rosenblum, Nancy, ed. 1989. *Liberalism and the Moral Life.* Cambridge: Harvard University Press.

———. 1998. *Membership and Morals: The Personal Uses of Pluralism in America.* Princeton: Princeton University Press.

Sandel, Michael. 1982a. ed. *Liberalism and Its Critics.* New York: New York University Press.

1982b. *Liberalism and the Limits of Justice.* Cambridge: Cambridge University Press.

———. 1984. "The Procedural Republic and the Unencumbered Self." *Political Theory* 12:81–96.

———. 1994. "Review of *Political Liberalism.*" *Harvard Law Review* 107:1765–94.

———. 1996. *Democracy's Discontent: America in Search of a Public Philosophy* Cambridge: Harvard University Press, Belknap Press.

———. 1998a. *Democracy's Discontent.* Cambridge: Harvard University Press, Belknap Press.

———. 1998b. "Reply to Critics." In Allen and Regan 1998.

Schmidtz, David. 1990. "Justifying the State" *Ethics* 101/1:89–102.

———. 1998. *Social Welfare and Individual Responsibility.* New York: Cambridge University Press.

Shapiro, Daniel. 1995. "Liberalism and Communitarianism." *Philosophical Books* 36:145–55.

Shapiro, Ian. 1996. *Democracy's Place.* Ithaca: Cornell University Press.

———. 1999. *Democratic Justice.* New Haven: Yale University Press.

Shapiro, Ian, and John Chapman, eds. *Democratic Community.* New York: New York University Press.

Sher, George. 1997. *Beyond Neutrality: Perfectionism in Politics.* New York: Cambridge University Press.

Simmons, A. John. 1999. "Justification and Legitimacy." *Ethics* 109, no. 4.

Sinopoli, R. 1992. *The Foundations of American Citizenship: Liberalism, the Constitution, and Civic Virtue.* New York: Oxford University Press.

Skinner, Q. 1992. "On Justice, the Common Good, and the Priority of Liberty." In Mouffe 1992.

Taft, William H. 1906. *Four Aspects of Civic Duty: Yale Lectures on the Responsibilities of Citizenship*. New York: Scribner's Sons.

Tamir, Y. 1993. *Liberal Nationalism*. Princeton: Princeton University Press.

Taylor, Charles. 1985. *Philosophical Papers*. Vol. 3. Cambridge: Cambridge University Press.

Theiman, Ronald. *Religion in Public Life*. Washington, DC.: Georgetown University Press.

Thernstrom, S., ed. 1982. *The Politics of Ethnicity*. Cambridge: Harvard University Press.

Thompson, Dennis. 1996. *Democracy and Disagreement*. Cambridge: Harvard University Press, Belknap Press.

Tocqueville, Alexis de. 1996. *Democracy in America*. Translated by George Lawrence, edited by J. P. Mayer. New York: HarperCollins.

Tomasi, John. 1991. "Individual Rights and Community Virtues." *Ethics* 101, no. 2.

———. 1992. Review of *Liberal Virtues*, by Stephen Macedo. *Ethics* 102, no. 1.

———. 1994. "Community in the Minimal State." *Critical Review* 8/2 (Spring).

———. 1995. "Kymlicka, Liberalism, and Respect for Cultural Minorities." *Ethics* 105, no. 2.

———. 1996. Review of *The Idea of a Liberal Theory*, by David Johnston. *Political Theory* (December).

———. 1997. "Liberalism, Sanctity, and the Prohibition of Abortion." *Journal of Philosophy* 94, no. 10.

———. Forthcoming 2000. "Civic Education and Ethical Subservience: From *Mozert* to *Santa Fe* and Beyond." In *NOMOS XLIII: Moral and Political Education*, ed. Steven Macedo and Yael Tamir. New York: New York University Press.

Urmson, J. O. 1969. "Saints and Heroes." In Feinberg 1969.

Waldron, Jeremy. 1987. "Theoretical Foundations of Liberalism." *Philosophical Quarterly* 37, no. 147: 127–50.

Walzer, M. 1984. "Liberalism and the Art of Separation." *Political Theory* 12, no. 3: 315–30.

———. 1989. "Citizenship." In *Political Innovations and Conceptual Change*, ed. Terrence, Ball, Farr, and Hansen. Cambridge: Cambridge University Press.

———. 1990. "The Communitarian Critique of Liberalism." *Political Theory* 18:6–23.

———. 1992. *Just and Unjust War*. New York: Basic Books.

Wilkins, Burleigh. 1997. "A Third Principle of Justice." *Journal of Ethics* 1:355–74.

Williams, Bernard. 1993. "A Fair State." *London Review of Books* 13 (May): 7–8.

Wolf, Susan. 1997. "Meaning and Morality." *Proceedings of the Aristotelian Society* 97, no. 3: 299–315.

Wolfe, Alan 1998. *One Nation after All: What Middle Class Americans Really Think about God, Country, Family, Racism, Welfare, Immigration, Homosexuality, Work, the Right, the Left, and Each Other*. New York: Viking.

Wood, Gordon S. 1969. *The Creation of the American Republic*. Chapel Hill: University of North Carolina Press.

————. 1992. *The Radicalism of the American Revolution*. New York: A. A. Knopf.

Wright, Roy, and Eliza Wright. 1938. *How to Be a Responsible Citizen*. New York: Association Press.

Wuthnow, Robert. 1988. *Restructuring of American Religion: Society and Faith since World War II*. Princeton: Princeton University Press.

INDEX